Yo Tookie, I've b___ ___ __ __ __ ___ __ eally Wanted To Thank You For Settin' Me Free, Cuz. I Mean You Were My Idol, And Now I See All Tha Pain I've Caused People Who Never Deserved It, Over A Color And What It Stood For. Thanks To You, I Now See How Wrong I Was. I Needed To Get My Life Back, And You Gave It To Me.

I would like to share the effect your books, movie and website are having on the juveniles in my rehabilitation program.
1) Dictionaries are going off the shelf faster than I can buy them.
2) More books are borrowed from the library than before.
3) Juveniles are telling me and writing me that they are changing their ways, that they are working harder at school.

"Thank you for writing me about Tookie Williams and sending me information about him. It encouraged me to pay attention to my school work while it lasts and get my mind focused on my weak points. My teacher tells me I'm the fastest worker in class. My comprehension skills are above average."

Thank you for changing lives. You may be saying the same things I tell the inmates, but when you say something, it reaches so many more.
Juvenile Rehabilitation Officer, Florida

We, the GD's (Gangster Disciples) and the VL's (Vice Lords), have found peace in our small town. The reason why we came to this peace is Mr. Williams. I changed his peace protocol from tookie.com just a little and it works. I think about the 52 Gangsta Disciples and the 40 Vice Lords that walk our town in peace. We don't worry about being shot or jumped no more. Sometimes we all see each other at a game or party and look at each other and nod and throw up two fingers that signify our peace.
From a 16 year old who doesn't have to worry about being shot anymore.

I am a college instructor who teaches race and ethnic relations. I watched your movie last night. It was powerful. Each semester I read a quote that you gave to an interviewer from *Mother Jones* who asked about anger being at the core of a lot of street violence. You stated: "That anger that we talk about is self-hate. On a daily basis these youngsters digest negative stereotypes about blacks, and eventually end up believing them and acting them out in life." It is important for my students to hear this and to understand the consequences of prejudice and discrimination that wounds and pierces the soul of an individual.

As a former Crip, I want to say the main reason why I left the Crips was because I read Tookie's book, "Life In Prison," and he inspired me to no longer gang-bang.

I understand the gravity of gang life firsthand. I would be glad to sponsor Mr. Williams if he was released. He has personally been instrumental in salvaging many youths that I know, including my son.

Reverend E. T. D.

Ah brah, God bless you as you blessed so many of us. Your testimony has made an impact on my life.

Thanks, b

Tookie, I'd like to say thank you for saving my friend. He watched your movie and broke down. Good men can get lost. They can also find their way to the road to redemption. I truly believe that my friend had only another year before he was on death row, or dead somewhere in an alley because of a fight. I'm so thankful to you. And through your words, and people like my friend who has gotten out and others like him, and people like me who truly believe there can be a change, we can stop this madness. I love you for all that you have done. I thank you, Mr. Williams.

Tookie, i have showed about 6 people that are in the Crips your movie they have been in the gang for almost 4 years n' they are hard core people. they are no longer banging. the gang is now no longer a gang. they have jobs n' are going to school n' most of them get A's n' B's. i am proud of them, n' it is because of you. you are a great person, cuz, you have touched every ex-gangbanger's heart.

Hello, Tookie. I have recently seen your movie, *Redemption*. I could strongly relate to it as I have for the past few years been running with a local Blood set called South Tre-Six Piru. After seeing your movie I visited your website and did a little research on you. All of what I discovered motivated me to leave my set and throw away my rag. I dont want to live and die by the gun anymore and I have seen too many friends die over this red and blue nonsense. Well, I really just wanted to write to tell you how you changed me and to thank you.

Tookie, my son and I watched your movie the other night. The impression it made on me from long ago bangin (I'm a police officer in the military now) and the impression it made on my son . . . all i can say is, thanks for the wisdom and courage you put into your work. My son is at a very impressionable age. If it wasn't for your movie i think he would have gone the same route a lot of us did at our age, back then. He has even stopped playing violent games. GOD BLESS YOU.

I'm a 15 year old girl. Awhile back, me and some of my friends got arrested for auto theft. I am going through a lot of stuff right now behind all that. Along with me reading some of your stories and watching the movie "Redemption," I have a whole different perspective on life. I realized that gang life is no kind of life to be living at all. I was worried and so was my family about where this stuff was leading to. I was told that I could go to prison and I'm deathly scared of that. I would like to thank you and let you know that you have influenced my life.

I was a gang member until today after i read about Tookie, it takes alot of courage to turn your life around, and tell your members you are out, but a real survivor would do that. So, thanks Tookie, you saved me and 100's of my friends.

Mr. Williams, I first heard about you while in my second year of repeating grade nine. At that time I was a resource student [a school category classifying students as slow or stupid]. Hearing about you made me realize that if you could achieve goals for yourself behind bars, I had no excuse for failing in my life. I was a kid of the system [a product of society], in and out of group homes, foster homes, psychiatric wards, shelters and the streets. No one was looking out for me, so i had to look out for myself. i did what i had to do to survive. To make a long story short, i dropped school, started home teaching myself, learned about the law in my province in order to protect and defend myself, and became actively involved in helping my community. At seventeen i got a youth worker position and did that for eight years. Although i left the youth work field, I continue to be an outspoken active advocate for young people. What is sad is that so many young people will end up like you, and although they can change, learn and achieve, they will never be given a chance by society. I thank you for influencing my life and for being a PERSON that i admire. I will continue to inform young people about you and your situation and i hope that they will learn and get inspired by the man that you have become, just like i was.

Stanley Tookie Williams, I would like to say thank you. You have been such a major inspiration in my life since I was 14. Growing up I would always hear that being in a gang was the best. Then I read your books, watched your movie, and done some studying of my own. I feel as tho you have saved my life. Without hearing your life story and all, who knows where I might be. It's because of you that I pulled my grades up in school. I'm now a senior in high school. I know that I want to be successful in life. No amount of thank yous can tell you how much my friends and I thank GOD for you.

I used ta be a crip but I watched tha Redemption movie. It helped me a lot in seeing that bangin blue aint nuthin. I can do without the trouble. Tookie kept me from bein behind barz. I'm stayin out of jail and keepin my head up all cuz of him . . . He helped people stay off the streets.

Mr. Tookie, wut'up? I seen your movie and read your books. I really learned alot. I see being a gang banger is really lots of evilness. I had wanted to be one like that at first, because I seen how people was living large. But at the same time dying over crazy stuff. Like money, girls, cars and whose gang is bigger and better. I had took the wrong path trying to fit in with others. But it didn't get me anywhere but in trouble and behind bars. None of them write me or come and see me, send me money or accept my phone calls or anything. I sit in my cell writing poems or drawing things. I wrote a poem in here on my birthday about being in here. I come from a place where people sat on there porch selling and smoking drugs in front of little kids and around babies. Thank you for showing me the light.

i just want to let you know the impression you have made on my life. i have lost several friends to gang violence, one whom was particularly close to me. i wanted revenge, i wanted to join up with my friends and go after the people that killed her. then i stumbled upon your book "life in prison." i read it, and looked at myself and decided that i did not want to do that. after all. if i had tracked them down and hurt them, or worse, what good would that do? i'd probably have ended up incarcerated, and it would not have brought my friend back. YOU are my HERO. thank you for all that you have done for the countless other teenagers all over the world who you have touched. you are in my prayers.

Tookie, your work has convinced six members of my family to not involve themselves in gang activities. Thank you for everything that you've done to help stop the violence that is tearing not only the Black community to pieces but other communities around the world.

Mr. Williams, I am an 8th-grade history teacher in California. I have read each of your books to over 300 students. We were the first school group to ever speak to a death-row inmate – you – over a speaker-phone. Your books have had a positive effect on my students, many of whom would be classified as "at risk."

Tookie, I was a member of a Los Angeles street gang. I would just like to let you know how big of an impact your story had on my life. Your works have made me realize the self-destruction that my involvment in a gang was causing. I love you for that. Thank you for saving my life.

REDEMPTION

REDEMPTION

From Original Gangster
to Nobel Prize Nominee

Stanley Tookie Williams

MILO BOOKS LTD

First published in Great Britain in November 2004 by Milo
Books Ltd.
Published in the USA as *Blue Rage, Black Redemption*
by Damamli Publishing Company, 25A Crescent Drive,
Pleasant Hill, CA 94523.

Cover Design:

Photographs:
Stanley Tookie Williams

ISBN 1-903854-34-2

Typset in Sabon by Avon DataSet Ltd,
Bidford on Avon, Warwickshire, B50 4JH.

Printed and bound in Great Britain by Cox and Wyman,
Reading, Berks.

MILO BOOKS
The Old Weighbridge
Station Road
Wrea Green
Preston
PR4 2PH

About the Author

In the early 1970s, many young people of South Central Los Angeles were members of small gangs. The youngsters roamed South Central, taking property from whomever they chose, including women and children.

Stanley Tookie Williams, 17, was then a high school student with a fearsome reputation as a fighter and leader of South Central's west side neighbourhood. To protect family members and friends, Tookie – with Raymond Lee Washington, also 17 years old, who lived on the east side – created the Crips street gang for black teenage males.

By 1979, the Crips had grown from a small Los Angeles gang of boys to an organization with membership of boys and young men who claimed the streets in many cities throughout Southern California as their "territory." They had become like the gang members they had once sought to protect themselves from – they had become gangbangers who terrorized their own neighbourhoods.

A rival gang member murdered Raymond in 1979. That same year, Tookie was arrested and charged with murdering four people. In 1981, he was convicted of those crimes and placed on death row.

Over the coming decades, to Tookie's surprise, the Crips gang would spread across the nation and around the world.

Since 1989, Tookie has worked to redeem himself from a Crips legacy of black-on-black crime and community destruction. He has authored nine anti-gang books instructing youth how *not* to follow in his footsteps. These books are in schools, libraries and juvenile correctional facilities in the United States and Europe as well as parts of Africa and Asia. Tookie also created the Internet Project for Street Peace, an international peer mentoring program for children. He regularly provides "live" mentoring via the telephone when he calls schools and juvenile correctional facilities to steer kids away from gangs, crime and violence. He has also been nominated four times for the Nobel Peace Prize and three times for the Nobel Prize in Literature.

Tookie's accomplishments have all been made from his 9-by-4-foot prison cell, without a chair, without a table.

At the time of writing, Tookie is awaiting a final court ruling on his case, which will determine whether he is executed by lethal injection by the State of California or given a new trial. He has always maintained his innocence of the crimes for which he was convicted.

Tookie can be contacted through his website at http://www.tookie.com. His email address is Tookie@Tookie.com.

Contents

Foreword

The two halves of this book represent two extreme phases of my life.

Blue Rage is a chronicle of my passage down a spiraling path of Crip rage in South Central Los Angeles. *Black Redemption* depicts the stages of my redemptive awakening during my more than twenty-three years of imprisonment on California's death row. These memoirs of my evolution will, I hope, connect the reader to a deeper awareness of a social epidemic that is the unending nightmare of racial minorities in America and abroad.

Throughout my youth, I was hoodwinked by South Central's terminal conditions, its broad and deadly template for failure. From the beginning I was spoon-fed negative stereotypes that covertly positioned black people as genetic criminals – inferior, illiterate, shiftless, promiscuous and ultimately "three-fifths" of a human being, as stated in the Constitution of the United States. Having bought into this myth, I was shackled to the lowest socioeconomic rung, where underprivileged citizens competed ruthlessly for morsels of the American pie – a pie theoretically served proportionately to all, based on their ambition, intelligence and perseverance.

Like many others, I became a slave to the delusion of capitalism's false hope: a slave to dys-education (see Chapter 3); a slave to nihilism; a slave to drugs; a slave to black-on-black violence; and a slave to self-hate. Paralysed within a social vacuum, I gravitated toward thughood, not out of aspiration but out of desperation to survive the monstrous inequities that show no mercy to young or old. Aggression, I was to learn, served as a poor man's merit for manhood. To die as a street martyr was seen as a noble thing.

In 1971, I joined Raymond Lee Washington (may he rest in peace), uniting with our homeboys to combat neighbouring street gangs on the west and east sides of South Central. (An erroneous grapevine has the Crips' formation in 1969, or even as early as the 1950s.) Most Crips themselves are unaware that the original name for our alliance was "Cribs," a name selected from a list of many options. But the short-lived label of Cribs was carelessly mispronounced by many of us and morphed into the name Crips, our permanent identity.

Most of us were seventeen years of age.

The Crips mythology has many romanticized, bogus accounts. I never thought it would be necessary to address such issues. But I can set the record straight – for Raymond Washington, for me and for others who fought and often died for this causeless cause.

I assumed that everyone in South Central knew that Raymond was the leader of the East Side Crips, and that I was the leader of the West Side Crips. A few published chronicles have Raymond attending Washington High School and uniting the neighbourhood *west side* gangs where he supposedly lived. In fact, Raymond attended Fremont High School on the *east side*, where he lived. A fundamental inquiry would have revealed that I lived on the *west* side, where I attended Washington High and rallied our homeboys and groups of local gangs. Even our former rivals have a better understanding about the Crips' origins than many social historians.

Most of the public misinformation has been fostered by academics, journalists and other parasitical opportunists, stool pigeons and wannabe Crip founders who shamelessly seek undue profit and recognition for a gang genocide.

There is no honour in insinuating yourself as a player in this legacy of a bloodletting where your feet have never trod.

Another version incorrectly documents the Crips as an offshoot of the Black Panther Party. No Panther Party member ever mentioned the Crips or Cribs as being a spin-off of the Panthers. It is also fiction that the Crips functioned under the acronym, C.R.I.P., for Community Resource Inner-City Project or Community Revolutionary Inner City Project. Words such as "revolutionary agenda" were alien to our thuggish, uninformed teenage consciousness. We did not unite to protect the community; our motive was to protect ourselves and our families.

There are people who say it was karmic justice that Raymond and I, who impinged on society in 1971 with our violent pact, deserved our exit from society in 1979 – Raymond to the grave and myself to San Quentin Prison. They cry out that I am incapable of redemption. Would God have it that everyone has the right to transformation and to redemption – except for Stanley Tookie Williams? I cannot believe this is so.

To avoid damaging others, certain names, nicknames and quite a few well-known incidents have been excluded. For the same reason I have used pseudonyms for some of the people I depict in this book. Otherwise, the story I tell is true.

"[President Nixon] emphasizes that you have to face the fact that the *whole* problem is really the blacks. The key is to devise a system that recognizes this while not appearing to."

– H.R. Haldeman
The Haldeman Diaries:
Inside the Nixon White House

Part One

Blue Rage

ONE

Born in the Bayou

On December 29, 1953, in New Orleans Charity Hospital, I entered the world kicking and screaming in a caesarean ritual of blood and scalpels. This being 1950s, pre-Civil-Rights Louisiana, my 17-year-old mother, a "coloured woman," was deprived of anaesthetics as her torso was slit from sternum to pubic bone. Over and over again, she sang the Christmas carol "Silent Night" to distract herself from the pain.

I was christened Stanley Tookie Williams III: I would mostly be referred to as Tookie.

Perhaps my laborious birth – and a seizure I suffered before the age of two, requiring a spinal tap – foreshadowed tragedy to come. But I've always felt that the real adversity fell on my teenage mother because of her station in life: a black woman living in the South, and with very little money. Morbid conditions of poverty were eager to devour us. Being exposed to this apocalyptic society, my thin skin of innocence began to peel slowly away as I grew to adolescence.

In my life, the natural progression from maternal weaning to paternal guidance was absent. My father was the weak link in the family equation. He abandoned us before I reached my first birthday. My memories of him were so remote that I could not have recognized him in a jailhouse line-up. He was a stranger, showing up once in a blue moon bearing gifts and an uncertain smile. His attempts at playing part-time Santa Claus and spreading good cheer failed to win me over. As far as I was concerned, my father was an unwelcome visitor whom I watched until he left the house.

My mother was the backbone of the family. She was hard-working, serious, tough, soft-spoken and had the foot speed of a cheetah. I can attest to that quickness through my many failed attempts to escape punishment. Before my mother's pregnancy, she was well known as a track star. Her genes were passed down to me: I could outrun my peers and many older youths. Standing at 5'2", she was a vision of loveliness with chocolate skin, a shapely physique and long silky black hair.

But my mother's beauty attracted a lot of unwanted male attention. Though her no-nonsense expression held most men at bay, a few boldly approached. Their foolhardy advances compelled me, for a while, to carry a sharpened 7" butter knife concealed in my waistband. To protect my mother, I would have happily become a Ninja mercenary.

Unknown to my mother, I later stashed that knife beneath a slab of rock in the backyard. Had she discovered it, I would have been severely beaten, or "disciplined," as she called it. My mother adhered religiously to the Judeo-Christian Bible, in particular Proverb 13:24: "He who spareth his rod hateth his son. But he that loveth him chastiseth him betimes". Yes, my mother loved me deeply, and I regularly felt her love's sting. But compared to the beatings some of my friends received from their parents, I got off easy. I will admit the Biblically inspired punishment did make me tougher. On the other hand, it failed to derail my misbehaviour.

The frequency of beatings aged me considerably. I became more unruly, distant and indifferent to the predictable consequence of my actions. By no means was I born a criminal. I understood the penalties for my actions all too well. Though my mother tried to instil in me the fundamentals of right and wrong, the development of my conscience was shaded with different meanings. I learned from the street culture that criminal activity was an economic necessity and violence a means to a desired end. Plain and simple, in my neighbourhood, if you wanted something, you had to take it – and then fight to keep it. I clashed often with my mother over my mindset and incorrigible behaviour.

Whatever was physically possible for a mischievous youth my size to do, I did. Motivated by greed and envy, I took to stealing little food items and toys from stores. If my mother happened to discover any item unaccounted for, she would march me back to return it, or would destroy it. Although I didn't completely understand this, my philosophy was hardening: adapt and survive. That was the street rule.

Sometimes my partner in crime was Rex, my brown and white mutt dog. The entire neighbourhood was in an uproar over my letting Rex run through flower beds and chase chickens and roosters. Time and time again I was warned about unleashing Rex, but it was all fun and games to me. Eventually I had to watch teary-eyed as Rex was hauled away to the dog pound. If there was a lesson to be learned, I didn't grasp it.

Being mischievous, hyperactive, and with a short attention span, I had to find something to do. My older cousin Walter and I used to slide and tumble on a gunnysack down a nearby dirt hill. Too poor to afford baseball equipment, we liked playing stickball with rocks and would play for hours before dinner. That stopped after Walter hit a rock that smashed into my forehead. Blood gushed everywhere. My grandmother, "Momma," patched me up with some Beech-Nut chewing tobacco, a trusted home remedy, and I was good as new. But my stickball days were over.

I believe it was the lingering racism of Jim Crow – the systematic discrimination against Southern Blacks during the period following the Civil War – as well as my incorrigible behaviour that fuelled my mother's desire to migrate to California. She first planned to leave me behind and then send for me after she got settled, but I was too hyperactive for my aunts and Momma, my ageing grandmother. If you recall *The Beverly Hillbillies* and the woman called Granny, you will have a pretty good notion about Momma's stature and style of dress. A beautiful Cherokee Indian, she was five feet tall, about ninety pounds, with whitish-grey shoulder-length hair and a copper-penny skin tone. She was also a devout Baptist who had served as a deaconess for seventeen years in the New Salem Baptist Church in New Orleans. Momma spoke softly, her melodic voice often issuing quotations from the scriptures. Her religious influence was evident in each of her sixteen children – nine daughters and seven sons.

Momma's gospel sermons of fire and brimstone held my attention for hours. I enjoyed sitting on the porch with her, drinking ice-cold lemonade, listening to her preach. After-wards, I would bombard her with questions. But I could not fathom why the religious figures in drawings and paintings were all white – and most of them *glowed*. I remember trying to sneak a peek whenever I saw white men, women or children, just to see if they really did glow. They did not.

In all of the religious children's literature I was given to read, there was an obvious absence of black people. Every-body was white: angels, Jesus, Adam, Eve, Cain, Abel, Moses and Noah. Only the devil was red. I'd ask Momma: where were the black people like us? Did God only make white people? Momma always seemed to be holding back. The more I'd ask, the more she would say, "Boy, you're tiring me out with all your questions!" Though I never did get a straight answer, I still believed something was not right with all those pictures depicting white figures as divine. Decades would pass before I'd be able to uncover the answers to those questions.

I relished Momma's home-cooked meals, especially her gumbo and sweet potato pie. The gumbo consisted of crabs, shrimps, oysters, clams, crawdads, chicken, mild and hot link sausages, okra and gumbo fillet. The taste was heavenly, etched forever in my taste buds. Her sweet potato pies were better than any store pies I ever tasted.

There were rare times when Momma would fall silent – the mention of my grandfather inevitably stopped her. He was a huge, muscular, loving, pensive man who worked tirelessly on the railroad and held other jobs to support his large family. He died from exhaustion; he worked himself to death. He left behind no pictures of himself – he didn't like anyone taking them. My mother said he would fight if you tried to take his picture. Often she would tell me, "If you want to know what your grandfather looked like, just look in the mirror." Since he loved Momma as I did, there is no doubt I would have loved him too.

I guess I didn't realize how much I loved Momma until my mother and I were on the Greyhound bus waving goodbye to her and our other relatives. Fear and curiosity had me wondering what was in store for us in California. I could see the sadness in Momma's expression mirroring the tears streaming down my face.

TWO

South Central

My mother and I were silent throughout most of that long bus ride to Los Angeles in 1959. Neither of us talked much anyway. It was difficult for us to express our feelings, probably one of the reasons we weren't in tune with one another. Still, our bond was evident. My mother struggled hard to clothe, feed, and provide for me. She was a fighter who had to wade through incredible obstacles to her progress. In more ways than she cared to admit, we were alike: determined, stubborn, demanding, quick-tempered and fastidious. Besides our characteristically serious expression, each of us had a black mole on the upper left side of the nose.

I adored my mother, and I regret never voicing my feelings to her.

As she slept on the bus, a beam of sunlight shone through the window onto the smooth dark brown skin of her face, and I wondered if she was as worried as I was about our destination.

After several days the Greyhound bus finally reached the bus terminal in downtown Los Angeles, California. It was like being on another planet. People dressed differently, talked fast and moved fast, as did the cars and trucks. I saw a small crowd of men who seemed to mirror comedian Red Skelton's portrayal of hoboes. It was the first time I had ever seen a hobo close-up. This was the so-called City of Angels, where my mother hoped to find prosperity. If she had foreseen the path I would follow, no doubt we would have quickly re-boarded the bus to return to New Orleans.

After several days and nights in a motel, my mother found an affordable, furnished place to stay. It was a white duplex apartment on 43rd and Kansas on the west side, now called South Central, and was set back behind two larger duplexes. Three rickety steps led up to the front door, and immediately inside was the kitchen. To the left was a small living room where I slept on a couch that unfolded into a bed. To the right, in the middle of the living room, was a door leading into my mother's bedroom. Inside her room was a mini bathroom. The place was tiny, but it was home.

We lived in a predominantly black area of private homes, apartments and duplexes. As I grew older, I realized that it wasn't the typical urban ghetto – it had a deceptive look of prosperity. It was a west side colony of poverty behind a façade of manicured lawns and clean streets, of Cadillacs, Fords and Chevys. The neighbourhood was a shiny red apple rotting away at the core.

I was the new six-year-old on the block, soon to undergo the ritual that would determine my position in the pecking order. The scenario was no different than one between nations, corporate executives, siblings, animals, or anyone else vying for status. The first day, outside the duplex, I was presented with a fight-or-flight option. Monroe, a stocky black youth about my height, strolled up and asked my name. I was about to say "Stan" when, without warning, he rained a barrage of punches on my head. Caught off guard, I began to swing wildly in defence. Whether from a lucky punch or a slip, Monroe fell to the ground. I jumped on top of him, and spurred by fear and instinct, I whaled away at his head.

Abruptly, I was snatched up. Monroe's heavy-set mother, smelling of cheap wine and cursing as bad as any man, held me by the head with one arm, vice-like, while holding in her free hand a jug of wine that was spilling over me. Mrs Monroe marched me down the narrow walkway to the duplex and knocked on the door. My mother opened it, a puzzled look on her face. Rocking back and forth, Mrs Monroe released me and began to complain loudly about how I beat up her son for nothing.

The evidence against me seemed overwhelming: Monroe stood there with a bloodied nose, big lip and black eye. I wanted to believe that my mother would not take the word of this foul-mouthed woman when she flashed her trademark accusatory look. There was nothing I could say. As soon as they left and I entered the duplex, my mother was all over me with a leather strap, quicker than Monroe with his fists. I learned two valuable lessons that day: remain silent in the face of controversy – whether guilty or not – and be prepared to strike first.

Later, Monroe and I became friends. His family lived directly across the street. I could tell that my mother disapproved of him, though she never uttered a word, and preferred to meet him at his family's house, a poor child's Disneyland. The front yard was cluttered with junk: broken toys, tyres, hubcaps, refrigerators, television sets, car engines, radios, mattresses and bicycles. There were also dogs, huge white chickens and roosters that Monroe and I chased around the yard.

Sometimes we positioned ourselves on the top of his house, armed with a BB rifle, to shoot at the old TV picture tubes that exploded with a satisfying bang. Our mischievousness led us past other boundaries of curiosity and trouble. We had several brushes with the law for minor offences. Once, Monroe and I were accused of stealing Oreo cookies out of their small sack in a liquor store. The older of two Asian-looking men claimed to have seen one of us do it, but he didn't know which one, since we looked alike. They threw both of us in the back of the store and then left. The back door was locked but I saw a window behind some stacked boxes. As I climbed the boxes, I felt a sharp blow to my back, knocking me to the floor. I was pinned on my back by the younger Asian with the butt of an axe handle across my throat. From the corner of my eye I could see Monroe creeping away like a thief in the night, only to reappear standing between two white cops. They were beaming with exaggerated pride, as if they had captured a vicious killer. The shorter, pudgy cop joked about how he should have fired a shot, just to scare the hell out of the "little nigger". There was a chorus of laughter from the two cops and the Asians.

The younger Asian snatched me up by the collar and shoved me down on a box next to Monroe. For a moment the cops and Asians stood in a huddle, whispering. I was scared. I had heard that white cops were notorious for cracking black skulls in the neighbourhood. When the huddle broke up, the cops tried to elicit a confession from us with the good-cop, bad-cop routine. It pissed me off that two complete strangers would try to get me to snitch. My own mother, deadlier to me than any cop, was never able to get a word out of me, yet these cops thought they could. Plus every child in the neighbourhood knew that cops were the enemy.

When the good-cop routine failed, the pudgy cop tried the "bad" routine. He threatened to bust me upside the head if I didn't tell him who ate the cookies. My silence infuriated him. He pulled me forward within inches of his face. His foul breath smelled like uncooked chitterlings, bad enough to curl my eyebrows. I held my breath for so long, I thought I would pass out. The other cop snatched Monroe by the collar and held his nightstick in a threatening gesture above Monroe's head. I believe the cop would have cracked his skull wide open had Monroe not fallen to the floor and gone into convulsions.

Both cops and the Asians stood there dumfounded, their smiles gone. I was shocked to see Monroe lying on the ground with his eyes rolling back into their sockets, saliva dribbling from the corner of his mouth. Though I didn't know what to do, I dropped to my knees and placed a hand underneath his head to prevent it from banging on the floor. After rolling Monroe over onto his back, I rubbed his chest in a child's attempt to comfort him. His eyes closed and I thought he had died. I began to cry. But seconds later, Monroe regained consciousness. I struggled to help him back up onto the boxes.

Meanwhile the cops and our captors had huddled. They shook hands, then tried to save face by saying they were willing to let us go. The pudgy cop asked Monroe where we lived. Despite his seizure, Monroe answered clearly.

During the short ride home in the back of the squad car, I asked Monroe what had happened. He said he had experienced seizures since he was a baby – he was epileptic. I prayed that it would never ever happen again when I was around. As the patrol car pulled into Monroe's driveway, the pudgy cop asked, "Is this where you really live, boy?" Monroe said yes, and the cop burst out laughing at the bizarre, cluttered front yard. It was like the Munsters.

From the car I could see Mrs Monroe staggering out of the house wearing a black ruffled dress, red stockings, a long, red, feathered boa, and a red flower in her hair. She looked like a 1920s harlot. The two cops nudged one another and again broke into laughter. The pudgy one leaned his head out of the window and told Mrs Monroe his distorted version of what had happened. He ended by pointing at me, then asking her if she could "take the mute boy home." He thought I was mute because, other than shaking my head, I hadn't uttered a word. Though puzzled, she agreed to take me home. She muttered a few words of profanity and ordered her son into the house, then whirled around and gave me a hard look that clearly said I was responsible for leading her son astray.

To me, Mrs Monroe was a female Jekyll and Hyde. When sober, she was an amiable soul who liked me and didn't curse that much. But drunk, her facial expression became a scowl, her speech foul, and I became like a red cape to a bull. She actually enjoyed marching me home to tell my mother lies about my getting Monroe into trouble. As usual, I prepared myself for another Biblical beating. It was no more a deterrent for me than prison is for most criminals.

I didn't enjoy getting into trouble, I just found the streets more interesting than home. It felt liberating to be able to face the street adventures and to make my own decisions about what I should do. Though I loved my mother, I wouldn't listen to her. There were many things I kept from her to avoid punishment. There was nothing I had witnessed or experienced that I wished to reveal to my mother. Nothing!

She is not responsible for my actions. Any of them. My mother exhausted every effort to raise me properly, but she could not stand guard over me 24/7. She was in thrall to some handed-down black version of a Euro-American parenting philosophy in conflict with the environment I saw around me and its stringent requirements for survival. Not even my mother's intentions and religious guidance could have compelled or prayed me to conform to society's double standards. Her cordial instructions conflicted with "the colony's" exploitation of the underclass. I was a member of that class. (What I call the colony – commonly known as the ghetto – is a modern urban version of the plantations on which African slaves lived in America. *Colony* is a more accurate term than ghetto, i.e. a group of people who have been institutionalized in a distinctly separate area.)

As a boy, I was incapable of articulating the contradictions I saw, or of dodging confrontations with the ominous influences outside my home. Each time I stepped out into this society – rife with poverty, filth, crime, drugs, illiteracy, and daily, brutal miscarriages of justice – I inhaled its moral pollutants and so absorbed a distorted sense of self-preservation. I was duped into believing that this toxic environment was normal. I was unaware of the violence being done to my mind. Lacking any knowledge of African culture, there was a black hole in my existence.

More than 500 years of slavery had left me with only scattered remnants of a broken culture. Exposed to a multitude of ambiguous, mostly negative influences, I would pass through my young life with cultural neglect and a profound identity crisis. Though I knew I was black, I had no real perspective on being black. I absorbed common negative black stereotypes that eventually made me despise my blackness. Yet despite my envy of the privileges, wealth and comforts held by many white people, I never fantasized about being one of them. Without the cultural knowledge I needed to shape my identity, I was unable to give my mother the respect she deserved. Since I respected neither my mother nor myself, it was inevitable that I would grow up, as I did, to disrespect other black people.

I blindly moulded an identity that was a classic product of corrupt influences and my own vivid imagination. Though I was no angel, neither was I a child demon. Life deprived me of the blood of freedom and an equal opportunity to succeed. I was guilty by reason of colour, convicted and sentenced at birth.

Like most of my peers, I stumbled through life "dys-educated," a very different quality than being merely *uneducated*. My options and opportunities were restricted. For me there were no Rotary Clubs, Yacht Clubs, Explorer Clubs, Boy's Academies, or any other privilege-bound associations. I was afforded equal opportunities on society's underbelly among street thugs, ex-cons, pimps, gamblers, con men, thieves, prostitutes and hustlers. Here, the prevailing motifs were violence and the daily battle to survive. Might was right, always.

Seen through my adolescent eyes, everyone was at war: fathers battled their wives, neighbours were at each other's throats, criminals fought criminals. Sometimes at night I would see birds of fire soaring through the sky or crashing into a fence; I learned that gamblers were setting homing pigeons ablaze and then releasing them, wagering on which one would come closest to its destination. And we kids would imitate them. This was our culture: casually brutal, unspeakably cruel.

The most popular bloodsport for money was dog fighting. Men would show up with different breeds – pit bulls, Great Danes, bull terriers, Labrador Retrievers, Chow Chows, Dobermann pinschers, Saint Bernards, bulldogs, German shepherds, huskies, bull mastiffs, and many others – in the hope of winning a cash pot. The gamblers would pay us a couple of dollars to water, feed, or patch up a mauled dog. In most fights a dog would lose an eye, tail, nose, ear, a plug of skin or part of a jaw. At first the sight of the blood, gore and loss of body parts was sickening, and I felt pity for the injured dogs. But I became hardened to the gruesome scenes. Whenever a particular dog was beyond patching up or was no longer wanted, one of the men would pull out his pistol and shoot it, or simply beat it to death with a baseball bat. Since most of the dogfights took place in abandoned houses, garages, or in pits dug out in vacant lots, the dogs were buried there, or discarded somewhere in the neighbourhood.

These hustlers would bet on anything – even who could spit, urinate or throw a rock the farthest. I witnessed cockfights, cricket fights, fish fights, and pay-per-view street fights among individuals between six and fifty years of age. Older hustlers would bet on children to fight. To earn money I would put on smelly, ragged boxing gloves and swing wildly until the other boy fell to the ground, and even then I wouldn't let him up. Some of the hustlers who wanted me to win would give me pointers on how to cheat. They would advise me to hit an opponent of equal height and weight while he was taking off his jacket, tying his shoe, putting on the boxing gloves, or when he wasn't looking. Win, lose or draw, everybody received chump change – a small amount of money. Though I won my fights, I didn't always come away unscathed.

Often my mother would catch me trying to sneak into the house with a black eye, cut lip, swollen jaw, or blood on my shirt. To her, fighting was a cardinal sin and whether I had initiated it or not, I was due a Biblical beating. But for me, fighting was part of growing up in South Central. My mother, bless her soul, didn't have a clue what was happening to me, nor to what I was being exposed.

THREE

Sibling Feud

I had no idea a storm was brewing, one that would turn into a raging rivalry – with a sibling I didn't know I had. But in 1963 my mother told me Momma would be arriving... accompanied by my new sister, Cynthia! What sister? I couldn't remember my mother ever being pregnant. How could I have a sister? Then again, no one ever explained to me the fundamentals of childbirth, so I probably thought that my mother's pregnancy was her normal shape.

Seeing Cynthia for the first time was traumatic for me. I racked my brain to figure out what was going on. Yes, Cynthia was supposed to be my sister, but were we truly related? She resembled no one I knew – not my mother, Momma, aunties, uncles, or me. Cynthia was a dainty and extremely light-skinned girl with shoulder-length hair and a vulnerable shyness. But the moment we acknowledged one another's presence, it was pure hatred. I would come to call her "cow," which earned me plenty of Biblical beatings.

During the few days Momma stayed with us, she cooked some of her famous sweet potato pies and delectable gumbo. Her cornbread melted like butter in my mouth, and her fried chicken, catfish, potato salad, collard greens and sweet corn were good enough to eat for breakfast. The presence of Momma had a tranquillizing effect on me. I tried to convince her to stay longer, but she had to get back to New Orleans.

When it was time for her to leave, we hugged and she whispered in my ear, "Tookie, be nice, you hear? Be nice." That was the first inkling I had that she knew of my antipathy to my sister.

It didn't take long for my mother and Cynthia to bond like two peas in a pod. My mother's preferential treatment of Cynthia allowed my sister to manipulate the situation to her advantage. It was obvious from jump street that our sister-brother relationship had deteriorated before it got started. We went blow for blow, pain for pain, curse for curse. We even emphasized personal ownership by saying, "*My* mother said for you to . . .", etc. We acted like our mother belonged to only one of us, never both.

The battle lines were drawn, but the struggle for my mother's attention was a lost cause for me. I fought for the sake of fighting, out of spite, and many of my beatings were due to my attempts to keep Cynthia out of my space and from getting on my nerves.

One day I was sitting on the couch trying to heal after a beating for going outside when I wasn't supposed to. I could see Cynthia in the single bedroom she shared with our mother, giggling, jumping around, and pointing at me. Angered, I wanted to throw something at her that wouldn't break. I reached underneath the couch pillow to retrieve my hidden yellow dart. I focused, aimed and threw the dart with the accuracy of a sharpshooter. Before Cynthia could duck, I hit her right between the eyes. She screamed so loud that I knew there would be hell to pay. But that beating wasn't too bad, knowing Cynthia was in pain, too.

Cynthia had everybody but me fooled with her sweet little girl act. The nursery rhyme about girls being "sugar and spice and everything nice" was not applicable to her. She was a crafty instigator, fabricator and manipulator. Whatever she said I had done, my mother believed. She saw me, compared to Cynthia, as aggressive, vindictive and devious.

As a black male in a ghetto microcosm, I had to be either prey or predator. It didn't require deep reflection to determine which of the two I preferred. I was the predator and Cynthia was my prey. I was a quick study and Cynthia didn't stand a chance. She was more devious at buttering up our mother and causing trouble for me, but to avoid corporal punishment I learned to finesse and out-fox her.

At home Cynthia held a superior position; she was our mother's third eye and ear. She would spy on me like the CIA and report back when our mother returned home from work. On rare occasions Cynthia could be bribed with nickels to keep her mouth shut. I led her to believe that a nickel was worth more than a dime because it was bigger. I used to charm her with magic tricks, making black cough drops appear out of my ear, or with the matchbox trick, where a coin disappears into the matchbox. She enjoyed eating the cough drops, which helped to silence her. I guess magic appealed to Cynthia. She also believed in the tooth fairy, Santa Claus and the Easter Bunny.

We never had any affectionate sibling moments. Perhaps neither of us had any to give. We were as unlike as night and day. Our differences were sealed forever when I saw her naked the first time. I did not yet know the biological distinctions between males and females and I was shocked to learn that Cynthia did not possess the male organ. I was tempted to question my mother about this, but such discussions were taboo. I just chalked it up as more of Cynthia's weirdness.

I noticed that sibling rivalries in the households of friends were tame in comparison. Yet though I hated Cynthia, I discovered that there was a limit to my malice. On the other side of our fence were a construction site and a huge dirt lot with deep trenches, a place where neighbourhood children often played. On any given day, children would have rock fights, play marbles, wrestle, or play war games with BB guns or wooden swords. Here and there lay piles of lumber, pipes, wires, nails, large buckets and heavy machinery. Some of the trenches were too wide to cross and over one I constructed a makeshift bridge out of several long wooden planks. I booby-trapped this bridge to collapse, so a person could fall into the six foot deep trench. Below I placed heavy planks with long, thick, spiked nails pointed upward. This bridge of doom was a payback for **anyone** I despised.

Along came Cynthia. One day I spotted her skipping her merry way through the lot. Like a trap-door spider, I was hidden behind a high mound of dirt. The moment she stepped onto the boards, I was ready to snatch the rope and send her tumbling onto the bed of nails. Cynthia was halfway across, and I was about to yank the rope – but something stopped me. It was neither fear nor concern about a beating that stopped me. I just couldn't do it to her. Perhaps it was a moment of conscience – though later in my young life I would readily snatch that same rope to harm would-be enemies. But as much as I despised Cynthia, the booby trap was something I could not execute. Yet our feud continued well into our teenage years.

FOUR

Hallelujah! Hallelujah!

Long before I enrolled in school, I was familiar with the holy
ambience of the Baptist church. It was a place where broken
souls were mended, sins forgiven, troubled minds calmed
and incorrigible children corrected. My mother may have
thought I was a little anti-Christ; certainly she recognized
my shortcomings and tried everything to correct them. But
nothing worked. I would sit in an old wooden church pew,
most of the time unreceptive and steaming with anger at
being made to be there.

Occasionally, though, this house of worship was a place
of wonder and excitement. I was mesmerized by the melodic
voices of the choir and the rhythmic beat of the piano. When
people were enraptured by the music, they would rock, clap
and stomp their feet, scream, holler, or jump up and do a
holy dance. The sweltering atmosphere was so charged with
spiritual ecstasy that the ushers were kept busy trying to
revive fainting women. There were no air conditioners, so
people sweated like melting ice cream. Most of them held
paper fans with pictures of a white Jesus, and pumped their
fans like pistons to generate cool air. Many of the women
who fainted or were inspired to *glossolalia* – speaking in
tongues – sat next to us. Once a woman lightly patted my
arm, said, "The Lord is with you," and then jumped up and
down speaking in tongues. I was scared to death! I thought
the woman was going crazy. I turned to my mother for

support, but she was chanting, "Hallelujah! Hallelujah! Hallelujah!" I sat rigid as a statue, hoping the woman wouldn't go off on me. It was always women who seemed to be spiritually touched by God. I prayed, crossed my fingers and toes, and hoped that neither my mother nor Cynthia would faint or speak in tongues. I would have run out of church in a flash.

The church barbecues, Easter egg hunts and Christmas candies given to us made it worth my showing up. At the barbecue, everyone took a paper plate overflowing with barbecued ribs, chicken, hot links, potato salad, and corn on the cob. These were the moments I really enjoyed; all other activities were adult in nature and too serious. I wondered why I sat watching a preacher point his sanctimonious finger at everybody while spitting out his fiery sermon, looking down on his parishioners from his pulpit high above the congregation.

We visited a different church for my baptism. I had to wear an ankle-length white gown, underwear, no shoes, and stand in a long line with other children and adults. "Why am I here?" I asked. My mother's menacing look and a lightning-quick backhand shut me up.

Inside this gigantic church was a well-lit square structure for baptizing that seemed to me to be a large glass swimming pool with steps on both sides. Thus, the audience had a clear view of the baptism. In the pool were a preacher and several ushers, all dressed in white gowns, waiting for people to walk down single file into the pool. I watched as each person, one by one, was held under water for a few seconds by two ushers. The preacher would mumble a few words, and then the person was raised out of the water, beaming. When I stepped down into the ice-cold pool, it came up to my chest. I stood there, frozen. The ushers had to guide me to the preacher. He recited a prayer then the ushers dunked me backward so quickly that I must have swallowed three pints of chlorinated water. I didn't even get a chance to hold my breath. I struggled desperately to free myself, but the ushers kept me under. I was waving my arms and kicking my legs like a drowning victim. When they let me up, I emerged gasping for air, choking, coughing and spitting up water. Then and there I swore that my mother would have to straight-out kill me before I let someone baptize me again.

It wasn't all bad, travelling with my mother from church to church, singing gospel songs. In our family all three of us had the ability to sing with fine-tuned, high-pitched voices. People enjoyed hearing me or my mother sing a solo. When I sang "How Great Thou Art," the elderly folks clapped and shouted, "Amen!" or, "Hallelujah!" Mostly, I enjoyed singing because I believed it made my mother proud of me. I overheard her telling someone that I possessed a beautiful, angelic voice. There was always debate about whether my vocal range was first or second soprano. It didn't matter because my mother loved it, and I enjoyed singing more than sitting around in the pew listening to the preacher.

It was in church that I first became interested in girls, after a couple of them showed an interest in my singing. Valerie and Shelia lived a few houses down from our house. Sometimes I would sit with them on their porch, crooning out a couple of songs, gospel or soul, that earned kisses afterward. Soon the word was out that I could sing, and other girls on the block began admiring my voice. It didn't go down too well with the envious young men on the block, but the abundance of kisses made me feel tingly and warm all over.

Away from the adults, I managed to do a lot of kissing at church. I was surprised to learn that some of these girls knew hiding places where we could kiss and explore each other's bodies. In church I was always getting into something. Though I'm not proud of it, I would show up at church, stay for the offering, duck out, and then return before the service ended. When the usher passed around the offering basket, I'd drop a few coins into it and palm two or three dollars, sometimes with Cynthia or our mother sitting beside me. As a child of poverty I justified my theft as a need far greater than the other people in church. I knew the difference between the haves and have-nots. The preacher, his family and cohorts were living high on the hog. They had fine homes, fancy clothes and jewelry, and the preacher sported a new Cadillac each year. Our family was broke, no car, no bicycle, no TV, and limited clothing. I figured the few dollars I pocketed wouldn't be missed. Hamburgers cost twenty five cents, French fries twenty cents, sodas fifteen cents, and candy bars were five or ten cents. Each Sunday that I attended church, my stomach stayed full.

Clearly, my baptism was no more effective than being dunked in a local swimming pool by some homeboys, but my mother refused to give up on saving me. One sunny morning we rode a bus to a religious revival at, I believe, the Shrine Auditorium. The building was spacious, huge, with numerous seats and a balcony. There were hundreds, perhaps thousands of people from different ethnic backgrounds packed inside the auditorium. We managed to find seats in the upper balcony. Everybody was there to see Kathryn Kuhlman, a female preacher and revivalist heralded as a miracle worker. She was rumoured to heal the sick, restore troubled lives, and perform other miracles. Her mantra, "I believe in miracles," was well known.

I dozed off and missed most of the service only to be abruptly woken. My mother stared at me. "Tookie," she said, "go down to the stage and get some help." I did a double-take as if she had lost her mind – but begrudgingly got up and headed down toward the packed stage.

The line was long. Standing under the bright lights, Kathryn looked pale white and quite frail. There seemed nothing extraordinary about her, but when she touched a man, woman or child on the forehead, that person appeared to faint and fall backward into the arms of waiting ushers. I could feel my mother's eyes penetrating the back of my skull. Failure here was not an option. I could only hope that whatever happened to those people would happen to me.

My necktie felt like a hangman's noose. I was sweating. When Kathryn placed her hands on my forehead, I felt absolutely nothing. Zilch. I was tempted to fake a fainting spell, knowing my mother was eyeing me like a hawk.

Kathryn removed her hand and mouthed the words, "Bless you, child." Nervously I searched her eyes for some plausible explanation to take back to my mother. But Kathryn had nothing more to say. There would be no miracles for me. Walking back to the balcony was like a death march. When I reached my mother and Cynthia, they were ready to leave. I could see my mother's disappointment, shame and God knows what else.

FIVE

The Art of Dys-Education

The time had come for me to enter a place of higher learning. But South Central's educational system was cloning and graduating students who could barely read, write or reason. It really didn't matter which elementary school I was enrolled in, because I was destined to be dys-educated. (I've coined the term "dys-education" to depict the abnormal, impaired, and diseased knowledge I received in life and from the public school system.) The first school my mother enrolled me in was Menlo Avenue Elementary, several blocks from where I lived. I braved the surroundings with a great deal of curiosity and eagerness to learn. My willingness to learn was somewhat hampered by Miss Atkins, the teacher assigned to the classroom. She and I would bump heads while I was there.

Miss Atkins was a rosy-cheeked, short, stout Caucasian woman, with her hair fashioned in a bun on the back of her head. She wore horn-rimmed glasses with a shiny silver chain hanging slightly in front, circling her head. She felt it was her duty to punish any child in the classroom. The most popular method of punishment at that time was called "ferule discipline" – a wooden ruler was used to repeatedly beat the inside palms of a child's hand. The child was told to stand before the entire class with hands held palms up and endure the pain without moving. If the child moved, the beating would start over. Just about every day I witnessed children squirming in pain as tears rolled down their cheeks. Just watching the ruler whacking a classmate's palm made me wince. Though I cannot remember a boy or girl crying out, not one of them refused to accept the punishment. When it was time to be punished, each one walked mechanic- ally to the front of the class and assumed the position.

It was inevitable I'd be called to stand before the class to be ferule-disciplined. One day a classmate asked if he could borrow some paper, and I said yes. Miss Atkins saw me passing the paper and assumed I was playing around. Her voice resonated like a megaphone when she yelled, "Stanley Williams, report to the front of the class." Now a Biblical beating from my mother was one thing, but a school beating I refused to accept; I would run if I had to. The room fell silent. I could hear my classmates breathing. I refused with a single, firm "No." Someone in the classroom gasped so loud I had to look around. Miss Atkins's face turned beet-red. Behind her desk, she used an even more authoritative tone.

"Stan, I want you up here in front of this class right now!"

Again I refused. My refusal was a stinging blow to her frail ego; I had defied her system of discipline. Visibly shaking, she pointed a stubby finger and ordered me to report to the Principal's office. I got up slowly and swaggered to the office. The Principal, a tall, slender man, was pleasant enough, but his lecture was about one hour long. I sat there listening without saying a word. He decided not to call my mother and told me to return to class.

After that clash with Miss Atkins, my classmates seemed to warm up to me. I began to make friends and was no longer just a new arrival. I was the hero who had challenged the dragon lady. From that day forward, she never attempted to discipline me, but we did butt heads over other issues. In her class, reading and writing seemed to be prohibited, but we were provided with mounds of clay, *papier mache*, puzzles and all kinds of non-educational items. Pencils and erasers were nowhere to be found. There were shelves of books that the students did not read; they seemed to be there just to decorate the classroom. I got on Miss Atkins's nerves, bothering her each day about letting me read a book. The more she refused, the more determined I was to read the literature on those shelves.

I was a darn good reader for my age. At home there was a box filled with books. Sometimes I would dump them on the floor and sit in the middle of the pile trying to read everything. Often my mother would help me with spelling and pronunciation. One of my favourites was an encyclopedia on dogs, with numerous colour photos. I could read for hours about different breeds. Reading was a way of escaping from my often-riotous thoughts. In my reading world, there was no poverty, no discrimination, no violence, no racism, no pain – and no Cynthia.

I started pilfering off the school library shelf to avoid being busted by Miss Atkins. My partner in crime was Shelia, a chubby black girl with a short, curly "natural", large brown eyes, dimples, and a contagious smile. Together, we pretended to be working on a project while taking turns reading from a book held in our laps. The first time Miss Atkins caught us reading, she thought there must be some hanky-panky going on. She made us stand and two books fell off our laps onto the floor. Miss Atkins had a fit, storming out of the classroom, shouting, "I'm calling your mother! I'm calling your mother!" This phone-your-mother scenario was played out with me twice a day, three or four times a week.

If Miss Atkins had her way, I'd have been handcuffed by police and escorted to jail. Perhaps because she sensed my potential, she was driven to hinder or obliterate my own intentions. To all who would listen to her outbursts, Miss Atkins would paint a false portrait of me, assassinating my character, behaviour, mental state and ability to learn. Perplexed, I watched in horror as she performed a masterful act of fake humility and concern for me in the presence of my mother. To parents, she was the epitome of what all teachers should be. But I had her number. I knew she was wicked.

All I wanted to do was become educated, not battle with a deranged teacher over my constitutional right to read schoolbooks. The odds were stacked against me. Miss Atkins's authority made her my nemesis. She had the Principal, teachers, parents, my mother, and even the janitor in her corner. Who would believe me? Whom could I talk to? The more my mother came up to the school to chastise me, the more it strengthened Miss Atkins's assertion that I was a very disruptive child.

Whether Miss Atkins busted me, Shelia, or other classmates who joined us in a clandestine study programme, she would call only *my* mother. For every minute my mother spent away from work addressing this, money was deducted from her paycheck. Perhaps the teacher was aware of that. Certainly, Miss Atkins viewed me as just another little darkie whom she openly predicted would fail in life. In her warnings to other students about examples of bad behaviour, she pointed a finger at me: "Look at Stanley – he is not what you want to be!" If ever a teacher needed psychological testing to be allowed to teach children, she was a prime candidate.

It was a surprise several months later when Miss Atkins implemented a reading and writing period in her class, but we were still largely on our own. As usual she sat behind her desk crocheting, head tilted down, looking over her glasses at us – mostly at me. She seemed to enjoy humming the hymn that goes, "…shall we gather at the river, the beautiful, the beautiful river…" It was odd that such an oppressive person would enjoying singing a church song. Fortunately, before she was able to have me expelled, I was transferred to another school. Although there were no farewells, I knew I would miss Shelia.

Now I was able to breathe fresh air. Cynthia and I were enrolled in Normandie Avenue Elementary School and the adjacent Day Care Center. Each school day after kissing our mother on the cheek, we headed toward the Day Care Center where Cynthia and I stayed before school and after until 4:00 p.m. The breakfasts and lunches tasted much better than the school's cafeteria food. All in all, the Day Care was a nice, clean place to be, with a lot of activities for children. Two memorable figures who worked there were Mrs Blue and Miss Davis. Both of these black women were exceptionally kind to all the children. It was Miss Davis who comforted me when I had run-ins with the door and with the monkey bars. She accompanied me to a nearby clinic, where I was patched up.

Miss Davis was in her early twenties, tall, slender, cinnamon-coloured, with a curly, brownish-gold Afro. She would drive up in a small black convertible sports car, usually wearing a brightly coloured tennis kit and a tennis bag over her shoulder. Her tennis dress was skimpier than a miniskirt, but I wasn't complaining. Watching her practise hitting balls off the wall raised my interest in female anatomy to a new level. Whether retrieving balls or sitting on a milk crate, I admired her sleek movement as her skirt hiked up to unbelievable heights. She had a preachy saying: "We sisters are black queens, and we have to keep our bodies firm and beautiful." Amen to that!

Mrs Blue was twice her age. She was short, with smooth brown skin and bluish, permed hair. She was sweet as pie and loved reading stories to us. When I did get into trouble, she tried to save me from expulsion. Mrs Blue would rather control me than threaten punishment. Her religious quotes and sermons were similar to my grandmother's and she always found something good to say about me. I once sat between her and my mother as Mrs Blue bragged about how smart I was. Her words were like droplets of honey poured down my throat. Encouragement was something I didn't receive enough of.

In school I maintained between a B+ and an A average. My ability to read, write and retain knowledge was evident with each passing year, and at first my efforts and behaviour were A-plus. I occasionally got into scrimmages, but what black man-child didn't rumble and tumble as a youngster? It was rare for me to fight a girl, but one named Janice was no ordinary female. I was about four feet six, and Janice was about six feet tall, broad at the shoulders, with a hairstyle like Buckwheat on *The Little Rascals* and a mean expression.

I was told she liked me, but she had a strange way of showing it. In class, she would throw books at me when I wasn't looking, or place a thumbtack on my chair. One day I placed several tacks on her chair and when she sat down she jumped up screaming like a banshee. She scanned the entire class and screamed, "Who did that?" The frightened classroom didn't have to say my name; I was busted the moment they all turned to look at me. That's when Janice threatened to beat me up after school. She wasn't fooling around; I had seen her beat a guy to a bloody pulp in the school bathroom. Janice could fight like a dude. She was tough, probably too tough for me to handle.

She stared at me from several rows away, pounding her fist in the palm of her hand. Then she drew her finger slowly across her throat. The general rule in our culture was never to strike a female under any circumstances. But Janice was no ordinary girl; she could fight. At that moment she frightened me so much that my mouth became dry and my heart jumped up in my throat. To further intimidate me, Janice started acting as if she was about to rush over and attack. Since I wasn't packing my trusty butter knife or a set of brass knuckles, I was a nervous mess.

Finally, the wall clock showed 2:45 p.m. School was about to end, and Janice had dozed off. It was now or never. I eased out of my chair and circled around behind her. Unmanly or not, I was on Janice like a wild man, knocking her and the chair to the floor. Fearful she would get back up, I was about to crown her with a chair when the teacher caught hold of it in mid-air.

To the amazement of the class (and me as well), Janice stayed on the floor, crying. For the first time I saw her as a girl, not as a bully or a beast. She was human after all. Though remorseful, I knew the fight was far from over. Janice had two brothers at the school – Vincent and the older Arthur. I later learned they agreed that Vincent, being bigger and taller, would restore their sister's honour. He bragged to classmates about what he was going to do.

It was on the Day Care's playground that I ran into Vincent and his stocky friend Frank. He gestured for me to come over, meaning only one thing: a fight. I was taking a risk because no one was around to intercede if they both attacked me or if I was on the losing end. As I approached, Vincent started taking off his sweater. When his face was completely covered, his arms held high in the air underneath the sweater, I attacked. Frank stepped aside like a matador avoiding a charging bull and I threw haymakers that drove Vincent up against the fence, until out of nowhere Miss Davis appeared and held me in a bear hug from behind. Vincent pulled down his sweater, picked up his glasses, and walked away, trailed by Frank. Miss Davis and I went inside, where she wiped my face with a wet towel. She asked why I was fighting such a big boy. I told her we were playing around. She smiled and said, "Maybe you were playing, but he sure wasn't."

In street fights, fairness was a moronic abstraction; it could get you killed. I learned from others to fight dirty, to cheat, and to look for angles, openings, mistakes. The prime rule of fighting was, there were no rules – anything went. In time I found ways to cut an opponent down to size, and if I lost, he'd better be prepared to fight me daily. Either that or suffer a nasty surprise.

Most opponents weren't willing to go the extra mile. To them it wasn't worth it, but to me it was. Fighting became my *modus operandi* for payback. Had I been aware of another reasonable and face-saving choice, I would have preferred not to engage in fisticuffs. Only a damn fool would do otherwise. For me fighting wasn't done for fun; it was a survival necessity. Yet I wasn't a born fighter; I had to become one. Even if you tease a peaceful elephant, eventually it will charge at you. A man of ill repute once told me, "Little brother, sometimes a challenge to fight must be met. You don't have to be good at it, just know what, how, where and when to do it, and the rest will take care of itself." It was a thug's maxim and it gave me an edge.

The strangest things can happen sometimes after a fight –
like the friendship that developed between Big Frank, Vincent
and me. Frank and I grew to be best friends. He lived with
his father, mother, and sister Judy, just two blocks away
from me. I noticed a sibling rivalry, but it was tame compared
to mine with Cynthia. Despite Frank's size and tough
appearance, he had a mild temperament. I never saw him in
a fight or an argument, in school or out. His height,
stockiness, bubble eyes and stern look probably intimidated
others, while I was as non-threatening as a butterfly. Most
everybody looked taller and bigger, so I was a sitting duck
for any bully looking for easy prey. Although I didn't act,
look, or talk like Erkel, the nerdy character on TV's *Family
Matters*, I could have been mistaken for that type of person
because I was small and mostly silent. But I was no pushover.

Through my acquaintance with Frank, I was briefly
introduced to the Cub Scouts, and then later the Boy Scouts.
I didn't have the money for my membership dues, scout
equipment, field trips, and other expenses – in fact, my
mother didn't have a dime to spare. But I had hoped to
explore scouting. Who can argue that a change in my
surroundings and activities might have altered my life? I was
envious of Frank and other children whose parents were
able to afford the Scouts and similar opportunities. I felt
deprived and sullen, but I drew confidence from my ability
to rebound from childhood disappointments.

When not at Frank's house, I was out hustling with
James, who lived with his mother around the corner from
42nd Street. James was a short, light-skinned brother with
freckles and a giant reddish-brown Afro. I met him during a
serious rock fight in a vacant lot that was filled with tall
mounds of dirt, trenches and tunnels where Monroe and I
had challenged everybody. Though James and his posse
outnumbered us six to one, we held our own and didn't get
hurt. Perhaps the combination of our giant homemade
slingshots and chunking rocks gave us an edge.

I would bump into James here and there, so we ended up
hanging out a lot. We shared one anti-social activity: stealing.

James was as slick as they come and knew the ins and outs of many local businesses. On weekends we would sneak on a bus to downtown Los Angeles with its smorgasbord of department stores, movie theatres, jewelry shops, and other places of business. James opened up a new world to me.

Together we roamed downtown LA, bootlegging clothing, food, jewelry and shoes. My mother's wrath became a distant memory the moment I replaced the black brogan shoes she always bought me with my first pair of Biscuits (a Stacy Adams-style shoe often called Southern Comforts). When we weren't stealing, we put our handmade wooden shoeshine boxes to work. As a street bootblack, spit-shines ranged from fifty cents to a dollar, with hopefully a tip to come. We earned a slow, slow $10 to $15 a day. Eventually a tall youngster named Michael moved to the neighbourhood and joined our crew and we became the Three Muscathieves.

Thugs and hustlers used to chant, "All money is good money" – but there are exceptions to any rule. One afternoon I was shining shoes downtown when a substitute teacher from school, Mr Eli, showed up wanting a shine. Lined up side by side, our shoeshine rags were popping in rhythm like an orchestra of Rice Krispies: "Snap, crackle, pop." Mr Eli was a substitute teacher who resembled the white guy with the thick moustache in the pop group Village People. He offered to pay us to shine a closet full of shoes at his house, if we were willing.

Mr Eli drove us to his home near a Santa Monica beach. He turned off an alarm and led us through a festival of flowers, to the back of his house. Mr Eli placed a gunnysack full of old, dusty shoes on a chair and then left. We were shining shoes for about fifteen minutes. He returned wearing a gold silk kimono. He dumped several coin bags of quarters and silver dollars on the floor in a pile, then suggested we play a card game I had never heard of called "strip poker". Although he explained the rules, I had *no* intention of taking off any clothing. Mr Eli managed to lose the first hand – and disrobed until he was completely naked! The hairs stood up on my neck and arms, and my eyes became big as silver dollars. What in the world was going on?

With each trip Mr Eli made to retrieve another bag of coins, we stuffed our pockets with as many coins as possible. He knew we were stealing the money, of course. When all the coins had disappeared into our pockets, he stretched out on a nearby bed and said he'd give us $20 to massage his back. His back was so hairy he could have been part bear. It was a nasty sight, but we agreed. As Mr Eli lay on his front, we each grabbed an item to substitute for our hands. I picked up a fly swatter, James a feather duster, and Michael had a fireplace poker.

Irritated, Mr Eli threatened not to pay us the $20 if we didn't massage him with at least one hand. When he saw us putting socks on our hands, he said, "Forget it. You guys don't want to make any real money." During the ride home, he tried to convince one of us to meet with him the next day to earn $100 – but he had no takers. I had him drop me off several blocks from home, and James and Michael bailed out too. I knew nothing about paedophiles at that time, but as I walked home, I knew I had shined my last pair of shoes.

Back at school my skills were growing, thanks to Miss Johnson, my sixth grade teacher. She was a master motivator. I'm reminded of how she looked each time I read *Ebony* magazine. Often it carried a photo of a black woman to whom a literary contest was dedicated, Gertrude Johnson Williams. The resemblance to our Miss Johnson was uncanny. Our teacher was a husky black woman who seemed always to wear black clothing. She sported black-rimmed eyeglasses and her shoulder-length hair was curled underneath, all the way around. She had an imposing presence with a commanding voice, but exuded a maternal sensitivity that made the entire class feel special. Miss Johnson devoted ample time to each student and had no problem repeating herself until a message was driven home.

Her classroom had no black curriculum, but when we were alone she talked about black greatness and the need for me to carry the torch. By then I needed more than Miss

Johnson's occasional chats. My cultural awareness was zero. I needed a complete black history course and a thorough deprogramming. I had been duped into believing that all black people were inhuman and inferior, that we had made no contribution to the forward thrust of civilization. Negative black stereotypes were broadcast or implied by the news media, magazines, institutions, television, newspapers, books, and every other medium you can think of, not to mention the countless deluded blacks I met who believed the myth of their inferiority. Their contempt for their own blackness was so ingrained they had subconsciously stepped outside themselves to assimilate with any cultural group but their own. Their dys-education was complete. The more I was indoctrinated with lies about my blackness, the more I grew to detest myself.

Miss Johnson did try but was unable to provide enough information to help me reassemble my mutilated outlook on life. She was restricted to the school's curriculum and forbidden any extramural teachings, in particular black history. She deserves credit for recognizing my potential and for trying to reveal it to me. Little did I know how much I would miss Miss Johnson's style of teaching. However, I sensed that when I did enter junior high, it would be a turning point in my life – with a downward trajectory.

During the summer after my elementary school graduation in 1966, I underwent a radical circumcision. I was twelve, and the procedure was a shock. The discomfort was inexpressible, and when aroused the pain was ten times worse than having one's member caught in a zipper. I couldn't help but wonder: why me? What did I do to deserve this? I knew nothing of traditions or rituals. The agony persisted throughout the entire summer vacation. I was a model son during this period of hell. Nothing compared to the pain, not even when my mother, Cynthia and I were struck by a car on the way to a movie theatre. The impact knocked my mother back onto the kerb, and I was left halfway on the curb and in the street. Cynthia landed underneath the drunk driver's car. Though my entire body was in pain, it did not compare to the soreness of circumcision. I viewed it as a form of punishment. It left a scar I drew strength from.

When the time came to enrol in Forshay Junior High, the pain had passed. At Forshay I went through the motions of showing up and performing each school task without understanding its purpose. I never harboured dreams of becoming a president, astronaut, banker, millionaire, doctor, fireman or lawyer. Such reveries were as absurd to me as Santa Claus. I was conditioned to anticipate a living hell. My future involved no fortunes, no dreams, no miracles, no hope and no peace.

Many of the teachers I faced at Forshay were really professional babysitters, there only to monitor behaviour and discipline or simply expel students from school. The first day I was singled out as someone who needed watching. Probably, my school files said I was incorrigible. Being under the school's microscope I believed I was expected to behave outrageously – perhaps standing on top of the desk, fighting in class, throwing books, or arguing with the teacher for no apparent reason. Perhaps they thought that at any moment I would jump up and start screaming like a mad child. Well, it never happened. Had I truly been unstable, a teacher probably could have pushed me over the edge. The teachers stood for authority and discipline. They were the school police.

There was no compulsion on my part to make friends in school. The few youths I befriended were usually the so-called miscreants: the aggressors, the loners, the defiant ones. All of us preferred being around one another, with no desire to make new friends. There was nothing antisocial about me, but I was selective in my social choices. I couldn't be a friend to everybody, nor was everybody willing or interested in being a friend to me.

I might have fared better in school if my hustling buddy James had not transferred to Forshay, but it is unlikely. Though ditching never entered my mind, I did try to avoid school by pretending to be sick. But any time Cynthia or I became sick, our mother would break out a steaming hot batch of castor oil with squeezed lemon juice and a dash of salt. She used castor oil or cod liver oil for just about every ailment and stood guard to make sure we swallowed every drop. The smell was so vile it made me want to puke. When forced to choose between school or castor oil, I chose school.

In truth, I really wasn't interested in going to Forshay. I felt that the teachers were insipid, and school was a bore. It was assumed I was a slow student, stupid, or had special needs. I received an "F" in all my subjects because I didn't do the work. In fact the school assignments weren't even a challenge, and when I did display my intelligence, I was accused of cheating. So for me, the eventual decision to ditch school wasn't difficult.

James and I would meet up at Forshay to catch a bus downtown to use our "poor-boy" routine, better known as panhandling. A sob story about having lost our bus fare to get back to school worked well. We'd end up splitting about ten dollars in a couple of hours. Then we'd buy junk food for lunch and sneak into one of the cheap movie theatres until school let out. Downtown Los Angeles became our institution of higher learning; its curricula of thievery, deceit and robbery promised a diploma in criminality. The even darker side consisted of the weirdos, psychos, sickos and other random twisted strangers we were exposed to. We braved these treacherous elements for mere pocket change. But to me, being downtown – or anywhere other than school – was worth the risk of getting caught or hurt.

At least once or twice a week, I stayed in school a full day for the sake of appearances. My attendance record was terrible, and my mother was always the last to know. The school Principal finally told her that I had been ditching for months. I know she felt like back-handing me right out of the chair, but when she turned to face me I was a good six feet away. I promised the Principal that I'd never ditch again but I knew the promise would be broken the following day.

During the bus ride home, I dreaded the inevitable punishment with a leather strap or electrical extension cord that left welts the size of a thick, braided rope. In silence I watched as my mother began talking to herself. She shook her head and asked, "Lord, what is wrong with this boy? Tell me what to do and I'll do it." Seconds later: POW! That swift backhand upside my head must have been God's response. Staring angrily out of the school bus window, I was convinced I could do better hustling in the streets than going to school.

This was the final straw for my mother. She decided to call in the big guns for help.

SIX

Voodoo Medicine

As a child I was content with my looks. I had no inner conflicts. I had never seen, heard, nor talked to an imaginary friend, dead relative, ghost, devil, angel or God. For me, there were no bogeymen or monsters beneath the bed, in the closet, or lurking in dark corners. I had no fear of the dark, needed no nightlight, teddy bear or security blanket for comfort. In spite of the cruelties I had witnessed as a child, the dogfights and burning pigeons, I had an affinity for animals. I was a normal child in an abnormal environment.

Although I was a quiet youngster who enjoyed playing with other children, I was also selective about who I would befriend. My silence and disruptive behaviour were only a show of independence. The lines of communication between my mother and me severed the moment I tried to step into the male position vacated by my father. I believed I was grown, making it impossible for any male to substitute as a father figure.

Though my mother was the parent, I established early that no amount of Biblical beatings could stop me doing what I wanted. I was willing to suffer the consequences. Through our lack of communication, my mother believed something was wrong with me mentally. I was then treated as being handicapped, impaired, or simply no good. She did not expect me to live past my late teens. But she insisted that

I receive some kind of outside help and found a psychiatrist
to treat me.

My mother had my best interests at heart, but it was a
mistake to seek help from a shrink, especially one who
lacked the racial empathy or experience to effectively
psychoanalyse me. The shrink's office was in a building on
the east side of LA, around 54th Street. I arrived there on
Monroe's bike and pocketed the bus fare. Inside the office
were shelves filled with medical books, and on the wall were
several framed academic degrees. On the other side of the
room was a long table with a buffet of assorted pastries,
candy, chips and beverages. The sweets were similar to a
paedophile's use of candy as a lure, to break down a child's
defences, enter their world, and then corrupt it.

I sat in a large brown leather chair with my short legs
dangling above the floor. There was a faint smell of cigar
smoke in the air. Seated behind the cluttered desk was the
shrink – a balding, yellowish-pink middle-aged man with
thick bifocals reminiscent of Mr Magoo, the nearsighted
cartoon character. From the first meeting, it appeared we
both knew to avoid one another's space. He was content
with my sitting there munching on pastries, as I was satisfied
with his reading a book and leaving me alone. Sometimes I'd
catch him peering at me like I was a lab animal, and then
he'd scribble on a notepad. Our verbal exchanges were
almost non-existent, with the exception of thank you, you're
welcome, hello and goodbye. On several occasions he tried
to inquire about two incidents when I was injured, but when
I exhibited my mother's stare, he backed down.

The two incidents in question had taken place at a day
care centre where Cynthia and I were enrolled. In the first, I
slipped while chasing a boy playing tag and smashed my
head against the side of a door, receiving a long, deep gash
extending from the upper right side of my forehead down
through my eyebrow and stopping millimetres from my eye.
I narrowly avoided serious damage and was rushed to a
neighbourhood clinic, where I was stitched up.

The second incident occurred less than a year later at the

same place. While playing softball, I was showing off in front of a pretty girl named Valerie, and ran headlong into the monkey bars. Blood squirted like a geyser from a gash on the left side of my forehead. Again I was rushed to the neighbourhood clinic for stitches.

Both accidents were due to clumsiness and inattention. I can only assume that witnesses thought differently, perhaps that I was intentionally running into objects to get attention. I've never been a masochist. I don't enjoy pain, whether self-inflicted or otherwise. If I'd truly craved attention, I would have broken a large store window and stood listening to the alarm instead of running away. That would have gotten plenty of attention from the store owner, police, and my mother.

It was too simplistic to diagnose me merely as a clumsy child. The decision was made to dissect my thoughts in order to get to the nitty-gritty of the problem. There was no way that a shrink could admit professional inadequacy or defeat; he could not simply say, "Mrs Williams, I don't know what's wrong with your son." Or, "Your son is clumsy as hell."

The colour barrier between the white shrink and me wasn't the only problem. He could have been black, brown, yellow or red and been equally unsuccessful. The problem, I now believe, was the absence of a valid psychoanalytic model for black people and the black experience. Meanwhile my mother was disenchanted with the failure of the shrink's voodoo to work its mojo on me. And he was clearly uninterested; months earlier I had stopped going to his office, and he neglected to tell my mother. The long distance bike ride to and from the shrink's office had become too boring. It was cutting into my playtime, and it wasted everybody's time, especially mine.

My mother might have fared better standing me before some of the street corner winos. It was rumoured that a few of them graduated *summa cum laude*. Some of their alcoholic rants and prophetic warnings were perhaps more learned than many academics. At least their analyses of racism, slavery, poverty, police brutality, politics, child psychology and other topics were gained based on grassroots experience. It's a shame they weren't able to climb out of those wine bottles.

SEVEN

Step Family

I was blindsided when I found out my mother had met a stranger at the laundromat. He was an ex-boxer, an amateur, five-eleven, brown-skinned, with a muscular build and close-cropped afro. His name was Fred Holiwell, and he was my future stepfather. He lived in an apartment on the corner of 41st and Kansas, down the street from the laundromat where he met my mother. Usually on Saturdays I accompanied my mother there, but this day I was at home cleaning the stove, piece by piece, a tedious chore that took several hours. Had I been with her that day, chances are that Fred and my mother may not have met. To stop any potential boyfriends, I would have brandished my knife in a foolish display of protective love for my mother.

The first time Fred showed up at our house, I recoiled into a defiant stance and refused to communicate. His cordial efforts to put me at ease fed my hostility. My mind raced with dreadful thoughts of being replaced by a dominant male. My world crumbled. Fred was the first man ever to enter our home as my mother's love interest and my potential rival. I was being dethroned by a stranger. I was furious.

Cynthia cozied right up to him, possibly in her need for fatherly attention, or because she saw the benefits of a new stepfather. But Fred's arrival was too late for me; I had already established a warped sense of male selfhood. When he moved to a house further away, on 69th between Denker and Halldale, I thought I'd seen the last of him, until one day he pulled up in his olive green 1962 Oldsmobile to take us to his home for a visit. Living there were his son Wayne and his three daughters: Vicky, Demetri and Bridget. It was an awkward moment, this meeting, with no greetings or exchanging of names. In a strange stare-down competition, we looked hard at each other for long periods without blinking. The hatred circulating around the living room suffocated any possible truce. We had invaded their home, and my mother was trying to replace their absent mother. They saw us as the enemy, and I reflected their sentiments precisely. As expected, Cynthia clung to my mother for safety while I engaged in a stare-down to the death against four sets of indignant eyes.

Almost from the start there were toe-to-toe scrimmages between Fred's daughter Demetri and me. Yet our hostility was really adolescent foreplay. We actually liked one another, and Demetri was cute really, but we still kept our distance. Her older sister Vicky was built like Josephine Baker, the singer, and could have passed for being a grown woman. At seventeen she could fight like a dude and knew exactly how to throw jabs, hooks, uppercuts and combinations. None of her boyfriends dared to physically abuse her; they knew better. Vicky was cool, except when she tried to talk back to my mother, who would have none of that. Vicky treated us fairly and never punched any of us. We stayed out of her space, and she did likewise.

Holidays and weekends were spent mostly at Fred's, because our divided families had merged. We spent a lot of time there; even the neighbours thought we lived at Fred's. The three-bedroom house was pretty much open to us, but the socializing factor was missing. At every turn we kids viciously degraded one another in an attempt to draw tears for blood. To them, our family was proper, meaning that because our speech patterns were devoid of ghetto vernacular, we were acting "white." Being called proper was a euphemism for being an Uncle Tom – the white man's black man. To me, Fred's kids were country bumpkins, acting like "niggers." I had picked up the derogatory term from the streets, where calling a black man the "n" word resulted in a fight or death.

Throughout the house we youngsters launched insults back and forth. Their stinging effects were camouflaged by loud arguments that often required parental intervention. Perhaps things would have been different if they had known that Cynthia and I had no choice in our diction. It was either speak clearly or suffer the consequences, issued by my mother. We had to attend a speech etiquette class outside of school. Day and night our mother stayed on us for using incorrect language. This regime was the only thing Cynthia and I shared equal footing for when punishments were meted out. Our mother's tenacity in correcting our speech worked, but we were certainly teased and tormented for it.

To avoid the others, I spent much of the time in the backyard playing with their dog Butch, a strapping, jet black Labrador retriever and German Shepherd mix. He was a loyal guard dog and a fighter. I felt more comfortable around dogs than humans. A dog would accept me for who I was. On a few occasions little Wayne caught me letting Butch out to chase after the many cats next door. Despite our feuding families, the little guy never told on me, and for that I respected him. My taking the dog for long walks didn't seem to bother anyone – perhaps because I was the only one willing to clean up Butch's defecation in the yard.

Taking Butch for a stroll was an opportunity to scout the neighbourhood. I discovered that any unleashed dog was a potential target for Butch: he was willing to fight any dog, any time. Once I was walking him and stumbled into a dogfight in an alley across Florence Avenue. It took all my strength to hold Butch back as he snarled and barked at the two monstrous pitbulls locked in battle. Men cursed and flashed money, while the dogs slung blood and drool everywhere. The larger black pit, Crusher, won the fight hands down and they had to use a wooden bar to pry his jaws loose from the other pitbull's throat. This gruesome sight was common at dogfights but there was more to it than the spilling of blood and gambling.

A fighting dog's chiselled muscles, its agility and its enormous jaw strength appeal to the testosterone of males of all ages. Being no exception, I viewed a dogfight with fascination – but was motivated mostly by the prospect of earning a couple of bucks. My mother would have been shocked to know that before the age of twelve I had been present at more than fifty bloody dog maulings. She would have hauled me back to a shrink, pronto.

Fred's neighbourhood buzzed with activity and I looked forward to each visit, but my future stepfather had other plans for his newly expanded family. He introduced to us the foreign concept of a family outing. I wasn't alone in thinking that the idea of our warring families going out to have fun was absurd. Our pouting faces should have been reason enough to reconsider. Even Vicky was upset, preferring to stay at home with her boyfriend. During the ride, we pushed, shoved and complained about the tight space. It was like being crammed in a foxhole with the enemy, unable to leave. My mother had to reach back and pop me a couple of times to get me to behave.

Each Sunday, like clockwork, we packed ourselves into the car and headed for the museum, for Griffith Park or Knott's Berry Farm amusement park, or for one of several public beaches. The family trip was like walking to the gallows. After a while I didn't care where we ended up, as long as it was far from home. The farther we travelled, the more home was forgotten. Almost instinctively, I tended to blend in with the surroundings and absorb the illusion of freedom. I hoped that somewhere in the distance was a utopian place to go and never return home.

Yet those family outings were the best form of rehabilitation for me. The therapeutic effect of escape made me temporarily obedient. But back in the real world, the cycle of hostility between Demetri and me continued. Our fights had more to do with our unfamiliar circumstances than personal grievances. No punches were ever thrown. We mostly wrestled, pushed, and tried to toss one another across the room. This was our way of touching without seeming interested or enjoying it. For about a week the house was peaceful. But the calm was shattered the day I returned from walking Butch to see a trail of blood leading up the sidewalk into the house. I found Cynthia stretched out on the couch with a blood-soaked towel on her forehead and a look of forlorn vulnerability on her face. No one was willing to talk about what had happened, not even Cynthia, and the incident was accepted by both parents as an accident. I later learned that Bridget had hit Cynthia in the head with a piece of wood. Accident or not, had my sister chosen to seek an alliance with me, despite our rivalry, I would have honoured it. But she kept her silence.

Eventually, there was an unspoken truce among us, but with lingering spite between our families. Cynthia still remained the enemy of Fred's kids and I was pretty much despised by everybody. The arguments, "accidents" and fighting went on and on. There was nothing Brady about our bunch.

EIGHT

Adolescent Blues

My young life continued to unravel. Although I wanted to be left alone at Forshay Junior High, it was inevitable that one of the several black male gangs would target me as prey. Whenever my friends Michael or James weren't around, I kept to myself and ate alone so that I could observe others. One day I was confronted by this curly-haired fellow named Lewis who hung with the Rough Riders gang, known for jacking other youths for lunch money. With the confidence of a bull elephant, Lewis demanded that I empty my pockets. I didn't say a word, just looked at him as if he were crazy. He reached to pat my pocket; I slapped his hand away and got up. We stood eye to eye, staring one another down to see who would look away first. Still eyeing me, Lewis backed away and said, "Okay, I'll see you later on."

Later, as I walked down the long sidewalk behind Manual Arts High School, Lewis appeared with five of his homeboys. Being outnumbered, I wasn't sure how placing my back against the wall would help, but I did it. Lewis stood directly in front of me, in my face, making a deliberate noise, sucking his teeth. The six to one odds made him feel invincible.

"How much money you holding?" he spat out.

To mask my fear, I bit down hard on the inside of my mouth to appear tough. My silence was interrupted when this guy, Earl, hit my pocket and the jingle of coins prompted these predators to smile. As they demanded I empty out my pockets, Earl sucker-punched me from the blind side. I stumbled into Lewis and held on for dear life while the others pounded away at my head and body. Both Lewis and I fell to the ground on our sides. As they kicked and stomped me, I held on as long as I could, then released him. My body imploded with pain and I felt hands ripping my pockets. The ruthless beating would have continued had not an elderly black woman hollered out, "Y'all leave that boy alone or I'll call the police!" The boys scattered like roaches.

I lay there, unable to move right away. "Get up, boy, go home!" shouted the old woman. When I was able to raise myself up from the ground, I started limping toward home. Most of the way, I leaned my body against the wall for support. My entire body was a wall of pain. I was spitting up blood and my pants were torn to shreds. Fortunately, my mother and Cynthia weren't home, so I discarded the pants and cleaned up the wounds as best I could with peroxide. Seeing myself in the mirror, with my fat lip, puffy eyes and swollen jaw, was embarrassing. The thought of having been beaten down frightened the hell out of me, and I felt emasculated. It sent chills through me to visualize being circled, surrounded, cornered like a trapped animal. I lacked the pugilistic skills of Joe Louis, the heavyweight boxing champion, or the might of a military leader such as Hannibal Barca, but despite my inexperience and diminutive size, I believed that being able to instil fear in those who had hurt me was possible, with the right motivation. That night, though I had no plan, I slept like a baby.

The next morning I woke up a bloody mess to a teary-eyed mother who told me to get dressed so Fred could drive us to General Hospital. One of the doctors shook his head and asked, "My God, what happened to this child?" There was no way to hide it; I looked terrible. Afterward, Fred said he was going to teach me how to defend myself in a fight. Had it not been for the pain, I would have burst out laughing. Boxing was cool, but I needed to instil fear in that gang beyond their imagination. Slowly, a strategy took shape in my head, a strategy that would form the core of my life for the next few years.

Though I was armed with a twelve-inch, pearl-white switchblade, the thought of returning to school terrified me. Through the school grapevine I heard that Lewis, Earl and some of their homeboys were in Juvenile Hall, or "Juvey," as it was called. The word was that they had gotten busted for trying to rob a liquor store. Whether true or not, I knew that eventually they would be back. It was unsettling, having to look over my shoulder continually, dreading being pounced upon again.

Months later, while emptying the trash, I heard a familiar voice on the other side of the fence. I peeped through a crack and saw Earl strolling by with several teenage girls. I decided to wait with a stockpile of rocks the size of softballs and toss them over the fence if he returned. After awhile Earl returned, singing, and when he was in range, I lobbed rock after rock over the fence. A few struck him on top of the head, and he let out a bone-chilling scream and ran away. There was no jubilation on my part in stoning Earl, the teenage giant, though it was a job well done.

Following the ambush, whenever I passed Earl on the street, he averted his eyes. Neither of us said a word, just begrudgingly nodded as we passed each other. I was certain he knew who had rained those rocks on his head. Rumours had me beating down Earl with a brick and chasing him home. Most of the local youth thought I had to be crazy to attack him. I gained a reputation as a quiet, tough guy who was also crazy. I had become the slayer of Earl, the muscular giant whose bullying days were buried under an onslaught of rocks thrown over a fence. More important, to my relief, Earl and his homeboys stayed away from me. That was all I wanted – to be left alone.

Meanwhile, my truancy at school escalated and my grades slipped to an all-time low. To compound matters, somebody got the bright idea of assigning me to the school hash line, where they sold hamburgers, French fries, hot dogs and other food items. Before long, I was pocketing money and passing James all the free food he could eat. The day the school security guard showed up at the science class looking for me, I knew why. My front pockets bulged with coins as I was escorted to the Principal's office. After the security guard patted my pockets and discovered the booty, I dumped about $20 worth of coins on the Principal's desk. He asked where I got the money. Selling newspapers, I said. The Principal suggested I have my mother and the owner show up to verify my story. For the time being, I was suspended.

Of course, I wasn't able to produce the newspaper owner, so I was expelled for theft and truancy. I was enrolled in Audubon Junior High, where I lasted a full week before being expelled again, for truancy and fighting. The next school my mother enrolled me in was John Muir Junior High, about ten blocks from home. The Principal was aware of my poor attendance record and had a truant officer keep an eye on me. This white dude took his job seriously. For two weeks he was like a hound dog following me everywhere, as if I was about to shoplift something. When I went into the boys' bathroom he'd come in and pretend to be washing his hands. Too bad he wasn't around to stop the fight I had in the cafeteria, otherwise I probably would not have been expelled.

To help me, my mother's instinct was to send me straight across town to live with Fred and his children. I would share a bedroom with Wayne until my mother was able to find an apartment in the area. Surprisingly, I was able to carve out a private niche in Fred's household while keeping to myself, minding my own business and avoiding everybody else's space. Meanwhile, I battled thoughts of meeting girls at school and the possible run-ins with thugs who underestimated me.

When I enrolled at Horace Mann Junior High, I was fifteen going on fifty. Wearing a black tam, a highboy shirt, heavily starched Levis, biscuit shoes, and a black fake-leather coat – called "pleather" – I was cooler than ice. When I passed a crowd of girls who were smiling and checking me out, I thought I was looking good until Demetri told me the pleather coat had to go. It was a kind gesture, her way of saying, "Don't embarrass yourself and me." I took the coat off and never put it back on again.

For a while, the nuances of a new school and the girls were enough to keep me interested. In each class I took care of my educational duties, but the affable teachers lacked the expertise to motivate me. Though the school material was interesting, my motivation level was zero. It was during those moments that I recalled how Miss Johnson made learning so interesting that I didn't want to leave. Now, I would literally get up and leave the room if the subject matter was weak or the teacher was incapable of stimulating my mind.

Still, I managed not to get kicked out of school, and my mother found a place on 83rd between Denker and Harvard. It was an apartment complex with one unit on top of the other, and we lived upstairs. There were two bedrooms and I had one all to myself, which gave me privacy from my snooping sister. Once we settled in, I ventured outside to assess the surroundings. Perhaps it was an omen when I noticed cop cars cruising the area far more frequently than anywhere else I had lived. No matter where I lived, though, the cops were considered by many residents to be the number one enemy of black folks. The more contact I had with them, the more they were a threat.

In spite of my being the most inconspicuous youth around, the cops swooped down on me because I was a "black youth walking." Two white cops jumped out of the car with their hands poised on their guns and demanded I stand still. One asked, "Are you a Panther, boy?" I didn't have a clue what he was talking about. I knew nothing at the time about the revolutionary group called the Black Panthers. I thought the fool was trying to call me an animal, so I responded, "Of course not." His rough pat-down search was a legendary law enforcement procedure known to virtually all black males in South Central and involving undue intimate contact in the groin area. "I'll be watching you, nigger," said the cop, smiling, as he prepared to leave. This was his attempt to instil the fear of the law in me. I feared neither the law nor him – only his gun.

The following day at a local liquor store I met Donald, a big dark fellow my age who didn't mind indulging in mischievous – and criminal – activities. At Saint Andrew's Park, Donald introduced me to some of his cronies: Bub, Erskine, Cuz, Ronnie, Ricky, Keith, and two tall, hulking fellows named Bob and Landry. They all eyed me with suspicion, not knowing what to make of such a little guy, but Donald told them I was game to hang with them. For whatever reason, while we sat on park benches Donald's homeboy Ronnie started "capping" on me. I didn't want to rock the boat so I bit my tongue and laughed along with everybody else, but being the butt of his jokes wasn't my idea of having fun. For the sake of the "homeboy 'hood," I hoped Ronnie had gotten the joking around about me out of his system.

A week later, while we were hanging out in the driveway of the apartments where Ronnie lived, he started cappin' on me some more. Then he tried to play the "dozens," a ritual verbal joust involving the trading of personal insults, by cappin' on my mother, which was something I didn't play. I can tolerate being talked about a bit, but to talk about my mother is to risk serious payback. Ronnie spat out just two words, "Your mother..." before I was on him like a Tasmanian devil. Donald and Bub had to pull me off. After calming down, I thought I had jeopardized being their homeboy and risked being jumped on. I watched Donald teasingly put his arm around Ronnie's neck and say, "Now see, I told you Tookie may not play the dozens." Unknown to me, this was a test to earn a place in their circle, but they hadn't anticipated my physical aggression. However, they agreed that I had *heart*. I didn't know what that meant, but I figured it had to be a good thing.

From that point on I never had any run-ins with Ronnie, and in time we blended like family. Often people outside our circle mistook us for cousins or even brothers. Though not a gang, we began to establish the missing link of camaraderie through common interests: partying, girls, fighting, kinship and hustling. School wasn't part of the equation; it had been reduced to a pitstop where we met girls, fought, or hung around when nothing else was happening.

Back then, ditching parties were the "in thing" at some-body's parents' home. The charge was usually 25¢ or 50¢ per person, but we'd crash the party, paying nothing. There'd be wall-to-wall teenage girls eager to give themselves to whoever caught their lusty eyes. Sex was as plentiful as food, alcohol and weed. There wasn't a school in California that could compete with a ditching party hosting from fifty to more than 100 youths. There were four times as many people at a ditching party than in a classroom, where all of us ought to have been.

When I did stay in school, I usually ended up arguing with a teacher or getting into a fight with someone vying for a rep. Though I wasn't fond of fighting, it was an on-the-job training ground where I picked up many little tricks to add to my pugilistic repertoire. One fight was with Ollie, a tall, thin youth, a bully who ran with a pack of his clones. He tried to talk to Demetri, but she ignored his advances. Ollie then made the mistake of patting her on the butt and she slapped him. If not for a teacher who intervened, they would have been fighting toe to toe. Ollie challenged Demetri to an after-school fight in an alley behind a café on Florence Boulevard.

As I arrived, there was a large crowd in the alley. I saw Vicky, Wayne, Bridget and Demetri heading my way. Ollie was standing there with a huge grin on his face while his homeboys stood off to the side. When he called Demetri out to fight, she was ready to throw down, but I stepped out in front of her.

"Who in the hell are you?" said a puzzled Ollie.

"Our brother," shouted Vicky.

I stood in silence, listening to Ollie build himself up by selling wolf tickets about what he planned to do to me. When he began to take his shirt off, my fists revved up like a lawnmower.

I used Monroe's rule of thumb and quickly took advantage. Behind me the crowd gasped in disbelief, while some of Ollie's homeboys had to be restrained. A couple of his homeboys yelled, "That punk cheated!" Then *I* had to be held back. Another of Ollie's homeboys, Lurch, stepped in between us. He was a tall, slender, dark-skinned youth wearing Eldridge Cleaver-style sunglasses. He calmed the crowd with a loud, "Shut up!" Lurch was the leader of the clique, and to appease them, he asked both of us if we were willing to fight again. I said yes, Ollie said yes – and then shook his head. He was accustomed to having the upper hand. Amazing how a bully's stance lapses into cowardice after getting a taste of his own medicine. Ollie respected me for flipping the script on him. Years later, he and Lurch became my loyal homeboys. The fight was also the ultimate show of kinfolk loyalty from my stepfamily. I was forever embraced as their brother.

In a short period of time, Horace Mann Junior High had become a popular place among youths from other schools to ditch and hang out. I saw people I knew from Forshay roaming around the school, trying to pick up girls. Often, flocks of male and female youth waited across the street for school to let out. One day my homeboys and I were hanging out there when a pack of youth showed, up eyeing us down. I recognized Wolf, Swig, Caesar and several others from the Brims street gang. I had grown up with most of them; in fact I knew Wolf's family and used to eat dinner at their apartment. So while he and I stepped off to the side to talk, our homeboys stood there eyeing one another. After some chit-chat, Wolf mentioned he had been hearing about us and wanted to know if we were interested in joining the Brims. In a polite gesture I said my homeboys and I were like family and weren't into gangs. I left it at that. After a few more minutes of reminiscing, Wolf and the other Brims drove away. Though it was a bold move to act as a mouthpiece for the group, I felt comfortable doing it. Any one of my homeboys had ample opportunity to object, because I made sure they heard every word. From the moment I stepped to the forefront, it was a position I would not relinquish.

My days of cavorting around Horace Mann were over. I had overstayed my welcome and the Principal kicked me out for truancy and fighting with some of the Van Ness boys. Back in the day, some of them styled a reddish-brown streak on the side of their Afro and were known for jacking other youths for their money. Some of them had cornered Bub and taken his money, then beat him down. We ambushed them at Horace Mann to send a clear message to all our opposition: *lex talionis*, an eye for an eye, for whoever dared hurt any one of us. My determination to retaliate and protect us from street gangs was absolute. I had appointed myself warlord of our tight-knit circle and was the first to jump into the fray. I was the crazy one. Try as I might, I could not turn the other cheek to expose myself – or my friends – to further harm. So I fought and fought hard.

There were just two schools left willing to accept my enrolment: Henry Clay and Brett Hart Junior High. I tried Henry Clay first but both teachers and students complained about my threatening them. The Principal's words to my mother were, "He prances around with an intimidating presence as if he owned the school." Neither my mother nor I could accept the intimidating part, especially given my boyish, innocent good looks! So Brett Hart it was.

NINE

Point of No Return

I felt trapped. My mother's attempts to rescue us from a disordered society took us from the pot into the fire. This time we moved to an apartment on 90th Street between Vermont and Budlong, an area alive with criminality. Society's underbelly was there to salute me the moment I set foot outside our home.

The only school in the city willing to accept my registration was Brett Hart. Having to rise each weekday morning to prepare for school was a ritual I despised and resisted. School had failed me and I had failed it. It would have broken my mother's heart to know my feelings, but no matter how much I yearned for help or how intensely sentimental I felt toward her, my world was closed to my mother.

At Brett Hart, I kept to myself and observed others from a distance. Though two of my cousins, Leroy and Roland, both of whom I cared about, attended this school, we didn't hang out together. The fact was that we were as different as night and day. Our interests differed; my cousins were bookish and dressed like so-called squares. I dressed to match the thug persona I had sculpted to mirror the territory. I wore Levis so starched I could've stood them in a corner; a highboy shirt or green army shirt; black leather coat; black suspenders; a black tam or gangster brim; and a pair of black biscuits, spit-shined well enough to see your reflection in the toe.

On occasion, I'd play football with my cousins and their friends, who also were the epitome of prey. Their mother, Delores, was my mother's sister, and she wanted them to stay far away from me, the black sheep of the family. But I was the iconoclast of bullies, someone they'd run to for protection from other bullies. One day at school, Roland nervously told me about two characters who, with some others, had ordered him and Leroy to bring their lunch money tomorrow before school, or get beat down. They may have looked square and vulnerable but they were my cousins, and I'd fight for them.

The next day we met on the corner of 90th and Budlong. I told them to walk ahead of me as though nothing was happening. While walking, I was distracted for just a minute by this girl – and when I turned around, two guys had my cousins trapped, their arms in the air and their pockets being rifled by the bullies. I ran toward them.

"Hold up, hold up," I shouted. "They're my cousins."

Both stopped in their tracks and looked in my direction. With an exaggerated cockiness, I demanded to know what was happening. The would-be jackers were members of a street gang called the Manchester Park Boys. Both of them were non-imposing and about my height, weight, and size. I felt the odds were even. I could tell they were sizing me up to determine whether or not to try me. Just in case, I had a concealed switchblade for an equalizer.

Maybe they recognized the fool in me, or saw themselves in me, I don't know, but I thwarted their jacking scheme. As we walked side by side toward school, one of them initiated the "Who's Who" name game, to draw out who I was. This was a thug inquisition, which could get me gang-rushed if they discovered I was a loner with no back-up. The guy running through a list of names was Lester; he had the biggest Afro I'd ever seen, about twelve inches in circumference. When I heard Terry's name, I said, "Sure, I know Terry, we're tight." It was somewhat of an exaggeration, but true. They both eyed me with suspicion, probably hoping they could catch me in a lie. Fortunately, Terry turned out to be the mediator in this conflict, because he wanted a fair fight, not a mob beat-down.

During the lunch period, Terry waved me over to where a crowd of hard-core gang members were standing. One of them was Big Earl, a mammoth human being standing six foot six and weighing more than three hundred pounds. I hoped I didn't have to fight that monster. As I stood facing this rowdy crowd, staring at me like vultures surveying a meal, Terry convinced Big Earl to let me fight either. He asked me if I was willing to fight one of them. I boasted, "I'll fight them both at the same time!" My cavalier response brought a roar of laughter from everybody except Harold and Lester. Neither of them wanted to fight, so we shook hands. The crowd roared again.

Within a short period of time I was accepted, and respected, by two formidable circles of homeboys from different geographical areas but identical in behaviour and survival mentality – the Brims and the Manchester Park Boys. It was an alliance unknown to either side. Both groups were willing, able and ready to fight alongside me, if necessary. At times I travelled back and forth on foot to where my homeboy Donald lived, or he'd pick me up in a beige Plymouth borrowed from an elderly white lady whose lawn he cut. Together we crashed local ditching parties and got so toasted on *ganja* we had to kick back until our high came down.

Between getting high and ditching school, my grades slipped off the map. The Principal warned, "If you don't buckle down soon, you won't graduate." I attended classes, did a little schoolwork here and there, and graduated by the skin of my teeth. Because of my low grades I wasn't afforded the opportunity to walk across the stage; instead I was handed my diploma out of sight of the class – and good riddance. Graduation for me was just another insignificant formality that pushed me toward another phase of dys-education. Pathetic but true: I was better educated about getting loaded than I was on scholastic topics.

I was twelve when I first started sniffing glue and smoking

weed with Wolf behind the 43rd Street apartments where he lived. Shortly after that, drugs developed into a weakness I employed to soar briefly into forgetfulness before crashing to reality. Long before high school, I was a user of street drugs. I had graduated from sniffing glue to smoking marijuana to dropping "red devils" – a barbiturate which is a depressant (downer). I became acquainted with downers by way of a pimp named Li'l Ron, a mean little sucker who beat down his girls with a heated wire hanger, a baseball bat, or his fists. He lived with Johnnie, his number one prostitute, in an apartment on 94th Street. Sometimes I'd be there nodding off on red devils, only to be awakened by the sounds of Li'l Ron beating one of his girls, chasing her through the living room. Often while ditching school, I ran small errands for him or one of his prostitutes, and was compensated with drugs and money. Li'l Ron's apartment was heavily trafficked. His side job was as the local street pharmacist.

Sometimes the apartment looked like the set of a motion picture, including a junkie's shooting-up gallery, a hardcore burlesque show, and a favourite spot for local criminals. The most horrific sights were of addicts overdosing and falling down, foaming at the mouth. Overdoses were commonplace, but most addicts knew how to revive a fellow who had passed out and was moribund. If an addict was beyond reviving, he or she was dropped off in a secluded area and an anonymous phone call was made to a hospital or morgue. I once got high with Mary, a beautiful black teenager whom I foolishly passed around like a marijuana joint to share. Somehow I ended up stretched out on the steps of Saint Andrew's park gymnasium with my head resting on Mary's lap as I slipped into overdose. Mary contacted my mother, who showed up with Fred and drove me to Morningside Hospital, where my stomach was pumped.

Still sick, the next day I was at the 77th Street police station being interrogated about my drug use. That evening I was transferred to Central Juvenile Hall. The facility festered with unwashed youth, chaos, hostile attitudes, random fighting, and the nastiest food I'd ever tasted. Each night I listened to the eerie sounds of other youth whimpering and screaming, "I wanna go home, I wanna go home!" If screaming was a sure way to get home, I would have outscreamed everybody daily. It was my first time in Juvenile Hall, and for awhile I felt sick, terrified and trapped as though the walls were closing in on me. I was claustrophobic. For seven straight weeks I prayed and read the Bible on my knees, hoping I'd go home any minute.

Like some of the urban schools I had attended, Juvey was a warehouse for incorrigible youth where they would vegetate and sink into ignorance and confusion. It also served as conditioning and preparation for a youth's inevitable step toward prison – as though it was a boot camp, training recruits for the next level of armed services. At the facility I learned absolutely zip, but it was very professional in teaching me to be more indifferent and embittered. Some of the turnkeys were more diabolical than gang members; they appeared to suffer from mental disorders while taking out their frustrations on us. The institutional setting aped a primitive version of a reformatory school where no parent could rush to your aid. As a ward of the court outside of parental jurisdiction, a youth could be subjected to involuntary psychotropic drugging and testing, prolonged isolation, bodily harm, degradation, sodomy, and even death at the hands of a turnkey or another youthful offender. Imagine me or any youth trying to explain to a parent about the facility's atrocities. We'd be seen as liars, plain and simple.

I was often in lock-up for fighting with juvenile J-cats (distraught individuals with serious mental health problems), gang members, and some of the turnkeys. After each clash, I welcomed the sight of a filthy bunk to rest and rejuvenate for the next encounter. It was during a brief stint outside of lock-up that I ran into Bunchie, a homeboy I'd met at Horace Mann Junior High. Bunchie was barrel-chested with thick arms and looked wider than a door. Though huge, he was a gentle giant and didn't fight unless roused.

One day I was bum-rushed in the gym by some Sportsman Park Boys when Bunchie emerged from his shell. He entered the fray, throwing bodies like rag dolls. His size and strength were revered and feared, even by the ruthless turnkeys who sometimes had to try to restrain him – like the time during breakfast when a J-cat, spaced out on medication, demanded that I pass the pitcher of hot cocoa. When I told him to wait, he tackled me to the floor, but within seconds Bunchie had picked him up in the air and slammed him hard to the ground. While the entire squad of turnkeys tried to control Bunchie, I was able to accommodate the J-cat with the pitcher and the hot cocoa. They ended up pampering Bunchie, but I was thrown in lock-up. After several weeks the courts released me into my mother's custody. Though relieved to get out of Juvey, I had a nagging suspicion I'd be back.

I fell back into the predictable rut of street activities. I was now going to George Washington High School, the home of several gangs, in particular the Sportsman Park Boys, the Denker Boys, a few Denver Lanes and the Figueroa Boys. At school or in the 'hood, the Sportsman Park Boys were our number one menace, known for bailing out of cars to attack any one of us. My road dog was Erskine, a stocky, bow-legged, quick-tempered youth with a flair for dramatic violence. His attitude was "I'll bring it to you!" Both Erskine and I gained a reputation at Washington High for our willingness to fight the street gangs head-up, or catch them off-guard in the school rest room or underneath the bleachers smoking *ganja*. In school, not many places were off limits. Both we and our rivals were deluded about who our true enemies were.

The classroom was a kind of sacred territory devoid of fighting. It served as a sanctuary where we could unwind until the next bell rang. Then it was time to tense up again for possible conflicts. Gradually, as a result of all the fighting on and off the school grounds, most of the known gang members transferred to other schools – Locke, Fremont, or Crenshaw High – to sidestep our mounting efforts to destroy them. We proclaimed Washington High to be *our* school.

This was our stomping ground, where my homeboys and I ruled. Yet we didn't financially own a centimetre of property.

During school days we'd meet up and plan the day, foolishly sacrificing an education for the forbidden fruits of drugs, unprotected sex, fighting, ditching, strong-arming and gambling. We could pretty much get away with anything, except murder. The staff knew exactly who we were and what we were doing at and around school, but they were too scared to stop us – or didn't care.

TEN

The Institutional Shuffle

In 1970 I was largely unconscious of the battle being fought on a higher level for black survival by civil rights organizations: the Black Panthers, United Slaves organization, the National Association for the Advancement of Colored People, the Student Nonviolent Coordinating Committee, the Nation of Islam, the African National Congress, and others in the United States and abroad. I was brain-dead about the Soledad Brothers, Huey P. Newton, Angela Davis, Nelson and Winnie Mandela, Malcolm X, Bobby Rush, Bunchie Carter, Bobby Seales, Martin Luther King Jr. and other black leaders.

Soon I returned to custody, this time for suspicion of burglary and being under the influence of drugs. I had made the mistake of being intoxicated and running out of gas in a stolen car, in a predominantly white area of Carson. While I was walking to the bus stop, the cops jacked me up for sticking out like a lone raisin in a bowl of rice. Before I knew it, I was back in Central Juvenile Hall, before being transferred to another facility called Los Padrinos.

The staff at Central Juvey had mentioned that I was being moved because I lived in the geographical jurisdiction of Los Padrinos, but my mother said, "Boy, those people didn't want you there because you acted like a fool." As it turned out, Los Padrinos was the Marriott Hotel of juvenile halls, with a swimming pool, clean rooms, and food that was gourmet compared to Central's. There were numerous peacocks strutting around with their plumage displayed and making shrieking noises sounding like a call for help: "Hel . . . . p, hel . . . . p!" Rumour had it that there was a donkey that enjoyed chasing people, but I never saw it. The judge who sentenced me decided, however, that I had to be moved. He stated, "In the interest of this court and for your welfare" – he was looking at me – "I order that you be sent to the Job Corps in Salt Lake City."

It was a long bus trip to Utah and I didn't have the faintest idea what to expect. When the bus finally pulled up, twenty or more youths were loitering inside the terminal. Half an hour later came a broadcast message requesting that all Job Corps recruits report to the bus outside. It picked us up and took us into grounds resembling an old army compound. I thought the judge had tricked me into enlisting in the armed forces. We were briefed on the rules and regulations, then assigned to living quarters in a quasi-military barracks. Like Juvey, there wasn't much privacy, only a partition separating each bunk.

In front of the large school building was a huge cannon, and across the street was the cafeteria. On campus was a wide spectrum of black youths, the descendants, as far as I was concerned, of a slave diaspora throughout the North, Central and South Americas. Though all of us were of the same genotypical black ancestry, many of them were Puerto Ricans, spoke with a Spanish accent and seemed stand-offish toward us, their darker counterparts. The racial tension was evident, with contemptuous stares and a better-than snobbery despite our common poverty, fatherless home lives, and not owning a pot to piss in. It was a minefield of racial intolerance between blacks and Puerto Ricans that had been primed for God knows how long.

Although I had no interest in the Job Corps' educational system, the archery programme was something different. I discovered that I enjoyed it. To stand and aim an arrow at a target attached to a haystack evoked some ancestral hunting desire. Out of the corner of my eye I caught sight of a guy sitting on top of my leather coat. I asked him to put the coat on the back of the chair and continued to shoot at the target. When I turned back around, the guy was still sitting on my coat, so I walked over and asked him again. I thought perhaps he didn't understand English. Though he was Puerto Rican and may not have understood English that well, his diction was impeccable when he said, "Shut up, nigger!" That was the first time I've ever used my foot in a fight, and I didn't even know karate.

The gym coach broke up the one-sided fight and marched me in to the Principal's office. The Principal admonished me for my behaviour without asking what had happened. After some time he told me to go to lunch and return afterward to continue the discussion about my incorrigible behaviour. Heading toward the cafeteria, I noticed two large groups squared off: blacks standing next to the cannon and Puerto Ricans across the street. As I cautiously walked toward them, an older black youth with an alarmed expression met me, stating that the Puerto Rican guy I sucker-punched and stomped wanted to fight me.

Standing in the middle of the street facing my opponent, I was confident until I caught sight of a shiny object flashing in his hand, slightly behind his back. Had not the sun been blazing that day, I would have missed the glint and walked right into a blade. I was able to unloosen my belt and then wrap it around my hand with the thick buckle dangling by my side. In Spanish, his Puerto Rican *compadres* were egging him on to attack, their warlike chants of "Get that nigger!" resonating loudly. The sheepish silence on the part of the black group was a powerful signal, suggesting, you're on your own, brother! There's no telling what might have taken place had not the campus guards rushed between us. Oddly enough, that's when the Puerto Rican exploded and started yelling, "I'm gonna kill that nigger." Several guards had to hold him while I was escorted to the campus jail, a place I didn't know existed until that moment.

Being behind bars was something I never became accustomed to. The walls were closing in on me when the Principal showed up, babbling excitedly about there being a possible racial riot and about my being dishonourably discharged, which I knew meant going home. According to the Principal, before my arrival there was racial harmony on the campus, and everybody got along. Having to shoulder the blame for everything was commonplace for me. No doubt the other guy was allowed to stay and graduated with honours. That evening the campus guard drove me to the bus depot, handed me a bus ticket and ten dollars and said my leather coat would be mailed to me.

When I arrived back in Los Angeles on my mother's doorstep, she simply shook her head, mumbling, "Oh, Lord." It was no surprise that the juvenile court judge didn't contact my mother and order me back to the courtroom. And since we weren't contacted, I went back to Washington High. Nothing had changed. The gangs still sought to make examples of me and others for defying their fiefdom over the school and neighbourhood. Personally, I was tired of negotiating the labyrinth of gang members' territories, where safe passage required sidewalk tariffs else a passerby would feel the gang's wrath.

By now, most of my homeboys were expert car thieves. We used the cars to impress young women and to track down Sportsman Park boys – who hung out in what is now called Jesse Owens Park – and beat them down. One night we were out cruising in a stolen 1963 Chevy looking for Sportsman Park boys. We stopped in Inglewood to get loaded while Bub and Adam argued about who should be driving. Adam tricked Bub to get out and come around to the driver's side, then locked him outside. They continued to banter until the Inglewood police drove up, and we scattered in different directions. I jumped through the car's back window, climbed a tall wooden fence, fell onto some thorny bushes, and rolled into a mud puddle. I jumped up, ran past a Dobermann pinscher and hopped another fence. On the other side of the block, I saw a crowd of teenagers in a driveway having a get-together, and joined in. Trying to look inconspicuous, I stood there for more than twenty minutes thinking the coast was clear and that Bub and

Adam had probably gotten themselves busted. When I reached the corner, several white Inglewood police cars with their lights out crept up. The cops already had their .38 calibre guns drawn, and ordered me to hit the dirt. I dropped to my knees and lay flat while I was searched and handcuffed.

At Central Juvenile Hall, two detectives showed up to question me about the names of my two homeboys who'd eluded capture. One of the white detectives said, "Look, Stan, if you tell us who was with you in that stolen car, you can go home today." I could not snitch under any circumstances, even if I were being accused of heinous crimes that others had committed. I was taught not to tell. I remembered vividly how when I was a little boy, Big Rock would become enraged when he talked about snitches being the lowest form of any animal. "Better for a mother to cross her legs during the moment of conception to choke the life out of that child than to give birth to a snitch," he declared. So when the cop asked again was I willing to give him the names of my homeboys, I said, "What homeboys? What stolen car?" Apparently I pissed the cops off, because they jumped up and stormed out of the room.

I was transferred to Los Padrinos Juvey, from which I would spend about three months going back and forth to court. While kicking back, minding my own thoughts, the muscular Los Padrinos gym coach approached me and wanted to know if I was interested in lifting weights. I thought he was crazy and told him so. After a week he again asked if I was willing to lift weights. "Lift weights for what?" I asked. He launched into a lengthy monologue about health, muscle body parts, vitamins, protein supplements, body-building shows and weight-lifting routines. I was eager to try the weights just to shut him up.

The coach's persistence in showing me how to back-arm, curl, bench press, and do pull-overs began to pay off big-time. Later that day, though sore, I felt good. The more I lifted weights, the more I became addicted to the feeling of being bigger and stronger. I can still hear the coach's words: "You have the body and bone structure to be enormous if you continue to drive iron and eat properly." I didn't believe a word he said, but he was able to motivate me to continue lifting weights. For me to find the raw power I never knew existed within me was a significant discovery. This was a discipline I could relate to and one in which I could see rapid results.

Meanwhile, the court judge had sentenced me to Camp Rocky, located in the mountains above San Dimas, California. Rocky was a fire-fighting facility with no barbed wire fences or guard towers, and there was nothing between me and freedom but air. A few times I thought about escaping but figured doing time there would be a cakewalk. Rocky was just another form of punishment I neither feared nor respected. Each incarceration taught me no life lessons. I simply entered into nothing, then was released, refined in bitterness and misdirection, to slip further toward ruin. Camp Rocky would prove to be no different than Juvey and the Job Corps.

It didn't surprise me to see an alliance between the whites and Mexicans at Rocky, because I had noticed it first in Juvey. Whenever a fight broke out between a black youth and a white youth, the Mexicans sided with the whites. It was odd because those same whites could not walk down the street in any barrio without being attacked. I had stumbled into another hotbed of unrest based on skin colour. There was a lot of back-stabbing, not with knives but with racial epithets ping-ponging through the air:

"You white devils . . ."

"You wetbacks . . ."

"You nigger . . ."

Most of the battles were verbal, but fistfights broke out here and there. I did manage to befriend some blacks from Los Angeles, including Tick, Anthony, Harper, Bobo and others who would become part of my circle.

All of us slept in a huge dorm room with steel bunks lined up on both sides of a slightly elevated control centre, where a counsellor stood vigil over us. At night, everybody kept a watchful eye out for possible "rat-packing": blankets would be thrown over a sleeping victim's head and he'd be beaten senseless. Though I'd only seen whites and Mexicans rat-pack the weaker ones among themselves, I still remained vigilant. I slept far in the back in a bunk next to the wall where I could see everything coming and going. The notion of sleeping with one eye open applied here – but it was next to impossible to do. I did become a light sleeper, however, and my ears were as sensitive to movement as a bat's echo-location system.

Each morning the camp programme began with us rising at 6 a.m. and washing, then meeting outside around the flagpole. There a counsellor would inspect our faces for any signs of facial hair. No youth was allowed to eat breakfast unless he was clean-shaven and washed. After breakfast, we dressed in fire-fighting gear and went out in a truck that seemed to stop randomly anywhere on the side of a mountain for us to work. We were handed tools to firebreak certain sections, hard labour for a measly 25¢ per day, or 50¢ for working at an actual fire site. I managed to get a position working in the kitchen where I eventually became the head cook. Most of my time was spent cooking and driving iron. In a short period, I had buffed up my fifteen-inch arms to seventeen inches. I was walking around with my chest raised up, arms stuck out to the side, and I strolled with my feet turned outward. I didn't care how my stroll looked to others – I thought it made me look tough, and it felt right.

I turned seventeen on December 29, 1970. I was bigger and stronger, but I lacked the discipline to stay out of juvenile correctional facilities. Though I looked forward to returning to the streets, my thoughts focused on counter-measures to conquer neighbouring gangs. No longer would my friends, relatives or I be afraid of harm. No more waiting on the so-called enemy. It would be seek and destroy. It was war.

Prior to my release date I was summoned for the customary re-evaluation. I sat inside the gymnasium before the staff's tribunal and faced a long list of questions. The last question was fair enough: "Stan, what are your plans once you are released back into society?" With an indifferent expression, I replied, "I plan on being the leader of the biggest gang in the world." My unrehearsed response was as shocking to me as it was to them. It was as if a ventriloquist had unexpectedly spoken through me.

The thought of joining a gang, or being a leader of one, was preposterous. I hated street gangs. But it was probably the first time the counsellors had been left speechless. While they sat there befuddled, I waltzed out, kicking the chair behind me for emphasis. One thing for sure: they were tired of my being there. I had given the staff hell. Two days later, Fred and my mother picked me up. I didn't look back as we drove away.

ELEVEN

Seeds of a Gang

I returned to the South Central colony to salutations all around from my homeboys. It was customary to pay homage to any one of us who had done time without snitching. Bub was the first to shake my hand and comment on how buffed up I had become. Mostly he was showing gratitude for my knowing how to keep my mouth shut.

The streets hadn't changed much. The gang problem still festered, and racial ferment was everywhere. The National Guard was called in to a riot in Wilmington, North Carolina. The Black Panther's Field Marshal, George Jackson, was shot and killed during an alleged escape attempt at San Quentin state prison. The political activist Angela Davis was still in Marin County Jail, and a rebellion was in full swing at Attica state prison in upper New York State. Not to mention the usual problems: poor education, few jobs, lack of youth programmes, broken families – all feeding the growing civil rights movement.

While funding for black economic programmes was cut, the gangs and their levels of violence surged. This was a growth industry. South Central was full of both visible and latent street gangs with parasitical appetites. Contrary to popular belief, black gangs were not new. The older ones – the notorious Slausons, Gladiators and the Business Men – had become ethnicity-conscious and were absorbed into the Black Panther party or other active political groups. A few remaining older black gangs still hung on: the Chain Gang, Low Riders, Avenues, Brims, Figueroa Boys and Van Ness Boys. These gave rise to newer, more predatory street cliques: the Sportsman Park Boys, Denker Boys, Manchester Park Boys, Hustler Mob, New House Boys and many others. However, despite our lack of numbers, I had several trump cards over the other gangs. As I had moved from school to school, juvenile facility to juvey, and hood to hood, I had established ties in each area with certain key youth who held influence over their circle of homeboys. Their homeboys became mine, and mine became theirs.

I was catapulted to the helm of my group not by force or referendum, but by opportunity, conditions and self-promotion. Simply, I stepped into a vacuum, an uncontested position tailor-made for me. My homeboys' acquiescence allowed me to follow through, to expand. We were not a gang in the traditional sense, but as our rivals raised the bar with their increasing aggression and strong-arming, we morphed into a gang without a title. There was no turning back, not really, because the more we fought, the more deeply entrenched our vendettas became. Though we saw the black images across the barricades as our enemy, we had no notion that our true adversaries were the squalid living conditions, the vortex of powers confining us to those conditions, and our own unwitting perpetuation of those conditions. Like countless other black gang members and criminals, we were unconscious accomplices in our own subjugation – our own worst foes.

Gang battles raged, and we picked up the pace in drive-by beatings. Often we'd bail out of a stolen car to beat down unsuspecting rivals and I'd let them know it was me, Tookie, who was doing it to them. If they didn't remember anything else, they'd remember my name. As long as the local gangs were at each other's throats and didn't unite, we could stand up against any of them, even though we were outnumbered. They came to despise us and the name they cursed most was mine. I became the neighbouring gangs' number one target, something I encouraged. I needed to be feared and known by all of them. It became a familiar sight for gangs to cruise the area and leave messages:

"Tell Tookie we're looking for him."

"Tell Tookie we're gonna kill him!"

One evening at a dance at the Saint Andrew's park gym, the Chain Gang caught a few of us off-guard. The guy who approached me was Daven, a twenty-something loudmouth who wouldn't bust a grape with cleats on. Surrounded by a mob of other grown men posing as his back-up, Daven was bold enough to thrust a finger in my chest and ask, "Are you Tookie?" It was *déjà vu* for me, reminding me of the time when Louis and his cronies stomped me in the dirt behind Manual Arts. This time I flipped the script and lunged at Daven, causing both of us to fall to the ground. The darkness in the gym allowed me to crawl out of the scuffle while Daven's homeboys continued to punch and kick him, thinking that it was me they were beating. Meanwhile, Bub, in the gym's kitchen, held other Chain Gang members at bay with a starter pistol, until they realized it was a fake. Like me, he managed to escape a serious beat-down.

We had constant reminders of our mortality, especially when shots were fired at us. Guns were replacing fists as the fastest way to earn a reputation for youths who lacked the ability to fight and needed an equalizer. It took nerve to fight with your hands – it's much easier to pick up a handgun and brandish it. A child could do it, with deadly effect. It's true that we had access to a cache of guns, **but we wanted to beat our rival gangs into submission, not kill them.** The horrors of gunplay disturbed me so much that for a long time, **I refused to possess one.** Guns represented death, and I feared their potential.

Nevertheless, even while hot lead was flying in our direction, I didn't give death a second thought. I had a false sense of invincibility. I wanted to live a full life but faced a meaningless future with no dreams, no tangible hopes. I lived each day with reckless abandon, not fearing tomorrow. God looks out for babies and fools, as the expression goes.

The fool in me was running amok: perhaps that's why death passed me by. Also, most of my rivals and enemies didn't even know what I looked like. I was said to be tall, with a scarred face and jet-black skin, a muscle-bound nut. I was pegged as a villain who harassed other gangs, didn't play fair, and needed to be taught a lesson.

My street rep continued to grow, surpassing the leaders of all other local gangs. Although I wanted the notoriety, I didn't anticipate the headaches. The police and school administration were receiving complaints about a student named Tookie who was causing trouble on and off the grounds. Both authorities wanted to identify this person. Even some parents of local gang members were up in arms about this mysterious troublemaker, but none of them could finger me. In school, gang members and everybody else knew me only as Stan, and I wanted to keep it that way as long as possible.

Our crew's fashion style was dissimilar to the other street gangs, but more and more we began to emulate them. My homeboys began to adopt gang names: Erskine became "Mad Dog," Terry was now "Bimbo," Big Bob chose "The Hawk," and Donald called himself "Sweet Back" after the main character in a Melvin Van Peebles movie, *Sweet Sweetback's Baadasssss Song*. Other homeboys did likewise. Soon, Terry and I got our left ears pierced to enhance our thug image. Again, our homeboys followed suit, styling the same kind of gold hook and cross, or a small gold hoop earring. We had gravitated toward the gang realm as if we belonged there.

Our persistent attacks – along with other street gangs destroying one another – began to turn the tide in our favour. Several of the larger gangs showed an interest in switching sides – extending an olive branch of compromise – while others reluctantly continued to fight. It was time to consolidate the friends and acquaintances I had cultivated for the past few years, to avoid making the divide-and-conquer mistakes made by other street gangs. It didn't take a mathematician to see that when a structure is divided, each individual part loses its potency and thus is exposed to possible annihilation. I didn't want to make that mistake.

The black community generally was blind to its defiant youth creating increasingly aggressive street gangs. Mislabelled by some as a "lost generation," we were instead forgotten prodigies who disappeared, children buried alive in a sandbox. We did what was necessary to exhume ourselves. Though we must share the blame, we were products of a culture that bastardized us.

TWELVE

Crip Walk

In the spring of 1971, the gang challenge took on new energy at Washington High. When the school bell rang for lunch one day, I went to meet Mad Dog in our usual spot, only to be abruptly distracted. The two strangers headed my way were clearly looking for me, perhaps for vengeance. This had become a prevailing motif of my life: I'd be confronted by an opponent and combat would begin.

Both strangers were extremely muscular. The taller of the two called out to me, "Hey Tookie," and stopped at arm's length. We faced one another while his homeboy stood to the side, watching.

"Are you Tookie?" asked the fellow.

"Yes, I'm Tookie. Why?"

I figured if they were here to fight, there was no need to be sociable. The guy's face had a scar running upward from the corner of his mouth. He smiled and extended his right hand.

"I'm Raymond Washington." Then he indicated his homeboy. "That's Bulldog."

We nodded, acknowledging one another. Raymond said his homeboy Clint, whom I had befriended, had told him about my willingness to challenge all the neighbouring gangs despite my homeboys and I being outnumbered. He talked about how he was experiencing the same problem with gangs on the east side of Los Angeles, and asked if I was interested in uniting. I had been approached with similar propositions on other occasions and turned them down, but this was different. What caught my attention was the way that Raymond and Bulldog were dressed. Except for my wide-brim hat, the three of us were dressed identically in black leather coats, black biscuits and heavily starched Levis. Had my enemies seen them, they would have been mistaken for part of my circle.

With Raymond and Bulldog dressing like we did, I was confident that neither of them represented my rivals; nor did Raymond say he was part of a gang. Had he mentioned any gang connections, I would have declined his offer, as I had with my childhood buddy Wolf, who was a Brim. As we talked, I made it clear how much I despised gangs. I told Raymond I'd give the alliance some thought and suggested we meet on Sunday at the Rio Theater on Western, off Imperial Boulevard. We shook hands, and I watched as they disappeared around the corner of the gymnasium. An alliance was possible, I felt, because it aligned with my agenda to consolidate the groups of homeboys I'd met over the years. I envisioned our being not a gang in the customary sense, but an unstoppable force that no gang in Los Angeles or the world could ever defeat. The thought appealed to my growing megalomania. I made up my mind right then that the alliance was on.

After apprising Mad Dog of the encounter with Raymond, I headed toward 113th Street, where Melvin lived in his mother's house, which was to become a regular hangout for us soon-to-be "Crips." He was driving iron in the garage – huffing and puffing while curling a set of barbells. Though Melvin was thin, he had the heart of a lion and was equally dangerous. He was the newest among my circle. I had met him under precarious circumstances: Melvin and about eight of his homeboys, armed with bumper jacks, crowbars and baseball bats, had Mad Dog and me surrounded in a tight circle on the school grounds of Henry Clay Junior High. We were held hostage for twenty minutes until it was determined that we weren't the ones who had jacked his brother and their homeboy. Mad Dog and I would have had to be Houdini to escape unscathed. After an apology for delaying us, they let us walk away unharmed. Melvin and I began to see one another often at the Rio Theater and established a connection. We later would fight alongside each other against numerous street gangs.

That Sunday at the Rio I was kicking back watching the movie *Al Capone* with my homeboys Mad Dog, Bub, Herc, Cuz, Lurch, Bimbo, Sweet Back and the Hawk. Midway through the movie, the theatre manager sent word that some people were outside, calling me. When I reached the lobby, I saw Raymond across the street with some of his homeboys. I waved them over.

"Ah, Tookie," Raymond whispered, "we don't have enough to pay for all of us."

"No sweat," I told him. "I've got it covered."

Raymond looked puzzled, but they all got in free. The manager and I had an arrangement: that as long as there was order inside the theatre, a few of us didn't have to pay.

In the lobby, Raymond introduced me to Fernando, Douhane, Chilli, Ichy and Little Sam. I also shook hands with Clint, who I knew. We went inside. Raymond and his cronies sat in front of us, and I sat directly behind Raymond. In order for us to talk, he had to sit sideways with his legs draped across the adjoining seats. Our homeboys kicked back as if nothing was happening, except for Mad Dog, who eyed every move. I had a sense that something new was beginning here, an alliance that would exceed our imaginations. Raymond and I had engaged in something I would read about decades later: a street version of an ancient African war strategy to hype ourselves before a battle, to visualize domination over our enemies. Our alliance would begin an urban cleansing of the gang element – or so we thought.

The chances of two strong-willed youth coming together from opposite geographical sides of South Central to create an alliance were – well, the odds were very long. Yet for reasons I can't fathom, Raymond and his homeboys integrated with us as if we had discovered we were long-lost cousins, kindred spirits. In fact, Raymond thought our circle consisted of relatives because we addressed one another as "cuz," short for cousin. Though none of us was related, we had a homeboy nicknamed Cuz, so it carried over from there. We avoided using "brother" as a salutation because it was no longer indicative of camaraderie. I knew that at least when a person called me cuz, he wasn't my enemy. Raymond and his cronies also liked homeboy, which, like cuz, eventually caught on with everybody.

Our meeting was not as newsworthy as the Appalachian meeting held in 1957 by more than 100 Italian-American Mafia bosses. But in the cloak of darkness, the stage was set for a new cousin-hood under the banner of street gang warfare. After the Rio closed, we agreed to meet at Washington High the following Friday to seal the deal and to bring together as many homeboys as possible.

I needed only to contact specific individuals who passed the word to their homeboys to be up at Washington High on Friday during lunch period. That day when the school bell rang for lunch, it was a bell signalling a gathering of the west and east side of Los Angeles's rebellious youth. By the time Bub and I reached the bleachers behind the gymnasium, Raymond was standing among nearly thirty of his homeboys. With just two of us – Bub and me – showing up, it called into question whether my word had much weight. Raymond asked what was happening. I told him my homeboys would be there, but I began to have doubts. Inside, I chastised myself for being dubious about my own homeboys, regained my composure, and looked confident.

I had been shaking lots of hands when Raymond's homeboy, Craig, shouted out, "Tookie, is that them?" I turned around to see the grand entrance: a smiling Bimbo strolling across the football field ahead of a battalion of his homeboys. I nodded to Craig, beaming, and assured him, "That's some of them." Then, as if choreographed, rounding the corner from the 108th Street side of the bleachers, Lurch appeared leading his homeboys in a military-style march, while four separate groups, headed by Big Curtis, Melvin, Fat Riley and Big Tracy came from the opposite direction. I filled with pride, knowing that my word meant a lot among my homeboys. They were dressed in a wide variety of styles: beige khaki suits, starched Levis, black leather coats, silk suits, army boots, black biscuits, suit coat vests and wooden canes carried for style but to be used mostly as weapons. (There were certain styling differences between the west and east. For example, in the beginning most of us West Side Crips wore an earring in our left earlobe and styled a wide brim hat. Not many East Side Crips wore earrings, but they often sported Ace Deuce stingy brims.)

It would have been a police photographer's Kodak moment to have captured all of us on film that day. Standing and sitting around on the bleachers was the largest body of black pariahs ever assembled. I'm convinced that had the Black Panther party still been recruiting, uninterrupted by the FBI, Huey Newton and Bobby Seale would have salivated over our untapped youthful potential. We embodied just one small division of a multitude of reckless, energetic, fearless and explosive young black warriors across the USA. Though often seen as social dynamite, I believe we were the perfect entity to be indoctrinated in cultural awareness and trained as soldiers for the black struggle. This opportunity to mould us into a valuable resource was never spotted by society, schools, churches, community programmes, civil rights movements, or other black organizations.

For me, the thin line between nihilism and warriorhood was blurred. I rushed headlong toward self-immolation. Little wonder that I relished the deafening, primal roar of our homeboys' approval when Raymond and I shook hands and then embraced. Finally, I belonged to something.

That evening, after the meeting, both the west and the east sides met up at Sportsman Park for the Tom Cross Record Hop. The dance was packed with young women, and my intent was to enjoy them and the scenery. However, in less than an hour, Raymond was prepared to go toe-to-

toe with Stanley, a giant Sportsman Park Boy standing about six foot eight inches. Some of his homeboys were also hanging around, not surprisingly, since this was supposed to be their turf.

Stanley got cute. "What do you little fools want to do?" he demanded.

Without any signal, Raymond and I hit him at the same time, and the giant stumbled to the side. I ran across the long row of seats, continuing to hit Stanley as he staggered toward the door, while Raymond also ran alongside him, unleashing body shots. But the giant wouldn't fall. When I reached the last chair and was about to jump down, someone blindsided me with a folding metal chair that knocked me and my hat in separate directions. Dazed, I crouched on all fours. Melvin and Warlock were beating down the Sportsman Park Boy who had crowned me upside the head. I found my hat and headed outside when my stepsister Demetri and some of her girlfriends noticed that I was bleeding. We went inside the girls' restroom, where I found my right ear had been split and blood was flowing from the wound.

Outside the dance, more than 100 of us headed down Western Avenue. In our path was a liquor store off the corner of 94th Street. We mobbed it and stole about half the store's merchandise. Eventually, we ended up at Jack In The Box on Western and 83rd, staying until the wee small hours of the morning, when I finally went home. The next morning my mother discovered a blood-soaked pillow under my head and took me to the hospital, where my ear was stitched up. At these moments my mother questioned whether I was the same child who exited her womb, or was I switched at birth.

Life seemed to accelerate after I met Raymond. Now we were talking about a "title" to best describe our campaign. In the school lunch area at Washington High a great debate took place over the title, and most everybody involved was excited about it – except me. It didn't matter what our title was, because for the west side I planned to have "Tookie" in front of it. Thrown into the hat were names such as the Black Crusaders, the Terminators, the Mau-Maus, the

Eliminators, the Rebels, the Annihilators, the Black Knights, the Warlords and the Black Gangsters. Raymond suggested the Cribs. The craziest title, the Snoopies, came from Melvin. In fact, he and some of his homeboys showed up wearing T-shirts with pictures of the *Peanuts* cartoon character, Snoopy the dog, on the front. Melvin abandoned the idea after it was ridiculed.

Not long after, my girlfriend Bonnie gave a party on 106th, in the garage at her mother's house. When we arrived she told me about two neighbourhood thugs, Buddha and Monkey-man ("Monk" for short), crashing her party and scaring some of her friends away. They had a reputation as a vicious tag team at Washington High, but we had not bumped heads before. That changed when Buddha and Monkey-man's arrogance brought them back to the party, drunk and boisterous. After being thoroughly battered and thrown into the street, they regained consciousness and left.

The next time I encountered Buddha and Monkey-man was in the school hash line. They approached me and were quickly surrounded by Bimbo, Bub, Mad Dog, Cuz, Lurch and others. Faced with a repeat of the battering they suffered at the party, Buddha told me that they were looking to join our circle. No doubt we appealed to their militant spirit by challenging their thug-hood; they had to join us or be smashed by our power. When I embraced Buddha and Monk, I sensed their fire to fight, but I had no idea Buddha and I would become inseparable.

The following day we gathered in the cafeteria area. Our quest for a title was narrowed down to three names. Bub liked the Black Overlords, Big Curtis favoured the Assassins, and Raymond still had that unusual title, the Cribs. In a unanimous vote, Cribs became our new name and epithet. Buddha asked me if I liked it.

"Cool," I said, "Tookie and the Cribs, what do you think?"

I'll never forget his expression of horror, and a genuine concern for my name being attached to the title. Buddha reminded me that such a title meant the police would hold me responsible for everything that happened. I begrudgingly listened because I knew what he was saying was true.

Though I dropped the idea of having my name before the Cribs name, the title itself was short-lived. Most of us, while intoxicated, mispronounced Cribs as Crips – and it stuck. Surprisingly, the mix-up didn't jeopardize anything: the alliance took precedence above all else. The word Crip replaced Crib, but neither had any underlying political, organizational, cryptic or acronymic meaning. Both titles depicted a fighting alliance against street gangs – nothing more, nothing less.

When Raymond and I became joint leaders of the Cribs, we functioned as a single federation. But during that period when our name, the Cribs, mutated into the Crips, tribalism developed. There were East Side Cribs and West Side Cribs. In our neighbourhoods we scrawled our names on our walls to differentiate ourselves from one another. Soon the Crips replaced Cribs across the board. Our two organizations were autonomous but were allies with the same agenda: war against street gangs. Each side competed to see which could conquer the most gangs, or take the most leather coats, cars, jewelry or money from those gangs. In spite of all the inflated egos, there was no tribal Crip warfare between west and east, not even fist fights. Occasional verbal fallouts between homeboys were always settled in full-contact football games held on Saturdays at Saint Andrew's Park. It was a magnificent scene, a collection of black talent on the field, although none of them would ever be offered an athletic scholarship or even an education.

It was Raymond whom I first heard jokingly say, "The west side is cool but the east side rules." My response was to reverse the phrase: "The east side is cool but the west side rules." Our light banter was taken out of context by some of our homeboys who, years later, would take the braggadocio to heart. In the meantime, Raymond and I held the alliance intact while I continued to solidify connections with other proselytized and defeated gangs.

Throughout the hoods we became notorious as a powerful fighting machine with a numerical dominance over the gangs. As we steadily multiplied and swarmed like ants at a picnic, no gang wanted to go head-to-head with the vicious Crips who vastly outnumbered them. No gang could match us strength for strength and the West Side Crips' swift rise to infamy was a traumatic blow to the older gangs. Instead they resorted to challenging us to meet at a designated spot, then ambushing us with a hail of bullets. Even a coward could chase fifty or more Crips down the street when strapped with a sidearm. On those occasions our marching orders became flight, not fight, because even our fists were no match for bullets.

The reputation of a black gang was usually built on its use of pugilistic success. Toting a gun wasn't our style – but we were getting shot at too often. One day after we had left a Jackson Five concert at the Los Angeles Forum, we mobbed our opposition of more than forty leather coats, and then Crip-walked down Manchester Boulevard en masse, more than 100-strong. Prowling in six cars, five in each car, were the Chain Gang, who opened fire on us. They continued to shoot even when an undercover police car passed.

Most of us ducked for cover inside Saint Andrew's Park. The air stank of potassium nitrate, and my heart pounded. All of us were half excited and half scared, except for Buddha and Mad Dog. The silence was broken from the other end of the park when the Chain Gang loudly challenged us to a fight. Even knowing they were packing guns, we strolled toward them with the audacity of men walking into a blazing fire wearing gasoline-soaked clothing.

As we approached, bullets zinged past my head, and we turned and sprinted to the opposite end of the park, then darted across Manchester Avenue into a car dealer's shop. Hiding behind brand new cars, we watched as the Chain Gang passed by and shot up the lot. Bullets ricocheted and smashed into vehicles and the wall. Some of us were trapped behind a row of cars and decided to make a run before they returned for another volley, but our route was blocked by big Bunchie, bawling like a baby, flatulent and refusing to budge.

The Chain Gang returned and their cars stopped. "We got your butt now, Tookie," jeered a voice, followed by rapid gunfire. In the midst of the hail of bullets, Buddha jumped up and ran toward them, cursing and shouting, "Over my dead body!" He brandished a gun, returning fire. Then Mad Dog appeared, also blasting away and causing the Chain Gang to screech off down the street. It surprised me that both of our homeboys were packing guns. We knew our tormentors would return, so I hollered at Hawk to move Bunchie out of the way. With one mighty kick, he rolled Bunchie to the side and we escaped into the darkness.

That event provoked many Crips to discard their right-hand leather gloves, used for fighting, and pick up guns. We were enraged, and strapped down for battle. Though I continued the old style of gang fighting and avoided toting a gun, I found security in knowing that those closest to me were carrying. Force and violence were a theme of our lives. The more we fought, the more we had to fight – a constant escalation.

Many of the Chain Gang members were grown men and had better access to weapons than we did, but they had to be taught a lesson, and it had to come swiftly. As the Chain Gang partied in their hangout late one afternoon, we surrounded the house. Big Curtis, Raymond and Fat Riley kicked in the front door and rushed inside with other homeboys. The house exploded. Chain Gang members were thrown out of windows, and those escaping through the back door ran into more of our fists and canes. Shots were fired, but our goal was to beat them into submission.

We met up at Saint Andrew's Park. I noticed blood trickling down Raymond's face; he had been hit in the head with a vase. But we knew the tables had turned. The Chain Gang had been eradicated on their own turf, although a few of them would blend into a new and deadlier foe, calling themselves the Inglewood Family.

Not long after, Raymond pulled up at Saint Andrew's

Park in a small caravan of black trucks with East Side Crips in the back. I recognized Head, supposedly a former Avenue Gang member turned Crip, driving one of the trucks. Raymond wanted to know if I'd accompany him to the Avalon Gardens (a public housing site) on the east side.

"There's this fool who lives there named Jimel who stole on me, then ran," he said. "I want to address that."

I told him no problem. With Buddha and the others we piled into the black trucks and caravanned to the east side of Los Angeles.

The trucks parked on the outskirts of Avalon Garden Courts, a housing project, were arranged in a half circle. The area was small in comparison to Imperial Courts or Jordon Downs, yet was exceptionally clean, with manicured lawns. We walked down the street and turned the corner, where I saw a small group of people standing on the grass in front of an apartment.

Raymond said, "That's Jimel with the lumber jacket on."

I saw a stocky, light-skinned guy with a large afro standing off to the side, looking guarded and uneasy. Raymond introduced Jimel to me. It was a tense moment. Raymond's homeboy Head had to be held back, and Jimel threw up his dukes in defence.

That's when Raymond asked Jimel, "Is it going to be Crip or what?"

Grudgingly, Jimel said, "Yes." They shook hands.

During the drama I scanned the area for a possible ambush while Buddha fidgeted with the .38 in his waistband. At one point Buddha whispered in my ear, "Cuz, when are we going to blast these fools?" I told him to be cool, let's see what happens. While Buddha paced back and forth behind us, another homeboy named Herc nervously looked around with his hand on a gun inside his jacket pocket. When we left, Head mumbled angrily, "I can't stand that dude, we don't need him anyway." But Raymond had a mischievous grin on his face. "Well, Tookie, that's more added to the east side," he said.

In the truck driving back to the park, Head told me Jimel

turned Crip because he didn't want to fight a war he couldn't win. Plus he was having too many problems with some of the neighbouring opposition like the Wall Nuts and Bishops gangs. Head mentioned it was the Wall Nuts who blasted Jimel with a shotgun, nearly killing him. Jimel did have influence over a small cadre of youths in the Avalon Gardens. They too would become a part of the East Side Crip regime. While Raymond was around, Jimel and company were simply East Side Crips. But later, when Raymond went to prison for a murder-related charge, Jimel and company became the Avalon Garden Crips. Raymond was the unchallenged leader of the entire East Side Crips regime, as was I with the West Side Crips.

At the Watts Festival at Will Rogers Park on the east side, Raymond introduced me to Mac Thomas, Mad Dog David, Little James, Eddie, Black Johnny, and a host of other Crips. There was an immediate rapport among all of them that grew through the years. Mac was beginning to build the infrastructure of the Compton Crips. Before long Little James and Mad Dog David established themselves as commanders of the east side, while Black Johnny would become the commander of the 43rd Street Crips.

Both Raymond and I were out constantly mobilizing and expanding our horizons without encroaching on one another's area. Shortly after recruiting Jimel, Raymond introduced me to a gang that had turned Crip. The gang he proselytized was the Compton Pirus, whose name became the Piru Crips. They were having a party in Compton to celebrate. I assumed Mac Thomas had sanctioned the alliance, since he reigned over the Compton Crips, who were growing quickly. But unknown to me, Mac and Raymond were in conflict over the alliance with the Pirus; Mac said they were his eternal enemies. The *entente* that Raymond had brokered was about to take a turn for the worse.

We arrived at the Pirus' party in a convoy of trucks and cars. Mac sat across the street on the hood of a car. After a long conversation with Tam, Puddin, and other Pirus, I walked over to where Mac was brooding. He launched into a tirade about not trusting the Pirus, complained about Raymond trying to compete with me for new recruits and said Raymond had no idea what was going on in Compton or with the Pirus. I listened as Mac talked about possible ambushes against his homeboys because Raymond had familiarized the Pirus with their hangouts. Mac gave an ultimatum: either the Piru and Crip alliance ended or he'd part ways, but remain allies with the West Side Crips, if I agreed. Mac predicted the Piru-Crip alliance would not last, even if he had to break it up himself.

The Compton alliance was flawed from the start. First, it was an offence to Mac, since Raymond didn't discuss it with him until after the fact. Second, the Pirus were Mac's nemesis. Third, the alliance could pit the Compton Crips against the Piru Crips and also against Raymond's East Side Crips. I would be placed in a position to choose sides or try to be non-partisan, which was next to impossible. If push came to shove, I'd choose whatever was best for West Side Crips.

I liked Mac Thomas. He was a short, muscular, brown-skinned powder keg that didn't take much to ignite. Thus far, the bad history between him and the Pirus hadn't been revealed to me in detail, but I understood how some scars were too deep to allow certain alliances. I continued to listen to Mac while greeting numerous Crips showing up late. Buddha, Herc, Bub, Raymond and others were inside the house party enjoying themselves. It was a gangster's *soiree*, Crips and Pirus in thuggish attire and women galore.

The festivities were interrupted by the sound of breaking glass, shouting, cussing, and Buddha's voice above it all: "Let's take it to the streets!" The house lit up, and people hurriedly scrambled outside, getting into cars and screeching off. Then Buddha stormed through the door. Mac and I jumped off the car and crossed the street. I could see Raymond and several Pirus following Buddha and Herc outside. They were arguing about some brim hat Buddha had taken from a Piru. Guns were drawn in hopes of restoring order. Raymond complained that Buddha was trying to sabotage the alliance, which Buddha said was a lie. It didn't matter to me whether Buddha was at fault; in my eyes he could do no wrong.

Then, to a stunned audience, Mac boasted, "I'm glad the alliance is broken. If Buddha didn't break it up, I would have."

"I don't want to hear that crap, fool," spat back Raymond.

For a moment Mac and Raymond stood eyeballing each other, then Raymond shook his head in disgust and continued trying to salvage the alliance. Mac was all smiles – he knew it was over.

The Piru Crips saga was the shortest pact in the history of black gangs. The Pirus became the Compton Crips' most deadly enemy. Mac was right – the Pirus were able to ambush Crip hangouts with regularity. But the West Side Crips, the Compton Crips, and the East Side Crips remained faithful allies with no internal warfare, but Raymond would always despise Buddha and Mac for what happened that night. And indirectly, he blamed me for the break.

A short time later, Bonnie and I were sipping fruit punch at a Washington High School dance and listening to a Buddha tirade about the aftermath of the Forum concert. He said he was tired of all the busters (cowards or squares) creeping up on us with guns, that we needed to fight fire with fire, wipe them all out. "I'm obligated to protect you, Tookie, and if I have to, I'll die trying," he raved. Bonnie's eyes widened in surprise.

Before I was able to respond, Mad Dog stormed in, angry about our homeboy Cuz being jumped on by some Figueroa Boys we had mobbed for their leather coats at the Los Angeles Forum. I rushed outside to see Cuz standing in a huge crowd of Crips with a swollen jaw, busted lip, torn shirt, and knots on his forehead. Cuz was a lanky, six-foot homeboy with the heart of a warrior. We moved out. When we reached the corner of 108th and Normandie, a caravan of ten low riders cruised by with Figueroa Boys hanging out the windows shouting vulgarities and challenging us to a gang fight. They parked their cars on 106th and walked toward us. We started walking from 108th, and picked up the pace to a slow trot, gaining momentum. As both sides neared the corner of 107th Street, gunfire rang out, causing everybody to scatter. Within minutes sirens were blaring and police cars were everywhere. It felt good to make it home safely and to avoid the police dragnet around the area.

Later that week, I was in class reading an essay entitled "What Would I Do If I Was Rich?" when school guards and several detectives entered the room looking for me and Mad Dog. We were led out of school, handcuffed, and driven in separate cars to Lennox Police Station, where they threw us in separate cells. I steeled myself for the inevitable interrogation while trying to figure out why we were dragged down to this hellhole. I was escorted to another small room and seated under bright lights across from two plainclothes police. One of them asked if I had attended a dance at Washington High Friday night. I shook my head. That pissed him off.

"Nigger, stop lying."

The other detective spoke in a milder tone and said that they had witnesses willing to testify that I was present at the dance and "the murder." The word "murder" resounded in my head: Are these fools kidding? In silence I tried to read their stony faces, hoping this was a cruel joke.

The two detectives huddled in a corner within earshot, discussing whether they would place me in a cell with adult murderers who would kill me. One of them eased behind me, then snatched the chair from underneath me. Hitting the floor hard, I gritted my teeth and tried to mask the pain. I was snatched up and shoved back in the chair.

"He's just a juvenile," said one.

"There's no age limit on charges of murder," said the other. "We have enough witnesses to charge him with first-degree murder. He'll get the death penalty."

Their psychological gymnastics to scare me into spilling my guts failed. I was returned to my cell, still in handcuffs, and before long Mad Dog was thrown in with me. Together we sat there cursing at the detectives, who occasionally peeped in at us. To ease our nerves, we laughed and joked around, but I said a silent prayer to be cut loose.

Mad Dog and I were released to our parents and I put the ordeal behind me. A couple of weeks later, my mother was contacted by the parents of Clint, an East Side Crip, and an attorney asking that I testify on Clint's behalf at juvenile court. Taking the witness stand seemed harmless enough. I confirmed his statements that we were together and didn't see anything. Clint walked away from his charges, but later I heard Raymond and Bulldog had been connected to the murder and were doing time. While Raymond was incarcerated, several Crips from the east side regime rose to become independent commanders but remained part of the east side collective.

The Crips was our vehicle for illusionary empowerment, payback, camaraderie, protection, thuggery, and a host of other benefits. We didn't want to be disenfranchised, dys-educated, disempowered, and destitute, but opportunities were scarce. We were seventeen-year-olds with polluted minds who wanted to be emancipated from the struggle against conditions that seemed to seek our extinction or emasculation. Regardless of hostile opposition or lack of social privilege, my vested interest, like everyone else, was simply to survive. The Crips became central to my self-destructive resolve.

This forgotten generation created a quasi-culture with its own mores, style of dress, hand symbols, vernacular, socio-economic qualities, martyrs, rituals, colour identification (blue for Crips), legends, myths and codes of silence. Words were coined for our madness. Buddha called it "cripping" or "crippin'." Our pride in the alliance gave birth to mottoes such as Craig's phrase, "Crippin' night and day is the only way." Melvin's favourite was, "Can't stop, won't stop." Buddha's brainchild was, "Crips don't die, we multiply." Raymond's favourite was, "Chitty chitty bang bang, ain't nothin' but a Crip thang."

"Do or die" was a common proverb among us, on both east side and west side. Crippin' was our reason for being. It grounded us in a way that nothing else had. It permitted us to lash out at gangs and at a world that despised us. This was an apocalyptic moment for countless black youth. Merely to survive each day was a personal victory. Our alliance was beginning to be noticed, and we were widely reviled.

Deprived by our colour and class of access to the American Dream, we began a Crip-walk toward self-destruction.

THIRTEEN

The Criplettes

In 1971, during the same month of the Crips' origination, there emerged a female version of ourselves, the Criplettes. They gained notoriety for indiscriminate attacks on both female and male opponents, overwhelming them with numbers and jacking them for their possessions. The founder of the Criplettes was my then girlfriend, Bonnie Quarles. She resembled a younger Aretha Franklin. Bonnie's close cousin Sheryl and I knew each other from school, and Sheryl wanted me to meet her. Though Bonnie wasn't enrolled at Washington High, I met her during a couple of my classes that she attended regularly, where a doting male teacher let her do whatever she pleased.

Before Bonnie, Sheryl and others were Criplettes, they were groupies hanging around us. Eventually they became girlfriends to some of us. They didn't fit the old profile of female gang members – masculine, dirty, scarred or nasty-looking. But in spite of their fresh, innocent good looks, they gained a reputation for fighting both in school and in the 'hood. Before long Bonnie's vanity and need to impress me led her to form a girl gang and try passionately to emulate us. They succeeded in deadly fashion.

I felt it was absurd for any woman to adopt the dangerous lifestyle of ganghood like hard heads. Some homeboys enjoyed watching women wrestling and fighting, but I was neither interested nor excited. In fact I was revolted by the

Criplettes' similar misdeeds. I strenuously objected to Bonnie and her friends' fighting and trying to follow us to gang fights.

A handful of them – Bonnie, Li'l Jackie, Black Connie, Bad Bessie, Goldie, Pretty Connie, Big Pam, Cookie, and others – etched their names in street infamy. Long life was no more promised to a Criplette than it was to a Crip. Drugs destroyed their lives and bullets penetrated their beautiful black skin like anyone else's.

Bad Bessie had a face and body that made her the spitting image of the entertainer Lola Folana. She was a throwback to a 1920s gun moll but willing to do her own dirty work. Like a black widow spider, she would lure the opposition into her lair, where Crips waited. Motivated by lust, our unsuspecting foe would follow Bad Bessie, the pied piper, to a beat-down, a robbery or their demise. Bessie often dressed in a beige khaki suit, brown suede boots and a brown Stetson hat. She was a trigger-happy gunslinger and a marksman. She practised with pellet guns, .22 calibre or a .38 calibre muffled by compressed steel wool, twine, copper wire, and other items she bragged about. Her silencers seemed to work. Everybody wanted one.

As a rule I kept Criplettes away during gang warfare. Females were a distraction to an undisciplined homeboy. I have childhood scars on my forehead as a reminder. But Bad Bessie was different. She hung around Crips instead of Criplettes and was respected for keeping her mouth shut under the pressure of cops. She could stroll right up to a rival, blast him, and then calmly walk away. Bad Bessie's "gun rep" made her a wanted Criplette, and she was shot a couple of times. In a shootout with the Figueroa Boys, Bad Bessie was caught in crossfire and was hit about fifteen times. Buddha and other Crips present told me she died on the spot. Rumours later had her paralysed from the waist down and living out of state. For a short while Bad Bessie was my best-kept secret, both from our opposition and from Bonnie.

Another one of Bonnie's homegirls, Pretty Robin, was

also beautiful: cocoa brown skin, a giant jet black afro and a statuesque body. She could've graced the cover of a magazine but aspired to be a Criplette. Although Pretty Robin did a lot of fighting and a little shooting, her favourite pastime was with reefer, bottle, or a glue bag. She was out to prove to any of us that she could out-drink, out-smoke, out-sniff and out-high any man. The new high for a while was a spot remover, ominously called Cryptonite, that fried brain cells like sausages. I tried it once and was zombified, scared straight – but to Pretty Robin, no high was too high. In her first experiment with Cryptonite, she died on the spot from cardiac arrest. She was seventeen.

The Criplette's legacy continues to serve as a deadly arche-type for other young black women who have abandoned hope.

FOURTEEN

Tookie's Law

Murphy's Law – "If anything can go wrong, it will" – could have been coined for my life. My struggle for order was constantly derailed by my desire for chaos. I couldn't help myself despite myself – that was Tookie's Law.

Washington High was probably the safest school on the planet while I was enrolled there – it became the West Side Crip capital, and every local gang kept a safe distance. Crips went back and forth to Washington High so frequently that they appeared to have diplomatic immunity. It was as if the school ceded its authority to us, resulting in a breakdown of control and order, and of the teacher-student relationship.

As far as I was concerned Washington High was Crip High. We were in control. There was no gang bigger or stronger, no gang tough enough to dethrone us. For a short while Washington was a Crip's paradise. We lounged around, got loaded, gambled, and pursued young women for sexual conquests. All was mellow until the day we entered the school cafeteria with shaved heads. This provoked snickers from a crowd of beefy football players and their women. Seconds later a few of the football players were stretched out on the floor, and the rest had fled.

After the cafeteria brawl the gloves were off. All guys were potential prey for us, in particular football players. It was a training ground for Crips, honing their thuggery at school and then venturing out to maraud, block by block and then mile by mile through South Central. Like locusts we swarmed and stripped people of their valuables, then melted away. Leather coats and jewelry were the hot commodities, as precious to us as ivory and animal skins were to blacks in Africa. We created schisms throughout the community, between parent and child, church and child, school and child, society and child. I'm certain that even the angels wanted no part of our forgotten generation. Everybody was caught off-guard by our rapid expansion. Even local black politicians who claimed to be in touch with the community didn't have a clue.

Crips were everywhere, visible day and night. Bonded by our shared poverty, the Crips became my family. I placed Crip above and beyond all else, even my life. Survival in this community meant slim pickings for a black youth such as myself, but as a Crip I could strive to be legendary. It was my intent to make "Crip" and "Tookie" synonymous, a matched set and a terrorizing force among every other black gang in South Central. Soon, however, my high visibility and obsession with being recognized led the school administration to identify me as the West Side Crips leader named Tookie, and to expel me. It was a blow to my ego to be thrown out of a school I was supposed to reign over.

The following week, when my mother and I entered Fremont High School for my registration, there were East Side Crips everywhere calling, "Tookie, Tookie!" My mother looked puzzled.

"Who in the world are all those hoodlums dressed like you?" she said.

"They're my cousins."

She shook her head and shouted back, "Boy, I know all your cousins. They aren't any of my sister's kids!"

I wasn't about to tell her that this school was the East Side Crip capital, that those hoodlums were my relatives of a different kind. The very next day, in first period, a counsellor escorted me out of class to the Principal's office. It had been brought to his attention that I was Tookie, a known troublemaker to most local schools, and that I was a close friend of one Raymond Washington, another unruly youth who hung around the school. The Principal said there were already too many problems at Fremont with Raymond and company to take on any more. So he politely apologized for the inconvenience – and then expelled me.

I was blackballed by Crenshaw, Manual Arts, Inglewood, Gardena, Los Angeles High and all the rest. The institute of learning supposedly tailor-made for me was California High, an all-boys' school formerly known as Reese School for Boys. California High near downtown Los Angeles, around 15th street off of Broadway. The school was a tall yellowish building with no windows, a steel mesh cage on top of the roof, and thick chains and locks on the doors. The front door was patrolled and heavily guarded by rent-a-cops.

A large yellow school bus started from Imperial Avenue and picked us up along Broadway Street. It was said to carry a bunch of degenerates and retards incapable of functioning normally in public schools. The bus didn't faze me; it was the school I disliked. There weren't any female students. It reminded me of the Job Corps, Camp Rocky and Central Juvenile Hall.

I managed to stay at California High for several months, though I did a lot of ditching. When I was finally kicked out, it was not for truancy but for trying to choke out a guy with a hoisting chain in auto shop. The teacher who intervened stammered with a Jamaican accent and jabbered about solidarity, unity, honour and black power. I couldn't tell the teacher the other guy had pulled a knife on me at lunch. After that, there were no more schools in the city willing to accept me.

I'm sure my mother missed the old days of Biblical punishment, but they had ended at fifteen when I was strong enough to catch her firm hand in mid-air. No more thick switches, leather straps, extension cords, or locking me outside the apartment. Now she ordered me to find a job – but where and doing what? Each morning when I left the house, it wasn't to hunt for employment. I was looking for gangs, leather coats and women.

The Crip evolution had me spinning in fast forward. While mobilizing and expanding, I'd forgotten that, back at home on 90th Street, I had befriended two brothers, Ronnie and Donnie, who had influence over thirty to forty other youths, mostly relatives and childhood buddies. They were jolted with excitement when I revealed that their buddy Stan was actually Tookie. Donnie whispered, "That's Tookie of the Crips, right?" I told them we were the West Side Crips and there were Crips on the east side and in Compton. When I said, "I want you both to be part of our Crip family," they looked at one another with huge grins. Then Donnie replied, "Of course, we've been waiting for this!" Ronnie, Donnie and their homeboys would become known as the Budlong Street Crips.

When my own recruiting efforts began to taper off, my homeboys had the good judgment to enlist whomever they felt worthy of being a Crip. Hordes of other youths would track me down to enlist in our youthful army. I walked down 90th Street toward Budlong with a group of homeboys when two youths approached us, identifying themselves as Big Bamm and Buck. Bamm asked which one of us was Tookie.

"That's Tookie right there," said Buddha, cradling his gun. "What's the problem?"

Big Bamm eyed Buddha for a split second, then like others before him expressed interest in being part of the Crips. En route to Saint Andrew's Park, I planned to take Bamm and Buck into our junta against other gangs. Recruiting was a natural process for me; I would observe the combination of a youth's street genetics, vibe, intuition or evil connection. We just clicked. Instead of the archaic gang tradition of "jumping in" a new member — giving him a group beating — I instituted initiation by battle, requiring a new member to test his mettle against the opposition, not against his own homeboys. Everybody I embraced was a mirror image of myself. We swaggered with a defiant arrogance that screamed, "No on can whip me, no one!"

That night, during several parties we crashed, Bamm and Buck initiated themselves into our Crip violence.

About a week later I met a youth named Alfred Coward, a.k.a. Whitey, a former Denver Lane gang member, at a Sportsman Park Boys' party where he and others were refused entry. After my homeboys and I demolished the Sportsman Park Boys, I introduced myself to Whitey: "By the way, my name is Stan but my friends call me Tookie. We are the Crips." Even in the dark I could see his eyes widen to the size of silver dollars. That evening Whitey participated in a Crip stomping of the Sportsman Park Boys that earned him his way into our youth army. Later Whitey would ask me to give him a new nickname. I named him "Blackie" for no particular reason, and it stuck. Later, the person I called Blackie, whose life I saved on several occasions, would become a Judas and lie on me.

Like most of my homeboys in this volatile microcosm, I didn't dwell upon death. Blind ignorance made me indifferent to its possibility. Though my homeboys began to be killed off, my inner self remained untouched. I shed no tears. Growing up I had seen enough ruthlessness to desensitize me. By lashing out at gangs and the world, I felt no empathy, no penitence for what I touted as the ultimate display of manhood. At seventeen I could not feel others' suffering or the loss they felt of a loved one. I stared at the corpse of each friend as if they were sleeping or in a drug-state coma. They were flashes of my future that I dared not face or feel.

There were Crips like Melvin's homeboy's fourteen-year-old brother Dee-Dee, murdered by the cops; Raymond's homeboy Craig, blown away by a vengeful adult; my homeboy Diver Dan, shot down because of his resemblance to me. I would have risked my life for them, but I lacked the humanity to mourn their deaths – even as I recognized that death would one day visit us all. I saw dying as the end of the losing equation in the scheme of survival. All of us Crips had witnessed death enough times to know it was inevitable. None of us wanted to die – but our haphazard style of existence was a form of *hara-kiri*.

If I wasn't undergoing near-death experiences in the gang area then I was clashing with those other maniacal foes, the hood cops, who could now identify me on sight. Like other blacks from my neighbourhood, it was instinctive for me to run from the cops to avoid harassment or getting set up, brutalized or killed. I knew that cops had *carte blanche* to violate my rights or blow me away, which made me nervous. Black people have known for many, many years that some white cops are racist, despite society's bland denials.

One evening, while leaving a liquor store on Century and Budlong with Buddha, Herc, Monk and Blackie, a lone cop car cruised by, then made a U-turn. They had seen us "walking while youthful and black," a serious offence. Two cops jumped out and hollered, "Halt, Tookie, halt!" I darted away, crossing the street under cover of darkness, and heard a volley of shots. Time slowed. I felt as if I was running in place on a treadmill. Bullets whistled by me as I ran through a vacant lot and cut into an alley. I stepped into a hole and flew out into the air, landed on my stomach, jumped up and continued to run. Soon the entire area was alive with Lennox patrol cars and a helicopter. I was cornered in a backyard.

The cops were doing door-to-door searches for a man who had allegedly shot at a policeman. It was only a matter of time before I'd be discovered hiding in an old shed. I didn't expect to make it out alive. I heard the cops enter the yard. I could see their flashlights shining through the tiny cracks in the shed. Seconds later the door swung open revealing shotguns pointing inside, voices ordering me to not move. It was chaos. Some cops were telling me to lie down, stay still, while others hollered I should walk toward them with my hands in the air. Each command was punctuated with, ". . . or I'll blow your black head off!"

An elderly black woman peeped her head through the screen door and turned on the light. I could hear her shaky voice asking, "Is that the dangerous killer, officers?"

One cop spat out, "Yes, that's him, madam, and he's going to jail."

She gasped, "Oh my Lord. Thank you, officers."

I was handcuffed and dragged through a gauntlet of flashlights, batons, fists, and kicks to the body. By the time I reached Lennox Police Station I was hardly able to walk. They dragged me along, then threw me in a cell. Buddha had contacted my mother, and she and Fred drove around hoping to find me before the cops did. The cops themselves spread the canard that I had shot several times at a cop. When they showed up at the station the desk officer said the charge was an assault with a deadly weapon on a peace officer. My mother was frantic.

The following day the cops stood outside the cell door threatening to pay me back for shooting at their partner. Since I wasn't handcuffed or incapacitated, their threats meant nothing to me. Later on I was told investigators were in the field looking for the gun they thought I had used. I knew in order for them to avoid a lawsuit and to justify the shooting, they had to play the charade to the end. The mysterious weapon was never found and I was released after seventy-two hours.

On my way out the sneering desk cop said, "You are one lucky nigger, because my partner is an expert marksman."

Out of my mother's earshot, I told the cop, "Well, that devil buddy of yours couldn't be too much of an expert . . . the cracker missed."

I had become the cops' prime target. It was a perilous badge of distinction. My mother feared that one day she'd receive a call that cops had murdered me. In South Central it was common for mothers to not only worry about street elements devouring their son, but also to worry about death-by-cop. Next thing I knew, my mother and I were on a Greyhound bus bound for Oakland, California, where my biological father was living with a new wife, son, and daughter. The plan was for me to live with them. They hoped this would change my life.

I sat in the back of my father's 1971 Eldorado Cadillac in the parking lot of some park and made noises, sucking my teeth, uninterested in anything he had to say. He blabbered about how I looked crazy wearing a wide-brim hat and a long cross earring, and then laughingly said, "Hell, only girls wear earrings." I had to press my hands together so as not to sucker-punch him upside the back of his head. I didn't know this man nor did I care to, and there was nothing he could tell me. When he decreed that I was going to school every day whether I liked it or not, I asked, "Are you man enough to make me?"

My mother intervened with, "Shut up, boy, and listen. That's the problem with you."

After this one-sided conversation, we headed back to the motel where my mother and I had spent the previous night. She gathered her suitcase, kissed and hugged me, and said goodbye on her way out the door. My father dropped six twenty-dollar bills on the bed and then left.

Meeting him was a moment of disconnection: his face was blurred, his words were academic and his eye contact was non-existent. His strategy to use a hardcore approach to reach me was as impractical as a cop's attempt to terrorize me into social reform. It was a weird father and son encounter – total absence of recognition and a reception cold as ice.

My father didn't return, so that afternoon I left the motel, returned to Los Angeles, and stayed with my homeboy A.C. and his mother near 112th and Budlong. Living at A.C.'s mother's house suited me just fine. It was the main Crip hangout for ditching school, getting high, and sexual pleasures. When A.C.'s mother was at work, the house was a revolving door for women. It was there I met Claretta, who came by looking for her seventeen-year-old daughter. We struck up a conversation, and were soon in her Lincoln Continental headed for her home in Gardena off of Vermont. Though Claretta was thirty-six years old and married with five children my age and older, she could easily have passed for twenty-one. She was attractive and voluptuous. After our first sex, Claretta tripped me out when she led me into another room that was red-padded and had three tables with two blender machines and a huge wooden bowl filled with fresh fruit. Standing in a corner in her panties and bra trying to look defenceless, she asked me to throw some grapes, cherries, and apricots at her. She told me not to use the larger fruits because they were for someone else who liked to get hit with them. I thought probably her husband. I obliged her, though I was edgy about Claretta's fetish. I couldn't fathom the connection between sex and being pelted with fruit. But I wasn't the weirdo – plus the sex was excellent.

On the eighth or ninth occasion, Claretta picked me up right after I had gotten loaded, sniffing glue and smoking weed. After sex we headed to Claretta's padded fruit room. She stood in a corner and while I was throwing grapes, Claretta started saying, "No, please stop, don't do that!" I stopped, and then she said, "Tookie, no matter what I say or do, don't stop!" As I continued to throw the grapes Claretta said, "Throw them a little harder!" which I did. But when she screamed out, "Harder, harder," I started firing those grapes and cherries at her with the velocity of a major league pitcher. When the bowls of grapes and cherries were empty, I pitched plums, oranges, apples and cantaloupes. Being loaded I seemed to be throwing the fruit in slow motion, but was actually moving at the speed of an animated cartoon character. When I ran out of fruit I even threw the wooden bowls and the blenders. After regaining my composure, I saw that Claretta was crouched in the corner, cowering and crying. We rode back in silence to A.C.'s place and I realized our sexual tryst was over.

When I wasn't kicking it at A.C.'s house, other activities kept me busy. Once a mob of us Crips from the west and east sides caught a bus downtown. After mobbing a couple of clothing stores for whatever caught our eye, I spotted a leather coat shop near a corner down the street from the Greyhound bus station. I knew exactly how to seize the moment and elevate my reputation. There were no less than twenty of us prepared to try on new leather jackets. I told everyone to find themselves a coat of choice. Once that was done, I said, "Let's go."

"Sir, how do you intend to pay for all of this?" asked the sales woman.

"Put it on the Crip bill," I replied, before kicking open the little wooden swing gate and walking out.

After gathering at a hamburger stand, Eddie, Archie and I took off ahead of everybody to get first crack at the merchandise. As we did so, several patrol cars pulled up. Cops jumped out with guns in hand and ordered us to raise our arms. We were cuffed, put in the back seat of a car and driven down the street to be identified for robbery.

Six youths standing outside of Clifton's restaurant on Broadway mistakenly identified us. Apparently there were other Crips around, because we got busted for something we didn't do at Clifton's. The three of us were taken to the police station and placed in separate cells.

Tookie's Law was firmly in place.

FIFTEEN

Boys Republic
to Factor Brookins

I was sent to Central Juvenile Hall, then to Los Padrinos. During my brief stay there, I had a fight with some Mexicans and some white dudes. In one instance I ran into a Mexican dude and knocked him down while playing football. He jumped up cursing and called me a stupid nigger, so I thrashed him. As I fought, I was hit on the head and back with metal belt buckles by his white and Mexican buddies. Standing on the sideline in a frightened, non-partisan stance were about twenty blacks who refused to budge.

Out of nowhere, a tall, skinny and blond-haired white guy stood back-to-back with me, knocking them down like I was. Afterwards while sitting in a classroom for a few minutes I thanked him for having the heart to assist me, but we forgot to exchange names. When counsellors brought in the group of white and Mexican dudes, all of them looked pretty bruised up. The white guy and I looked at one another, then burst out laughing. Though a truce was made, I knew never to turn my back because those guys could become super-dangerous.

When it came time for the court judge to make a decision between Youth Authority and Boys Republic, I was shipped off to the latter. Boys Republic was located in Chino, California, down the road from Chino State Prison. The entire facility was huge, with about five cottages, each two storeys high with a lot of bedrooms. There was a large church, gymnasium, school building, workshops, football and track field, weight room, refreshment store, cattle and other things I had never seen. I wasn't at Boys Republic a full week when I got into a fight in the wood-shop class with several Mexicans and whites. The blacks there had left me high and dry, but I got hold of a wooden table leg and chased my assailants out. No surprise: the only one ending up in the lock-up was me. Despite my own bruises, I guess it looked pretty bad, me standing there with a bloody table leg in my hand.

After being in the Central and Los Padrinos lock-up units, this was no different. I was isolated from other youths. There were no books, letters or any materials to occupy my time. When I wasn't sleeping, I did hundreds of pushups or shadow-boxing, essential conditioning for gang battle. There were moments in my solitude when I reflected on my existence, wondering if this was all life had to offer. Such thoughts really didn't matter. Tomorrow seemed aeons away. I lived only for today.

Isolation in the lock-up unit was designed to overpower a prisoner's mind with diffidence and fear, to shock a person into rehabilitation, nihilism, or psychosis. In the event this didn't work, there were plenty of prisons, asylums, and graveyards to accommodate the failed prisoner. This was something too profound for me to articulate or to write home to "Moms" about. But I resisted its subtle coercions.

Once outside of lock-up I was greeted as a warrior by a group of blacks who proudly shook my hand. The telling and retelling of the woodshop incident had been hyperbolized with Biblical overtones, as though I had beaten down over twenty enemies with the jawbone of an ass. A stocky black teenager of my age named Barker revealed that the dudes I beat with the table leg hated blacks and pretty much called shots on everybody. He went on to say the majority of blacks here were busters and didn't want any problems, but if need be, he, George, Psycho and others were ready to fight. Barker was from Los Angeles, on 90th Street, but had spent years in and out of state institutions since the age of twelve. When I introduced myself as Tookie, Barker's eyes lit up. He said, "Yes, I heard of you, the Crips, the Crips." He shook my hand for so long I had to pull it away. I ended up welcoming Barker and five of his friends into the West Side Crips, and awhile later, following his release, he became one of the commanders of the Budlong Crips.

Christmastime brought the annual Boys Republic tradition of making ornaments. Any youth wanting to earn a furlough home had to reach a specific quota of ornaments to attach to the wreaths. I reached my quota and earned the furlough. My mother and Fred came to drive me home – and the next day put Cynthia and I on a Greyhound bus to New Orleans. They intended to keep me out of trouble during my furlough by sending me to a place where there were lots of relatives and no hoodlum friends. Cynthia stayed in the front house with Momma (my grandmother) and Aunt Dorothy. I stayed upstairs in the back with my cousins Sonny and Turo. Both of them were amazed at my garb and asked did all California teenagers dress like I did. "Of course not," I said, "only Crips dress this way." I explained a bit to them about the Crips then changed the subject.

When I wasn't with Momma enjoying her company and her home-cooked meals, I was working out with a sixty-pound dumbbell I had tucked away in a travel bag. Once I ventured out to a seedy spot in New Orleans where the price of *ganja* was ridiculously inflated: $10 for an itty-bitty matchbox of weed, compared to South Central's three- or four-fingered dope bag for the same price. My cousins – who were not into drugs – convinced me not to jack the dealer for his dope because it would have brought heat down on them.

My stay in New Orleans was quite nice, especially after I met a young lady whose hospitality was downright accommodating. Though I enjoyed the visit, I couldn't wait to get back to California. Soon Cynthia and I were waving goodbye and boarding a plane to fly back. The next afternoon I was back at Boys Republic driving iron in the weight room with Barker. I briefly got involved in the football programme, which I enjoyed, playing wide receiver because of my speed. Playing against the public schools was interesting, although we lost every game, but a fight or two would break out afterwards, allowing us to end the evening with a win.

Presently, I gave the dorm leader a black eye for turning off the TV while we were watching it. I warned him not to snitch, but he did. The next day I was expelled and driven home. I warned the counsellor driving the van that he better not try to take me to Juvey because I'd cause him to wreck. He assured me that was not his intent.

I arrived home. My mother stared at the counsellor through the screen door and asked, "What did he do this time?" The counsellor told her I had attacked a white guy for no reason and gave my mother a number to call to find out what the courts planned to do with me. When he left I told my mother, "Don't waste your time calling those people. I'm not going back to Juvey. They'll have to catch me first!" There was no doubt in my mind the court's next step would be to send me straight to Youth Authority. I wasn't going willingly. My mother looked at me bleakly but didn't say anything.

When I called Buddha, he told me about a place called Factor Brookins in Banning, California, a little over 100 miles from Los Angeles. He gave me the number for Bob Simmons, the director, who told me he would contact the courts and have me assigned to his programme. After my mother called Bob, he called back to tell her that I was enrolled in his programme and to bring me on Sunday before 3 p.m. to the park on Willow Brook off of Compton Avenue, where a bus would be waiting. When we arrived there were two buses, a crowd of people – and Buddha standing next to his mother, grinning. While our mothers talked, Buddha told me that Banning was cool, that we'd get furloughs, and that several of our homeboys – Little James, Warlock, Monk, Melvin, and other Crips – were there. With all my homeboys around, I figured how bad could the place be? I hugged and kissed my mother goodbye, and the bus took off for a long drive.

Banning itself was a barren pastoral town with a single police station, a bank, a theatre, a club, a park and a hardware store. It was the polar opposite of the chaotic madness in the Los Angeles jungle. Factor Brookins was sponsored by a man known as Jake the Barber, a one-time associate of the notorious Al Capone. The facility consisted of four long rows of furnished two-bedroom duplex apartments and plenty of food. Buddha and I shared an apartment and put our weights in the living room. If ever there was a youth's fantasy of freedom, Factor Brookins was it.

Shortly after settling in I noticed tension between my homeboys and the local youths, since young Banning females often invited my homeboys to their picnics, house parties and other social functions. At one of these gatherings, jam-packed with my homeboys and plenty of local girls, an upset crowd of local dudes challenged us to fight. When we went outside, they scattered. At 10 p.m. when the gathering ended, some of my homeboys jumped into cars or into the back of a truck, but I decided to enjoy the night air and walk back to the boys' home. Though he knew I disliked guns, Buddha tried to slip me a chrome snub-nose .38 that I pushed aside. In typical Buddha fashion he stated, "Well, since you don't want my piece, I'll walk too." I grudgingly accepted the gun, shoved it down my waistband and walked away. As the truck passed by, Buddha and the others hollered, "Crip here," then stopped. Out jumped twelve-year-old Little Tee, saying, "Buddha suggested somebody walk back with you, so I volunteered."

It was therapeutic to inhale the crisp cool air and stroll down the street without a care. Nowhere in Los Angeles was I able to feel as close to being liberated as I did that moment. It was 1972, I was eighteen, the Crips gang wasn't even a year old – but we were the baddest human beings on this planet. I started doing the Crip walk taught to me by Dancing Sugar Bear, who originated it (it was later described by a magazine as "a tiptoe dance that some say looks like hopscotch on crack"). But thuds and sounds of glass breaking shattered my mood. Bricks rained down on us, and two of them hit me square in the chest with enough force to stun and knock me back. Instinctively I whipped out the gun and fired blindly into the darkness to scare my attackers. Tee and I trotted some distance until I stopped, bent over in pain. I told Tee to run ahead to tell the others what had happened.

I walked down the middle of the street peering around houses, vacant lots, and cars, anticipating another ambush, possibly with a volley of bullets. From a distance I could hear Buddha cursing and hollering.

"Who were those cowards? Let's go smash them."

As Buddha, Warlock, and Little James got closer I could see guns in their hands and rage in their faces. I told them it was too dark to see who it was, but I was sure it was the country bumpkins who challenged us earlier then ran off. Buddha swore up and down he would avenge the attack.

As I climbed into bed that night I noticed two nasty bruises. All I wanted to do was sleep the pain away, then come back strong for whatever. The last thing I remembered before dozing off was Buddha telling me, "This won't take long, cuz. I'll be right back." Around seven the next morning I heard the sound of a police radio and jumped up to see what was going on. Buddha was in the back seat of a patrol car, beaming wickedly. As I approached the car, Bob told me Buddha was accused of shooting up the movie theatre last night and that he'd blasted at some of the locals, hitting one of them. After Buddha emptied his gun, he calmly reloaded then started shooting at them again. He often acted as if he cared more about me than he did about himself. The car pulled away with Buddha in the back seat. I wondered how long it'd be before I saw him again.

Factor Brookins soon became co-ed. Bonnie was in the programme, along with a few other Criplettes from Los Angeles She became pregnant. Though I felt proud to be a father, I didn't know the first thing about raising a child. I had problems raising myself. My elation – and uncertainty – came to a halt a month later when Bonnie had a miscarriage. The baby would have been a boy. That week Bob and the counsellor, Kenny, suggested I become a junior counsellor with a salary. I could be a counsellor, get paid, and still be able to go out crippin'.

Bob then came up with an outrageous idea: we would attend Banning High and play football for Banning. What school in their right mind would accept a bunch of high school rejects with criminal records? But Bob pulled it off and began to train us like professional football players. Each morning before five we were up running wind sprints, obstacle courses, and laps around the track prior to breakfast. I trimmed down from 175 pounds to 160 in a matter of weeks, and though I had a lot of definition I felt skinny. By then Sweetback was in the programme, too, and joined the football team. We were in tiptop shape – a fast, vicious, talented crew of athletic misfits, the best players on the team, exceeding Bob's expectations. Here we were, Crips, playing team football, attending classes and actually doing schoolwork. None of us even thought about ditching class or school. I was attending school and enjoying playing on the football team, without pretext or profit. For the first time in my chaotic life there appeared a chance to uplift myself.

One day, preparing to run wind sprints, I caught site of Buddha in a football uniform, Crip-walking across the football field chanting "Crips don't die, we multiply!" He had been released, was enrolled in school, and on the football team. Everybody extended their cousin salutations to Buddha and went through our welcoming routine: a split-second hug, handshake, and a Kool-aid smile. In our practices we dominated so much that Bob told us opposing coaches from other schools accused Banning coaches of hiring ringers who played semi-professional football. Then it was discovered that we had criminal records and that no school in Los Angeles would enrol us. Pressure was placed on Banning High, and they kicked us out of school. This was not a surprise, since I had never experienced true accomplishments. I viewed everything through a negative lens, expecting only the worst.

Since we seemed destined to end up in prison, a rehab clinic, or a local graveyard, I felt the need to continue striking blows at anything in the name of Crip. In my mixed-up world everything was twisted: sin was my morality, immaturity served as my wisdom and war represented peace.

In spite of my Crippen ways I was still receiving a pay cheque of $125 every two weeks as a junior counsellor. I started saving money to buy a car so I wouldn't have to steal them all the time. Cars were vital to us. Sweetback had a stolen, cocoa-brown, 1963 Malibu. He was so possessive of it that he attacked our homeboy Cuz for spilling ketchup on it. Herc was so attached to his stolen 1964 Chevy that he bought new brakes and a new ignition for it. He kept that car for a year until he wrecked it during a shootout. The longest I held onto a stolen car was for two days, thinking that by then it would be on every cop's hot sheet.

I planned to give most of my pay to Bonnie to stash for me to attend a big dice game in one of the apartments. Buddha enjoyed gambling and was darn good at losing all of his money. Every youth in the programme received an allowance of $50 dollars twice a month and most of them gambled – but Bob or one of his buddies usually won. Whenever the sole Los Angeles Brim, Little Dodi, won the jackpot, everybody wanted to rip him apart, and I had to prevent it. But once in a while a novice would win the jackpot – and this time it was me. I left with $600 dollars! The next day I ran across a car outside of the area of Banning where we lived. Catching my eye was an immaculate 1963 metallic gold Lincoln Continental with snow-white leather interior and suicide doors. After a smooth test ride I paid $500 for it, then drove it back to the boys' home. Buddha said, "Cuz, that's you, that car fits you to a tee." Everybody commented on how sharp, classy, and gangster-esque the car looked.

During our next furlough to Los Angeles, Buddha and I scoured the area to appropriate a set of wheels with Crager rims for my car. Spotting this guy Odel with a brand new set, I convinced him to follow me to a vacant house. Once there I coerced him to take the wheels off his car and then place them on mine. They were a perfect fit. Next, we had hydraulic lifts put in the front and thick whitewalls from the House of Chrome that gave my car a 1920s gangster look. The Lincoln was a head turner, a modern army tank creeping through enemy territory ready to do battle. With a flamboyant air I would arrive on a scene, Buddha and me in the back seat and Herc driving. We'd step out in complete Crip attire with fancy wooden canes, ready to fight anyone. The arrival of the Lincoln had my rivals fleeing on sight.

The car also became a target for police harassment. I'd get pulled over several times within a radius of ten blocks. Under the watchful single eye of their revolver they'd hold me hostage until a search of my car was complete. Throughout the day I'd be tag-teamed again by the Lennox Sheriffs, the Los Angeles Police, or the Firestone police harassing and searching for contraband. In front of Bonnie, one cop scratched the serial numbers off my tape deck then arrested me for receiving stolen property. While I sat in jail, there was a seventy-two-hour investigation that culminated with the charges being dropped.

Plenty of times when the cops pulled me over and found nothing incriminating, they'd arrest Bonnie for truancy. She was seventeen and required by law to be in school. I thought marriage would resolve the problem. On our wedding day there were torrential rains, the window button on the driver's side was stuck, the window wouldn't close, and I got soaked. The wedding was simple and brief: no tuxedo, wedding gown, wedding ring, wedding cake, and no traditional honeymoon. Since Buddha wasn't on hand as best man, Bimbo substituted as witness and rice thrower. Being callow and unpolished, I didn't take the marriage seriously even though Bonnie was devoted and loving. I was loyal to crippin' and nothing else. Our wedding day was expedient and unsentimental. After the ceremony I dropped Bonnie off at her mother's house and went on my merry way.

The following day I was out caravanning with Buddha and other homeboys in a turquoise Lemans he had bought. We went to a self-service car wash on Western around 74th

Street. While washing my rims I saw a couple of carloads of dudes drive up and park on the side street. Two people got out and walked towards us, Buddha boldly confronted them and asked what they wanted, while trigger-happy Herc stood off to the side. I walked toward Buddha. The larger of the two introduced himself as Big James and the slimmer fellow as Michael. As I got closer I heard Buddha say, "Well, there's Tookie. What's up?" After introducing himself to me, James stated he'd been hearing a lot about the Crips and that he wanted to join us. He mentioned a dance at the YMCA behind the Crenshaw Mall where we could meet later that night. Buddha kept tapping me on the arm, whispering, "Cuz, I don't trust this dude." But I waved him off and told James we'd be there.

Buddha reminded me after they'd left that the YMCA was in the same area where we had raided several Rebel Rousers' parties a week before and seized a bunch of leather coats. But I didn't forget; I simply didn't care. I was no zip-zam fool. I did do some asinine things, but usually there was a method to my madness (except when I was loaded). I saw this as an opportunity to expand the West Side Crips and was going to take it.

That night we showed up at the YMCA after 10 p.m. and parked our cars across the street in the shopping mall lot. I left my keys with Bonnie in my car, while Li'l Jackie stayed in Buddha's car. I opted for just a handful of us to be there: me, Buddha, Herc, Blackie and Monk.

The YMCA looked deserted. There were no other cars nearby. I felt a little uneasy, wondering if this was a set-up. When we entered, the YMCA was jam-packed. People were bumping with the James Brown song "Pass the Peas." Big James was nowhere around so I decided to wait awhile to see if he showed up. A short time later this guy appeared, saying, "Big James is outside waiting for Tookie." Outside I saw James standing on the corner next to his homeboy Michael and another guy who had one hand in his coat pocket. As soon as we stepped out into the open, more of James' homeboys appeared, surrounding us in a semi-circle.

We stood in creepy silence. The breeze chilled me. Was this a setup? Was Buddha right? I sensed James was stalling, but for what, re-inforcements? I tried to calm myself, knowing that Herc and Buddha were packing, but was it enough to ward off the larger numbers? The silence was driving me crazy. I didn't like feeling trapped or vulnerable. As I looked eye-to-eye with James, anger began to well up within me and my patience wore thin. I could wait no longer.

"So what's it going to be James, Crip or what?" If something was supposed to happen, then let's get the show on the road.

Standing there at six foot two and more than 200 pounds, Big James was larger than me, but I believed in the legend that I was a giant killer. I saw indecision in James's eyes. I repeated my question with some heat.

"What's it going to be, Crip or what?"

Big James broke the silence: "Yes."

After a brief handshake the tension relaxed – until a squad of cop cars descended upon us from every direction. A helicopter's spotlight beamed overhead. They ordered us to get down on our knees and lock our fingers on top of our heads. Though the cops didn't find any weapons on us, several were found a few yards away. That was enough to take all of us to jail.

Bonnie had the presence of mind to follow the police car I was put in to the station. Inside, the cops interrogated us one by one. Since no one talked, we were charged only with possession of a deadly weapon. That's when James' homeboy Michael spoke up,

"There's no need to do that. The guns are mine."

Riding a beef was common among my homeboys, but to witness someone do it outside our circle was unusual. I was impressed.

Before being released Big James assured me they were ready to become part of my West Side Crips. He and his crew would become known as the Harlem Crips. Later, during a brief stint in the Los Angeles County jail, I ran into his homeboy Michael, who revealed that they were supposed to smoke me on that night. They also planned to smoke the madman Buddha because he was too dangerous to leave alive if I was dead. It was to be retaliation for our mobbing and Crip-stomping some of their relatives and homeboys at a party. Michael said, "Cuz, we literally mapped out a plan to smoke you, but Big James didn't follow through." They were now West Side Crips. That was all that mattered to me.

Driving back to Banning I relished the moment, knowing the West Side Crips were evolving into the dynamic force I had envisioned at Camp Rocky. While buffing iron in the apartment at Factor Brookins with Little James and Buddha, I rehashed the latest addition to the West Side Crips and how we would continue to grow. I jokingly told them, "The world will know exactly who the Crips are."

When it was my turn to work out with the barbell doing back-arms, I stood before the full-length mirror and boasted, "One day my arms will be so yoked up, no one will believe it!"

But Little James interjected and said, "That's cool, cuz, but what about a powerful chest?"

He was right. I needed a monstrous, powerful chest. Little James worked his arms but he also worked on his chest. He was the first Crip among us who bench-pressed more than 300 pounds. He was the one who encouraged me to start benching, and soon I was out-benching Little James and any other Crip. When I wore a short-sleeved shirt, my appearance had a noticeable effect on women. It was odd how I always felt twice as muscular as I really was.

Bob was increasingly aware of the gang epidemic spreading throughout Los Angeles and Compton. In addition to establishing more boys' homes, he wanted to bring public focus onto the serious youth problem. Bob published a small Compton newspaper with an article called "The Baddest," with Buddha, Little James, Warlock, Melvin, Sweetback, Monk and me on the front cover. It introduced the city to a gang called the Crips blowing up in Compton and South Central. Occasionally Bob would set up youth prevention workshops to expose this plague, but his warning fell on deaf ears. It wasn't long after his attempt to warn the masses that the Factor Brookins programme was terminated. Our refuge was gone. We were kicked back into the gut of South Central, and into full-time crippin'.

SIXTEEN

Mr Buddha! Mr Buddha!

His name was Curtis Morrow, a.k.a. "Buddha." He had Asian-esque, almond-shaped eyes that became slits when he was drunk, crowned by the bald roundness of his cranium. Buddha was five foot eight, about 180 pounds, stocky, with a baked-brown complexion. His Crip persona was atrocious. An angelic countenance disguised his nature; he could explode in a pico-second with rage capable of humiliating the devil. As a human being he was no better or worse than others, but as a Crip he defied imagination. Whatever anyone may have thought about him, good or blasphemous, for me he was Mr Buddha ... my friend, my brother.

The first time Buddha met my mother, he made a more favourable impression than any other friend of mine. To her, he was a consummate gentleman who spoke with the diction of a choirboy. My mother often said in earnest, "Son, why can't you be like Curtis?" Around her or any Crip's mother, Buddha was gooey-nice. He possessed humanity within his soul, but for an enemy – beware. I'm grateful he was on my side. Our rivals – or Crips themselves who had a legitimate reason – feared the hell out of him.

He and I met under violent circumstances. He was beat down and thrown into the street along with Monk. I believe Buddha squashed any thoughts of retaliation against us because he respected the force that dared to enter his world, his domain, and smash him like a fly. Tough as Buddha was, he recognized a collective might bigger and stronger than he was, and he joined it. I was the mediator between Buddha's wrath and the world. He knew only one way of doing things – with radical fervour. But if he had even an ounce of respect for you, then he'd listen.

The terror he unleashed in the name of Crip was widespread, but I cannot fully detail his ruthlessness lest some fool try to duplicate his misdeeds. Perhaps Buddha's actions in life will engender greater understanding, or at least expose what a black child can evolve into when he is ignored by society.

Shortly after the termination of Bob's programme, there was a problem brewing with another west side gang, the Hoover Groovers, who dressed exactly like the West Side Crips. Things got out of hand when Little Chocolate, a member of the Hoover Groovers, was murdered. The mysterious killing of Chocolate and the shootings of other Hoover Groovers were blamed on the West Side Crips, but mainly on one person, Buddha. The West Side Crips were ambushing the Hoover Groovers regularly, but neither Buddha nor any West Side Crips killed Chocolate. Buddha did hate him. While in Factor Brookins, Buddha had held a lit cigarette to Chocolate's forehead and dared him to move for such a long time that I had to snatch his hand away. Chocolate was not an innocent bystander. He couldn't fight a lick but he fancied himself as a pistoleer and was a known shooter for the Hoover Groovers.

Through Bimbo, I befriended some of the leaders of the Hoover Groovers when I attended Brett Hart. My homeboy Fat Riley came bearing an olive branch from the Hoover Groovers for a sit-down at Saint Andrew's Park at Manchester, a park we had anointed as our own. When Boo, Diamond, Donnie Boy and Big Chocolate of the Hoover Groovers showed up, they were surprised to see the large throng of Crips and Criplettes hanging out, some playing football. They had to walk past us to get to where Buddha and I were sitting on a park bench. Bonnie and a few Criplettes were watching, sitting in the children's swing set.

It was probably by design that Big Chocolate spoke for the group. Although he and I had known one another since Brett Hart, things were different now that his younger brother had been killed. He started off with, "Rumour has it that Buddha killed Little Chocolate."

Buddha jumped up and said, "What, fool? If I had smoked Little Chocolate, I'd tell you right here, right now. If you truly believed Buddha was the killer, you wouldn't be here. We'd still be at war."

I calmed Buddha down, then told Big Chocolate, "Buddha didn't kill Chocolate, none of us did. But time will reveal all."

Big Chocolate went on to say they wanted to establish an alliance but not until they learned who was responsible for the killing.

Buddha rudely interrupted, "Look here, dude, we're the Crips. We don't need anybody."

I could sense Big Chocolate was trying to be patient so I eased the tension by appeasing them both.

"Buddha is right, we don't need anybody, but Big Chocolate, you're right, too. An alliance will benefit all of us. We can seal the alliance when we smash whoever smoked Little Chocolate."

The mention of revenge brought a smile to Big Chocolate's scarred face and to everybody present, even Buddha.

Though no master strategist, I knew that a prolonged war with the Hoover Groovers would create chaos among any of my homeboys who had relatives in the Hoover Groovers. The last thing I needed was a division within our ranks, so I was willing to forge the alliance. As soon as I shook hands with Big Chocolate and his homeboys, they left.

Buddha smiled. "Cuz, you are a shrewd character," he said.

"And you, my cousin, are a crazy, crazy character," I shot back. I told him I needed him to calm down because his outbursts could mess up my plans. I understood his frustration. I too was tired of all the drama but more and more I was learning about the need for tact and diplomacy. This was a street war on a smaller level; however, there was no difference between our mind-set and that of a nation seeking to eliminate its enemies through whatever method – life or death.

The Hoover Groovers held the Figueroa Boys responsible for smoking Little Chocolate. The Figueroa Boys were already our rivals, and attacking them fit in with my strategy. But not only were they difficult to find, they operated with the stick-and-move ambush tactics of guerillas. The Figueroas were notorious for surprise attacks, popping up when least expected and spraying the area with bullets. Fighting hand-to-hand was alien to them. A pistol or rifle was more their speed. They were deadly until more Crips began to arm themselves. Then, things changed.

Wherever the Figueroa Boys were discovered, they were ambushed with a hail of hot lead, something they weren't used to. Then, fate dropped our enemy into our lap. Their leader, R.M., happened to be in a night club on Vermont where the West Side Crips and Hoover Groovers planned to meet up. When we entered the club, one of the Hoover Groovers recognized R.M. partying on the dance floor. For him to look up and see the room filled with enemies staring him down was a nightmare. His scrawny body bounced from fist to fist like a ping-pong ball till he bounced into Buddha's knuckles, which knocked him smooth out. He was Crip-stomped twice and riddled with bullets to his chest. The deadly sneak-up artist and gunslinger somehow survived but the Figueroa Boys seemed to fade away. Word had it that R.M. and some of his homeboys moved to Pasadena or Pomona. Either way, the terror of the Figueroa Boys was a thing of the past.

The alliance with the Hoover Groovers – now known as the Hoover Crips – had been cemented by violence. This was around the time Buddha rapidly rose to the top of the heap as a number-one terror, playing shoot-em-up, armed with two or three guns. If Buddha didn't have his gun, his fists or a baseball bat would suffice. At Saint Andrew's Park during a dice game, when he and some of his homeboys lost some money to a street hustler, Buddha hit the guy, knocked him cold and put him into a coma. Buddha also took all his money – for cheating. Months later, as I lay in bed with a female sack artist named Dianne, she told me that that hustler was her brother and he was no longer in a coma. That was the last time I visited her.

Though our rivals feared me above all, they feared me more because of Buddha and his relentless pattern of vengeance. One evening after leaving Buddha at his mother's house, I was on my way to pick up Bonnie when some Lennox policemen spotted my Lincoln and pulled me over to the kerb. They claimed there was a warrant for my arrest for attempted robbery. I was handcuffed, taken to the station and booked. The next day, I was booked in the Los Angeles County Jail, waiting for arraignment.

Several weeks passed. I was transferred to the old Los Angeles County Jail where I became a trustee. I was stuck for months with a bond over $100,000, and had to rely upon a public defender to get it reduced each time I appeared at court. When I was able to contact Buddha, he said, "Tookie, when you get out, we have a lot to talk about, and you won't like it." Sensing it was bad news, I brushed it off, teaching him about our West Side Crips homeboy, Black Dog, who was in the Old County with me. One day as I walked by the module where Black Dog was housed, he was engaged in a dispute over money. He and another guy stood face-to-face arguing, then the guy slapped the taste out of Black Dog's mouth. The slap sounded like a firecracker. I expected him to unleash a flurry of punches to down his attacker but Black Dog just stood there sniffling, tears streaming down his face. All I could do was curse out the guy who slapped Black Dog. I told Buddha, after that, "I refuse to talk to him anymore."

"Cuz, I would've done the same thing," said Buddha. "What is this world coming to when a Crip can't defend himself?"

To me even if a Crip lost a fight, he should return and fight again. For any Crip to accept being slapped was an insult to the Crip god. Hell, it was an insult to me! I had met Black Dog through Victor, a West Side Crip who was a formidable bully. In my mind's eye, Black Dog was now a speck, a non-entity, expelled from my consciousness.

With my bail reduced and my car sold to make up the difference, I bailed out of the County Jail. The first thing Buddha and I talked about was the divisions that had occurred during my absence and how he wanted to cremate those responsible. I surmised that it was natural for someone to assume a position of leadership when their leader was out of commission. Prior to the Crip regime I intentionally kept the commanders of different hoods incommunicado from one another to eliminate any possible subversion. But here, I was the only link to connect the chain of different hoods that I had established individually. As expected, when any Crip tried to assume my role, he was renounced, which caused the commander of each 'hood to recoil into autonomy. The first time I recognized this phenomenon was while I was away in Boys Republic. My homeboy Melvin tried to seize the helm of the entire West Side Crip regime but was quickly rebuffed. Disenchanted, he back-pedalled to his own hood, which he named the Block Crips.

Once at Factor Brookins, Buddha and I had Melvin hemmed up in the theatre restroom. I watched as Buddha, with his hand on his gun, demanded that Melvin reveal where his allegiance lay.

"Cuz, do you think you're Tookie? Do you think you can take his place? Is this block crap a sign of your being a leader?"

"No, no, no," responded Melvin.

He proclaimed his fealty to me, and though I accepted it, I despised him for even considering that he or anyone could replace me. There are four conditions with which to test a friendship: money, loyalty, women and a secret. To violate even one of them is a sign of an enemy.

While Buddha and I worked for Bob Simmons as junior camp counsellors in the mountains of San Diego, the unified West Side Crip regime started crumbling into factions.

Buddha fiercely reminded me that Raymond's East Side Crips broke into numerous splinter groups after his incarceration, as did Mac Thomas's Compton Crips when he was locked up. The explosion of the West Side Crips was matched by a kind of implosion, Crip cells splintering, reforming, splintering again. Factions began cropping up all over, and the West Side Crips became a cluster of autonomous sets: The Block, Underground, Harlem, Budlong Street, Sportsman Park, Inglewood, Hoover, Manchester Park, 83rd Street Gangsters, Raymond Avenue, Magnificent Seven, Payback, Rolling Sixties, Sunshine, Gardena, Hollywood and many others. Some of these were vying for supremacy. Prior to this set-tripping, it was unthinkable for Crips to be at war with each other.

The Crip factions muddied my masterpiece. Buddha remained fixated on a Valentine's Day style of massacre. But if Mac Thomas and Raymond could adjust to the changing times, then Buddha and I could adapt as well. I was still the arrogantly irreplaceable Tookie. Despite the new names, the Crip faction commanders I knew personally still held allegiance to me and were West Side Crips. I maintained a following and respect across the board, and I prided myself on never messing over another Crip.

The west side was always rocking with parties, picnics, dances, clubs, and especially concerts. There was a time when a crowd of us stood outside Sweetback's mother's house making plans to go to a concert at the Los Angeles Palladium. But the anticipation of going – for Buddha and me – was spoiled when Bob Simmons pulled up in his Ranchero and told us that we were needed back at the camp. We wanted our paychecks, so off we went with Bob. It was good that we didn't go to the Palladium that night. We would have met the same fate as some homeboys charged with murder. Bob told us it was in all the newspapers about a gang of Crips killing another youth over his leather coat. Of all the Crips accused of the crime, Bub was the most recognizable, an All-American high school track star (though it frustrated Bub when he tried to out-run Sweetback and me and wasn't able to, whether we were intoxicated or not). All those who were charged with that murder were homeboys I grew up with from the 'hood. Most of them ended up doing time – Bub, Hawk, Cuz, Jetson, Mad Dog, Eric, and a few others. The zeitgeist was changing. Cops were getting a lot of help solving crimes from people with diarrhoea of the mouth. The Palladium incident, where a black life was lost and other black lives ruined, had absolutely no effect on Buddha or me, for crippin' night and day was the only way.

Our lives were spared for a moment. The mountains, a stone's throw from an Indian reservation, were a peaceful refuge from the urban madness. It was mellow at the youth camp, yet we were restless and yearned to be in the thick of things. Sitting in a canoe in the middle of a small lake, Buddha and I cast our baited hooks into the water. It was an odd thing, two youths from our background, fishing. Buddha chose that moment to become sentimental, but warned me not to get a big head.

"Tookie, you are an older brother to me, and I respect you. I admire you, and as long as I breathe there's nothing I wouldn't do for you."

The words chilled me, like a last rite I tried quickly to dismiss from my mind. Not knowing how to respond, I told Buddha, "Ah, shut up Buddha, you're my Cuz, and you always will be!" It was a strange moment for both of us, trying to articulate a foreign emotion of brotherly love with that machismo thing in the way. He was the essence of a best friend, a brother I never had, always there for me. Even when I frequented a clinic for radiation treatments to stabilize my vitiligo – a disease characterized by unpigmented areas of skin – Buddha would always accompany me on the bus. I regret never telling him how grateful I was.

It was difficult for Buddha to express his emotions. I had always seen beyond his toughness and identified with his hidden humanity. He was the most unique person I ever had known. Under better circumstances his wit, fanaticism, and do-or-die spirit would have earned him an invaluable spot in any black movement. We had also discovered while attending

Banning High School that Buddha was a whiz with numbers, a potential mathematical genius.

On February 27, 1973, Bob Simmons called me into his office. We sat in silence for a moment. In the background, birds chirped and I heard children's laughter outside, but something was choking up Bob.

"I hate to be the one to tell you this, Tookie", he said, "but Buddha has been shot and killed."

The words ripped my heart from my chest. Buddha was invincible!

During the ride back to Los Angeles, I felt paralysed. Kenny Thornton, the driver – a counsellor and non-Crip mistakenly identified in the book *Do or Die* as a Crip – asked if I was all right. I couldn't respond. How could such a thing happen to Buddha? He was always armed with not one but two or more guns. My mind raced with all sorts of questions – and no plausible answers.

The day before Buddha's murder, he and Blackie had gone down to Los Angeles to pick up some *ganja* and return to the youth camp. Blackie's version was that they, along with some women, stopped off at A.C.'s mother's house to sniff some glue with A.C.'s brother Michael. Later Michael accused Buddha of breaking his stereo player. Buddha slapped him. Michael left the room and returned with a gun, threatening to shoot as Buddha taunted him, "Kill me, fool, kill me. This is Crip." Blackie said Michael shot Buddha and he fell to the ground. Michael stood over him and shot him again. Once assured that Buddha was dead, that he couldn't rise again to kill him and his entire family, he backed out the house and ran away.

That night we tried to locate Michael, but he had turned himself in to the cops. Some of the vigilantes wanted to blast Blackie, who was present, but he could not substitute for Michael.

At Buddha's funeral, while everybody else was seated, I stood in the back leaning up against the wall. What was happening to me was a total contradiction of my desensitized street conditioning. I wasn't supposed to feel anything, but

Buddha's death devastated me. It scared the feeling of invincibility out of me. I realized the rhetoric of our catch-phrase, "Crips don't die, we multiply," was a metaphor, not reality. I watched as a long line of family members, homeboys, and strangers made a march past Buddha's casket. There was no doubt in my mind that many who attended the funeral were there to make certain Buddha was dead. I watched as Buddha's girlfriend, Li'l Jackie, sobbed uncontrollably. I knew the foetus in her belly was probably Bulldog's or someone else's, but not Buddha's. Standing before Buddha's body, all eyes were on me, anticipating an emotional outburst of rage. I felt only numb. I stood there waiting for Buddha to leap up and prove to everybody he wasn't dead. Lying in the casket, with no expression, was my best friend, my partner in violence, my Crip enforcer, the deadliest of his kind – and there was nothing I could do about it. Our madness finally had a recognizable face, and it was the death of my closest homeboy.

While everybody seemed in a festive mood inside Buddha's mother's house, I sat on the porch wanting to be left alone. Later, Buddha's mother brought me a plate of food and placed it next to me. I didn't touch it. She stood staring into space as we shared a moment of silence. She put her hand on my shoulder and whispered, "Curtis loved you like a brother, Tookie. I know he wanted me to tell you." She turned and stopped at the door, then said, "You know, Tookie, you don't have to always be tough and hold it in. You're human. There's nothing wrong with letting it out." She came back, kissed me on the forehead, and went inside. I got up and walked down the street. The night, cold and extremely dark, hid the tears streaming down my face.

SEVENTEEN

Compton Ambassador

It was shortly after losing Buddha that I found myself in a Los Angeles County courtroom, accused of the attempted robbery of a black and a Caucasian, both of whom were broker than I was. Looking at these two characters, I wouldn't have needed a weapon or my fists to rob them. A simple "boo" would have sufficed. But being innocent made no difference. I was still charged with the crime. Luckily, my stepfather had a friend, a seasoned and skilled attorney, Johnnie Cochran. His brilliance in the courtroom had my two accusers tripping over themselves with so many obvious lies that the D.A. was shaking his head in disgust. Even though Johnnie told me not to worry and congratulated Bonnie for her splendid testimony, I was still worried about the unpredictable jury. The jurors reentered the courtroom in silence and the foreman read their verdict: not guilty.

If this trial was a warning, I failed miserably to pay attention to it and continued promoting the Crips and my reputation like a politician lobbying for office. I could see no further than my limited intellect allowed, and I relished the thug recognition even if it was for black-on-black genocide. My homeboys helped make me a street legend in their own *griot* recitals of my violent exploits. Mad Dog David, Madbull, Black Johnny, Peewee, and others boasted about my exploits to elevate me to thug royalty. Whenever Mad Dog David addressed his homeboys, he would cry, "My cousins, my cousins, let Mr Tookie speak. He is the Crip king." Black Johnny, an equal to Buddha in ruthlessness and the flamboyant commander of the 43rd Street Crips, who ruled with brass knuckles, would lay out the blue carpet when I showed up. When I ventured into most of the commanders' strongholds, I was greeted as though I wore a crown. The respect I received inflated my head to the size of a watermelon. I earned it for oppressing other blacks. There is no bigger fool on earth than a man who destroys his own people.

Meanwhile, the would-be king was castle-less and broke, and Bonnie was pregnant. So I went back to work with Bob Simmons in Compton. The boys' home where I lived and worked was a two-storey house with six bedrooms, two bathrooms, basement, dinette room, living room, and a garage with a half-moon circular driveway. The place was huge, located off Santa Fe on Pine Street next to a mini-mall which included a liquor store, barber shop, laundromat, Italian take-out, record shop, soul food restaurant, and a gas station across the street that also sold dairy products. Bob called this house the Ponderosa, but to the outside world it would become known as the Red House or the Crip House. Living there were mostly young misfits with Crip backgrounds, or an occasional Brim, Bounty Hunter, Van Ness Boy, Inglewood Family, or Piru. J.B., of the Inglewood Family, stayed there for a moment, only to be arrested for allegedly killing his father (according to Bob). Donald R. of the Van Ness Boys befriended me and even accompanied me on raids against Pirus. Thus, two violently opposed individuals fought side-by-side. The Red House was located in a clean, quiet residential area and several neighbours contacted their councilman unsuccessfully to have the programme moved.

I met Bob's wife Ethel and their children, and his parents, who welcomed me with open arms. His mother Edith and I had brief conversations about my future plans – though I couldn't speak about that subject with any clarity or conviction. Sometimes we talked about Bob's efforts to help troubled youths and how I could help him with the gang problem. But I was in no position to address the gang problem – I was a willing participant. As I recall, Bob was the first to initiate a truce between several Compton gangs. He consistently tried to alert mainstream society to accelerating gang membership, but they assumed he was crying wolf. In one such attempt, Bob set up a gang truce meeting in the backyard of the Red House. I attended with Blackie, Monk and D.N., the Oaks Park Boys leader. There were also some Bounty Hunters and Pirus like Puddin, Tam and others. No one appeared to be interested in or listening to Bob, but rather we sized one another up for future sightings. If stares could kill, all of the gang members present would have been dead. The meeting was a fiasco, producing not even a handshake among us.

It didn't take long for me to familiarize myself with the different factions of Compton Crips. The Grandee Crips' hangout was around a block full of two-storey apartments on a street shaped like a "J" and ending in a cul-de-sac. Though some Crips lived in the Grandees, most lived on the outskirts. My first day in the Grandees I met Frosty, Bitter Dog Bruno, Mr X, King Ning, Vamp, Salty, King Rat, Duck, Hoss, and Popcorn from the Park Village. Though Mac Thomas was incarcerated, he had established a Crip force as violent and destructive as the West and East Side Crips. When I wasn't kicking it with the Grandees, I was in the garage at the Red House driving iron with the weights I had collected. When word was out that I lived in Compton, Crips showed up to meet me, drive iron or both. The Red House was a quasi-Crip embassy and I was the ambassador. Finding their way to the Red House from long distances were Mad Dog David, Big James, Jimel, Big Curtis, Lurch, Fat Riley and plenty of others. A regular visitor to drive iron was Little James, commander of the 118th Street Crips. In fact, Little James was my first training partner. We urged one another to drive hard to blow up our arms. If he and I weren't driving iron at the Red House, then we worked out in his mother's garage, where there were weights, mirrors, and magazine cutouts of professional bodybuilders on the wall for motivation. One in particular was Cuba's Mr Olympia, Sergio Olivia, who was unbelievable in size. Tapping his picture with my finger, I told Little James, "Cuz, I am going to be bigger than this cat."

At the time, there were quite a few Crips and non-Crips who pumped iron and who were bigger than me: Seals, Pancho, Head, Bulldog, Raymond, Donnie Boy, Jimel, Big Bear, and the biggest of them all, Munson. The first time I saw Munson at Roosevelt Park, I couldn't believe my eyes. Buddha shrugged him off as a Goliath ready to fall on his sword. Head told me once that Raymond idolized Munson and wanted badly to join the Avenues but Munson objected. As a result, Raymond decided to create a junior version of the Avenues and call them the Cribs. Whether fact or fiction, it was obvious Raymond respected Munson, because he spoke of him often.

One day a few of us drove over to where Munson, Bear and Donny Boy were driving iron in a garage on a U-shaped street off Avalon. Munson acted aloof, and when he did speak, he spoke down to Raymond. I asked Eddie H. what was the problem here, and he said, "Cuz, that's the way they trip all the time." Friend or no friend, I held no one in such high regard that I'd allow him or her to berate me without a comeback or payback.

After leaving that garage I was determined to become bigger and stronger than Munson – but without ever having to be in prison. A few of my homeboys used to brag about how they planned to get yoked up whenever they went to prison. I was convinced I could become yoked while on the streets. So I started driving iron obsessively, and with phenomenal results. Driving iron with Little James was what helped me pack on muscle and set the stage for more size. At the age of nineteen I had nineteen-inch arms that looked even larger due to my height of five foot ten. To be "yoked" was a new word in my vocabulary. I could stand in front of a mirror listening to any James Brown song while back-arming a 175-pound curl bar from afternoon till dawn.

Yokes looked intimidating and served me well in head-up fights – and life.

My desire to fight was never for the sake of fighting, but rather to set an example for my homeboys and any opposition foolhardy enough to try me. When fisticuffs ruled in gang primacy, a Crip could boldly roam into forbidden territory relying upon his fists, win or lose, to back him up. Although I was a traditionalist in street gang fighting, I wasn't a fool. I bought a 12-gauge riot shotgun for safety.

It didn't take long for the Lynwood cops patrolling in their all-white cars to target me with their petty harassment tactics. Bob said the cops had mentioned having received word from the Lennox Sheriff's Department and the Los Angeles Police Department about me being the leader of a gang called the West Side Crips. According to Bob, one cop had said, "Tookie's kind can never change. He's anti-social, among other things." That statement was the general consensus of many other cops on the west side but their opinion never mattered to me. I was never anti-social. I was selectively social and refused to socialize with just anybody.

The cop's trite statement reminded me of the time when a County "voodoo" doctor had labelled me anti-social and a fifteen-year-old revolutionary. Odd, because back then, I couldn't even define revolutionary, yet alone comprehend its concepts. His analysis of me was a typical racist stereotype used to describe every homeboy I knew. Instead of defining me as a defiant teenager, his amateur opinion tagged me as a revolutionary. At fifteen, my actions were anything but revolutionary, but were instead the prototype for future Crips.

Living in Compton, I needed a car bad, and Bob had an old buddy sell me his white two-door 1965 Chevy with a 396 engine and a four-banger stick in the floor. With my Compton Crip homeboy, Killer Carl, we drove to the west side and appropriated a low rider's Chevy car, boldly stripped it in the Grandees and left it there. A week later I had hydraulic lifts put in my car and I had a small black pirate's flag on the antenna to signify danger. The car quickly became recognizable by rivals, and by both Lynwood and Compton cops.

With access to wheels, I entered the PJs (a.k.a. the Imperial Courts Projects) where I was introduced to Anthony "A.B." Braylock, commander of the PJ Crips, and his right-hand man, Poindexter. It was also where I met Beverly McGowan, the future mother of my son Stan. A.B. stayed in one of the many PJ apartments along with a family who practised the religion of Islam. Though only four foot nine and of medium build, A.B. was game for anything and was at war with the Bounty Hunters and the east side Bishops. By Crip association, they were my rivals, too. His low-rider station wagon, a '57 grey and white Nomad, was a magnet for enemy potshots whenever he travelled near Nickerson Gardens, where the Bounty Hunters lived.

During several other trips over to the PJs, A.B. told me that all around the gymnasium were Crips, but on the other side they weren't interested either in Crips or in *becoming* Crips. Fist fights were still in vogue, and that's what took place despite the visible guns. The scenario was a trip, because on the opposite side there were youths our age partying with their older brothers, uncles, and fathers, but most of them were rowdy and willing to fight. They had no qualms about betting on themselves, relatives, or on any of us. Though most of the burly dudes I fought were unknowns, driving them into the dirt only increased the myths about me. I was known as a knockout artist with one punch and was dubbed the dirtiest fighter on the continent.

By no means was I comparable to Joe Louis, Muhammad Ali or Mike Tyson. But back then, winning was required for me to set a standard in the name of Crip. High on arrogance, I'd drive to the opposite side of the PJs, stop my car in the middle of the street, get out, and challenge whoever was present. If there were no takers, I'd stroll up to a crowd of dudes and start sucker-punching them. They thought exactly what I wanted them to think: Tookie is crazy. I was a spectacle, sporting a shiny bald head with sideburns and a goatee, dressed in blue overalls, army boots, no shirt, and with an oiled-up body too slippery for an opponent to grab. It was A.B., Poindexter, and their homeboys who applied consistent pressure that turned the other side into Crips. With the PJs under the control of A.B., they concentrated on battles against their rivals.

Whenever a potential attack was rumoured, the PJs morphed into an armed fortress suicidal for any rival to attempt to drive-by. It was like trying to attack the Nickerson Gardens, a deathtrap. One of those false alarms was the first time I had seen nearly 100 Crips *en masse* with guns and rifles out in the open. It was unbelievable. On other nights when we hung out getting high, undercover cops would do a drive-by and holler out "Bounty Hunter!" or "Bishop!" and let off shots, then peel rubber chased by a hail of bullets. Minutes later, the PJs would be surrounded by an armada of patrol cars and helicopters hovering above with spotlights. It was never a surprise seeing the same undercover car that drove by earlier showing up alongside the others.

"Those cops pull this crap off and on because they want us to ride down on the Bounty Hunters," A.B. told me. "It keeps them busy. Plus, the cops were shooting blanks."

I looked at him like he lost his mind and said, "Blanks? Hell, blanks don't ricochet off walls and put holes in cars."

Yes, as unbelievable as it may seem, 'hood cops, with impunity, committed drive-bys and other lawless acts. It was common practice for them to abduct a Crip or Bounty Hunter and drop him off in hostile territory, then broadcast it over a loudspeaker. The predictable outcome was that the rival was either beaten or killed on the spot, which resulted in a cycle of payback. Cops would also inform opposing gangs where to find and attack rivals then say, "Go handle your business." Like slaves, the gang did what their master commanded. Had they not been fuelled by self-hatred, neither Crips, Bounty Hunters nor any other black gang would have been duped.

The 'hood cops were pledged to protect and serve, but for us they were not there to help, but to exploit – and they were effective. With the cops' Machiavellian presence, the gang epidemic escalated. Gang warfare actually fuels funding for the so-called anti-gang units. Without gangs, these units would not exist.

In the midst of the madness, my name reverberated through much of Compton, offending members of opposing gangs. One night while I was in the PJs, a well known Piru named J.B. and several of his homeboys paid the Red House a visit and threatened the youngsters there. J.B. boldly left a message: "Tell Tookie I'm looking for him."

I had to take J.B.'s threat seriously because he showed up on my doorstep, calling me out. He made it personal and offended my ego. I had to find him and make an example. While cruising with Norwood around Compton, I spotted J.B. and two females going into a liquor store. We parked and I approached J.B. and asked if he was looking for me.

He responded, "Look here, brother, I don't even know you."

But the moment I said, "I'm Tookie," his eyes became as big as golf balls. Moments later, he was stretched out on the cement while the two females ran back inside the liquor store screaming for help.

Later that night, Beverly and I were asleep in my recently obtained apartment across the street from the Red House when I was woken by loud noises and people hollering, "Tookie!" Thinking it was J.B. and his Piru cronies retaliating, I jumped up and looked out the window. There were about six low-rider cars parked. Still groggy, I was able to make out Black Johnny, so I hollered down to him and his homeboys to hold down the racket.

Although it was night, I could see Black Johnny's teeth shining with a devious smile. He was a darker, taller version of Buddha, and to say he was crazy was an understatement. He was so mean it was said that when he went to prison his own homeboys celebrated and prayed he'd never get released. Locced out (unpredictably crazy) or not, Black Johnny was the commander of the east side 43rd Street Crips and would go to war at the drop of a hat.

When I told him about what happened earlier, his reaction

was, "Well, I'll come back with an army so we can destroy them." Then he asked, "Is the man loony? Does he know who you are?"

"It makes no difference," I told him. "Whatever the problem is, I can handle it."

After a few hours of bantering, snacking, and reminiscing about the Watts festival, Black Johnny and his homeboys were ready to go. As they left, they chanted out loudly, "Crip here" and all threw up the C-shaped hand symbol. Black Johnny's eyes had a tendency to turn blood red when angered. He was hardheaded, combative and argued often with Raymond, Pitbull, and others. He used to annoy me intentionally – until I began putting him in headlocks and applying pressure until he ceased. Yet he was one of the most reliable homeboys I knew. I recall thinking that Black Johnny would one day completely lose his mind because he was already beyond crazy. It was similar to my thought about Buddha not living long because of his extreme cruelty. Either way, Black Johnny was a true-blue Crip and had a cache of weaponry second only to Little James's.

The following night around midnight, Killer Carl and I were sitting at the kitchen table smoking weed while Beverly prepared a meal. I heard a loud noise outside and someone repeatedly calling my name. I thought it was the madman Black Johnny and his homeboys again, but knew better when I heard glass breaking and a chorus of, "Piru, Piru, fool!" I opened up on them with an M-1 rifle that sounded like a firecracker going off with each shot. It jammed, and I had to feed the rifle one bullet at a time. After the crowd of Pirus dispersed in all directions, I saw J.B. slowly cruising by in his dark blue Chevy low-rider without a care in the world. I took aim, pulled the trigger, and the rifle jammed again.

Killer Carl and I ran downstairs and crossed the street to the Red House, where we found the youngsters were unhurt but my car window had been busted out. The Lynwood cops swooped down on the Red House while I was cleaning and ordered me to hit the dirt, and everybody in the house to come out. They were responding to the dairy on the corner having been burglarized earlier, and a trail of spilt milk led from the dairy to the Red House garage. The cops managed to get a confession from a thirteen-year-old runaway. Two days later, they came back to the Red House to question me, with Bob present, about the firebombing of J.B.'s mother's house. They thoroughly searched my car and the garage looking for incriminating evidence. The cops acted as if I was the only Crip in Compton, assuming it was me who firebombed that house because someone had hollered out, "Crip here!" I denied knowing anything about it or being anywhere near that house. Later, there was a single-shot drive-by at the corner of Sante Fe and Pine directed at a young Crip named Shotgun. The Red House was immune to any more violent disturbances, but Compton got hot for everybody.

I was still making the rounds, like an ambassador on a public relations tour, meeting more and more Crips throughout Compton, on the east side, Centerview, and other places. During that period I met Peewee, commander of the JD (Jordan Down Projects) Crips on the east side. There were two sides to these projects with a dilapidated factory separating the two sides. When I started hanging out in the JDs, Crips existed on both sides and their numbers were equal to the PJs, if not slightly higher. Peewee was dark brown, short, and thin, with an aggressive heart. He wore the longest cross-and-chain earring of any Crip; extending from his earlobe to his waist. It was his way of being flamboyant and showing off, as all Crips were known to do.

Whenever I showed up at the JDs, Peewee rolled out the blue carpet and introduced me to all sorts of women. Sometimes he'd jokingly say, "Cuz, there's this woman such-and-such who's well built, but she's real ugly. Any problems with that?" Then he'd start smiling in anticipation of my response: "It's not the beauty, it's the booty!" Peewee would burst into laughter at that, especially when he was loaded. The JDs, PJs and the Grandees were like second homes to me. I'd visit each one often, sometimes all three on the same day.

Three other Crip spots I frequented were Boothill, Park Village and Centerview. Boothill was several sets of two-storey apartments located on Alondra, next to a liquor store and directly across the street from the Park Village Crips. Less than three Crips actually lived in Boothill, yet thirty to forty of us Crips and Criplettes briefly commandeered the property. Most of the time, you could find Crips getting high or sitting up in second-storey windows taking potshots at Piru cars – which triggered the Pirus' notorious sneak attacks.

A lot of Crips hanging out at Boothill were from the Grandees; they should have been called the Grandees Boothill Crips. It became an active spot for Crips such as Big and Little Hancho, Mister X, Popcorn, Tick, Yeayea, and Bitter Dog Bruno, who was a character-and-a-half. If Bruno wasn't warring against the Pirus, he'd be challenging any Crip foolish enough to think they could out-drink him. Bitter Dog Bruno would turn up a fifth of "Mad Dog 20-20" with several giant gulps and finish it. The Boothill Crips lasted only for a few months, which was how long it took the owners to get fed up with our presence and have the Compton cops make numerous arrests then evacuate any remaining Crips from the premises. Things had gotten so petty around Boothill that the Compton cops arrested me for spitting on the ground.

The other spot where I made my rounds was a huge area with many fine homes called Centerview, on the outskirts of Compton. Mad Dog Wilson was one of the commanders of the Centerview Crips, though he often hung out at the Grandees and in Boothill. To get to where Mad Dog Wilson lived, I had to drive down an extremely long street with a wall on both sides extending over half a mile. The Centerview Crips lived on the left side and the Pirus on the right. As far as I knew, there was only one way in or out of Centerview on either side.

Sometimes Mad Dog, his homeboys and I would attend parties on the rivals' side, looking for trouble and having no problems finding it. I never had any qualms about participating in any Crip feud, because I felt it was my duty as King Crip not to kick back but to be in the forefront of our wars. Plus, if I got hurt or MWGB (murdered while gang-banging) it would be in the name of Crip. Smash or be smashed! Mad Dog Wilson's nickname reflected his actions perfectly. He was making a name for himself using mad-dog tactics. It was said that he was too bold for his own good, but then that was true of all of us.

EIGHTEEN

Straddling the Fence

Perhaps it was a strategy of Bob and his partner, Shaw, to steer me away from gang life by making me a full counsellor and announcing I'd be operating my own boys' home within a week. But my mindset could not embrace the legitimate precepts of being a counsellor. I was too dys-educated and self-absorbed to be concerned with adolescents confessing to the world they were baby Crips, Brims, Pirus, whatever. I wasn't ready for this – but surely I could fake it, having been a thespian in my personal drama, called "survival," most of my life? I was as ill-prepared to be a full counsellor as I was when I was thirteen and having sex with a forty-two-year-old woman.

I was set up in a plush area with a two-storey house that had five bedrooms, a swimming pool, and a huge garage for all my weights. It didn't take the neighbours long to discover who we were and why we lived there. The second day in the house, two Crip youngsters, Tiny Man and Guy, got the bright idea of robbing one of the merchant booths up the street, at El Segundo off Avalon. After robbing the booth with a gun, they high-tailed it back to the boys' home, followed by the man they robbed. They were probably kicking back counting their loot when the cops banged on the front door and demanded over a loudspeaker that everybody in the house come out with hands up. I was in the garage driving iron and slowly raised the door to see the familiar squad of snarling white faces with badges, guns, and the desire to blow me smooth away.

"That's right, Tookie," barked a cop, "walk slowly towards us with your hands in the air. No quick moves."

As I emerged from the garage I probably looked like a huge black beast to them, shirtless and sweating from my workout. Then Tiny Man and Guy walked out the house looking guilty as sin.

A black man hollered out, "That's them, officers, those are the two boys who robbed me."

I shot an angry look at the two youngsters, who bowed their heads as if in earnest prayer. They were placed in the back of a patrol car but I knew they'd be back in a week or two, since they were minors. Meanwhile, this cop with his gun pointed at me said,

"Of all people, what are you doing in such a fine, upstanding neighbourhood? You don't belong here. We should just blow you away and get it over with."

I remained silent. I felt defenceless but I sought comfort in the fact that without his gun I could have snapped his neck like a twig – and he knew it.

Another cop approached and told his buddy who was pointing the gun at me, "He doesn't have any warrants, so we have to cut him loose. It's a shame. We know the boys' home is a front for criminal activities. Tookie, you're free to go – but we'll be back."

They kept their word and returned with what appeared to be FBI agents who never spoke a word but only observed. Neighbours gawked as I was handcuffed and taken downtown to the Glass House (an LA jailhouse), where I underwent several lie detector tests. This time I was accused of having burglarized the Compton military armoury to steal a large arsenal of AR-15s, rocket launchers and ammo. In their minds either I did it, ordered some Crips to do it, or had knowledge of it. This was the beginning of the mythical "super-nigger" stigma that the cops branded me with. In their minds I could perform the impossible, even steal their guns while they were looking at me. For the first time in that neighbourhood, cops patrolled and surveillance was established to watch my movements. The following week we were out of there after a petition was filed against us to leave.

The next house we moved to was off Compton and Avalon, in Swamp Boys territory. They were allies of the Pirus, and it didn't take long for the Swamp Boys to find out who I was and cruise by in snail fashion, "red-eyeing" me and flashing their guns. Often as I washed my car, Killer Carl stood guard with a visible weapon, and several times I had to restrain him from blasting the cars. I knew it wasn't kosher for a counsellor to be openly involved in gunfights.

Shortly after, a homeboy of mine, L.C., from the east side Back Street Crips, started visiting me at the boys' home. Years earlier, before he became a Crip, he and his homeboys had stumbled into the Rio Theater and been stomped and relieved of their leather coats, hats, money and dignity. Though he knew I was the one who had taken his white wide-brim and decked him, we became tight over the years. Around that time, regular sneak assaults were launched against the Swamp Boys, and the cops blamed me, L.C. and Killer Carl. During the short period we lived in that area, the Swamp Boys converted into the Swamp Crips. In fact, some of them began to visit and drive iron in the garage with Killer Carl. I don't know what he told them, but they used to darn near salute with excitement whenever they saw me out and about in the 'hood.

Killer Carl and some of the Swamp Crips went out to a party in another neighbourhood and turned it out. The next thing I knew, the cops were looking for all of them, and the community had posted fliers throughout Compton with photos and descriptions of Killer Carl accusing him of rape. By then, some of the Swamp Crips had been busted. I saw Killer Carl a few times before he was arrested. He didn't seem the least bit worried about being the subject of a growing manhunt, but he finally succumbed to his mother's pleas to turn himself in.

Not long after Killer Carl was locked away, Bob suggested that I enrol in Compton Junior College. What motivated me to enrol was that I'd be getting paid for going. In class I alternated between boredom and vague interest. I would look around and wonder what in God's name I was doing among all these busters. Many of them were struggling to get an education to obtain a vocation, but I was already employed without an academic degree. Plus, the extra-curricular school activities were fashion, gossip and sex. I was trying to balance an educational impossibility, an alliance between stupidity and wisdom, and trying to straddle the fence between crippin' and counselling. My school odyssey lasted for only several months – then it was *sayonara*.

A couple of weeks later, an English teacher from Compton College called and tried to convince me to come back.

"You're quite intelligent, Stan. You should rethink coming back to school," he said.

I believe he heard the loud, "Hell, no!" before the click. With school out of the way, I was beginning to settle in where we lived until Bob told me we had been petitioned to move once again. We were relocated in another fine-looking house on Slater and Stockwell. It was beautiful inside, with thick cocoa-brown carpet and matching shades of wood panelling; ceiling-to-floor mirrors covered an entire living room wall, with the same kind of mirrors on the closet doors. The place had two baths, three bedrooms, a large breakfast nook, a large patio with artificial turf, flowerbeds, floodlights, a huge pool table and security bars around the entire house. There were two backyards separated by a brick fence and a large garage. It was tailor-made for me.

I had two full-grown Dobermann pinschers for each yard and a pitbull puppy named Cuz. Under my guardianship the house was kept immaculate. The youths were well-fed, clothed, clean and attending school. Odd that I could play father to them but was too trifling to take care of my own sons, Travon and Stanley, whose mother was my then girlfriend, Beverly. Being irresponsible and low-minded, I convinced both Bonnie and Beverly to not list me as the father, to say they weren't sure who the father was so I could avoid paying child support. I had stooped low but didn't feel the slightest discomfort about my lack of ethics. Yet, I was at the same time the paternal figure for a house full of youngsters: Cross, Guy, Tiny Man, Dennis, Leroy and others. Though it was hypocritical of me to try to convince them not to live foul when I was living fouler than foul, I tried anyway. It didn't matter that I was unreachable, unsalvageable and unethical, there was still something inside of me that wanted better for them than I had for myself.

I expected these youths, confronted by damned conditions and caught in the cycle of ganghood, to get educated, uplift other blacks, and live productive and peaceful lives. My hypocritical message was: do as I say, not as I do. They ignored my words and held the worst in me as the paradigm to which they aspired. It was difficult to disguise the Crip aura that exuded from me like liquid fire. These boys heard my name resonating throughout the streets, a name associated with ganghood above and beyond anyone else's – and they loved it. Unfortunately, so did I.

Outside the door of the boys home I was engaged in a war where the "illusion of victory was won with a great loss." I fought for three years alongside the Compton Crips and was so recognizable that I was often mislabelled as their leader. Though I was in the forefront of much madness in Compton and elsewhere, I was merely doing my duty to represent Crip and myself to the fullest. It made no never-mind where I represented Crip. It was West Side Crips today, tomorrow, and forever!

I still managed to travel to the west side, where the Los Angeles Police Department and Lennox cops quickly learned I now drove a 1965 white Chevy. It was during my crisscrossing from Compton to the west side that I suspected I was being followed. There were occasions, looking through the rear view mirror, that I'd detect a car following me but then would veer off. I later found out that I was under close surveillance.

The cops were fanatical in their harassment of me. My being black was in part their justification; my being a Crip exacerbated matters. There were times when I was stopped, frisked, and held at gunpoint. Sometimes cars showed up with official types looking on while others took pictures of me. My homeboys dubbed me "super-hot," meaning I was the focus for the cops' harassment. This also brought unwanted attention to those around me.

Back then, a thirtyish woman named Bessie, who was like a mother figure to the Avalon Garden Crips, warned me about a police plan to set me up or to murder me. She had relatives working for the Los Angeles Police Department who'd told her that my name and Raymond Washington's were on a roster called the Alpha List. From what she gathered, the list consisted of blacks who were a menace and merited extermination. She cautioned me to immediately leave town, but although I believed her, I was too foolish to listen. Before long the American Civil Liberties Union, better known as the ACLU, got wind of the Alpha List. On December 13, 1974, the Los Angeles Times ran an article headlined, "ACLU Sues To Kill Police List of Allegedly Dangerous Blacks."

A black man in his twenties had first told us about the Alpha List. He used to show up at the gym in one of the Watts housing projects to teach us karate. He claimed to be a member of the Black Stone Rangers in Chicago. The Alpha List, he told us, was a well-kept official secret, a list of black male youths and adults who were systematically bumped off by the cops and then had guns planted on them. The cops, he said, were mostly setting up black Chicago gangs like the Black Stone Rangers and the Disciples. I dismissed him as a nut. I thought that whatever happened in Chicago couldn't possibly happen to me here in South Central. Short of killing me, they had pretty much covered all the bases in violating my civil rights.

It was better for me to stay in Compton than to cruise on the west side where I caught all the hell. At least in Compton I was living a poor man's fantasy: access to a palatial place to rest, an easy job and pay cheque, women, and several choice spots to get free gas and dairy products. During the gasoline shortage, I met several gas station attendants who assisted me with free fill-ups. One such gas station and dairy combined was owned by this guy Gerald's father. He wasn't a Crip but he knew who I was and what I stood for, so I could go there and load up on anything I wanted. On a couple of occasions, I took Cute's brother Mouse from the Magnificent Seven Crips to the gas station to fill up his car. Then one day while high as a kite, Mouse showed up trying to get gas from Gerald's father and destroyed that particular connection. You can believe my other spot remained a secret.

With one foot in the Crip life and the other in the counsellor realm, I decided to upgrade my image. I had to meet and talk with parents, particularly mothers, so I had to appear presentable. I located a clean, two-door, 1967, powder blue Cadillac and started styling slacks, dress shirts, suit vest, biscuit shoes, and a bald head without the thick sideburns. I still wore an earring, but I bought a Gruen watch with four diamonds inside, and a diamond ring. The only things thuggish about me were crippin' thoughts and behaviour.

Though I felt comfortable operating the boys' home, my mindset prevented total commitment. I had been inculcated into the streets, where neither employment nor millions of dollars could have altered my behaviour. I bought into the rhetoric about survival being based on the principles of accumulated wealth, force and violence. This was the American Way! Neither the Crips nor our rivals invented greed or violence, the basic capitalist theme of man-eat-man. No surprise that my foremost concern was self. Although I would have defended any diehard Crip to the death, my own survival was paramount. I bear witness to my own mindlessness.

After Buddha's demise, I really didn't care much about anything except crippin'. The most lavish aspects of that life were funerals for our dead homeboys. These mini-extravaganzas featured colourful wreaths, plush caskets, stylish clothing, and limousines so royal they made dying seem appealing. A dead, martyred Crip appeared to receive more kudos than he did alive. In Islam it's paradise, in Christianity it's heaven, but for Crips it was the expectation of an elaborate wake. Such was the case with a young Block Crip named Odie, murdered at Sportsman Park. Odie's funeral was the prototype for others. A Crip's death was the last hurrah, like a falling star kissing the universe before it fades into nothingness. People paraded past Odie's casket, dropping in jewelry, pictures, drugs, Crip bandanas, money and other memorabilia. Had Odie still been alive, many of those same people would not have given him change for a phone call.

After viewing Odie – who didn't look remotely like himself – I expressed my condolences to his surviving family and prepared to leave. The spectacle had turned my stomach so much I opted not to go to the gravesite with the long caravan that was being followed by a convoy of detectives and a cameraman. Instead I headed back to Compton to confront the cycle of violence, debauchery, treachery, death and other injustices received or dished out. I never expected nor cared if anyone else understood me, because the only ones who could were those involved in ganghood, and like me they had no solution.

Mine was a path of ignorance. I learned nothing, gained nothing, and had nothing of worth to offer anyone. I was trying to counsel teenagers not much younger than myself in age, mentality or behaviour. I was no more prepared to be a counsellor than I was to be President of the United States. Being a counsellor was self-serving. It provided me with a steady paycheck so I wouldn't have to be in the streets hustling or strong-arming people.

The fence I sat on could no longer hold the weight of irresponsibility. The chickens were coming home to roost.

NINETEEN

Invincibility Shot Down

I continued to go through the motions, play-acting the role of counsellor to look good. Because the Slater home was running smoothly, Shaw found a bigger place, a spacious double-duplex converted into a single unit with four bedrooms, two kitchens, two baths, two living rooms, and two yards. I immediately set up a mini-gym in one of the kitchens. An East Side Crips homeboy of mine, Jackie, called it "the sweatbox." The house was located on Palm Street off Compton Boulevard, behind Zorber's hamburger stand. Several blocks away was Compton High School, and hanging out down the street were Compton Crips – Movie Star, Ron Dog, Boo, Crusher and others.

At one time or another, I worked out with some serious iron drivers, such as Little James, Big Vertice, Marcellis, Bunchie, King Rat, Mouse, Big Jackie, Jimel, and Pretty Mike, who became a professional bodybuilder. My best training partner was Jackie. He was willing to drive iron anytime and anywhere. Jackie became like a brother to me; his family became mine and vice versa. If we weren't driving iron at the Palm House or in the backyard where his family lived, we'd drive out to different gyms like Babe's, Bill Pearl's, or Gold's Gym in Santa Monica. At Gold's Gym I met Mr Olympia, Arnold Schwarzenegger. Jackie and I strolled past Arnold and a female on the boardwalk at Venice Beach.

"See that guy there?" Arnold said to his companion, indicating me. "Those aren't arms – they're legs!"

Jackie was like Buddha, a true friend. He was my closest homeboy, a loyal sidekick who would defend me to the end. His favourite saying was, "Tookie, you are the first, the last and the only one. After you there will be none." He was six feet tall, brown-complected and big-chested, with huge arms with a lot of definition, skinny legs and long braids. He got a kick out of me taking off my shirt to flex and make my chest jump up and down for women or a crowd of children. We coined the phrase "breaking out" for taking off our shirts to flex. Like breakdancers competing against one another, Crips would break out and compete to see who was the biggest and the best built, especially for female attention.

When Jackie and I weren't hanging out, I was over at the apartments on Central, off Imperial, where a homeboy of mine, Godfather, was the manager. The place was a modern-day Sodom and Gomorrah, where fornication, gambling and drugs were rampant. There I was introduced to a variety of drugs, including paper acid, called blotter acid. I tried orange sunshine and microdot acid, but I preferred window-pane because it kept me hyped up without tripping out or seeing bizarre things. Admittedly, I did see traces, after-images like when I spit or waved my hand, but that was tame in comparison to seeing monsters and other horrors. It was odd that acid didn't seem to affect my energy or my strength while driving iron, very unlike the lethargic feeling when I smoked weed, a rare event.

I hid my drug problem from everybody, even Jackie. There I was, King Crip, seeking comfort in drugs like a drunkard seeking salvation in a bottle. I needed desperately to escape the madness around me, so I used acid and other deadly stimulants to block out the living nightmares even though the blockage was temporary. My sharpness of wit was leaving me like water seeping through hundreds of tiny holes in a bucket. Though my chameleon role as a counsellor was working – I believed I had most everybody fooled – I was destroying my mind in the process. My life was a contradiction. I didn't really expect to die, but I didn't care if I lived or died. In the back of my mind was the delusion of invincibility. I continued to engage unrepentantly in secret night raids on my rivals, who knew darn well it was me though I left no calling card. To avoid the cops, we'd dress up as if going to church or a social gathering and creep around in an inconspicuous car, then park down the street. In the name of Buddha and other slain Crips, I had no compunctions about retaliation, nor did my rivals. Strange how we Crips, Bloods, other black gangs and the black street drug dealers were so gung ho to obliterate one another – but would shy away when it came to confronting poverty, unemployment, politics, cop brutality and other social inequities.

Throughout most of my life, I was psychologically scarred. I carried an inner loathing of self and my own culture. Since I wasn't psychotic – Bobby Wright's book *Psychopathic Racial Personality* confirms my analysis – self-hatred motivated me to seek a kind of accomplishment by hurting other blacks. That's why I could stroll through Will Rogers Park during the Watts Festival, eager to impress my fellow Crips by knocking unconscious any target they pinpointed. The Watts Festival was a knockout day for Crips. Most any rival who stumbled into the park was spotted, then pounced on. For me, the defensive necessity of fighting had been overshadowed by the desire to show off. I relished unleashing my raw, repressed power in a single punch that drew "oohs" and "ahs" from bystanders.

After one such display, the cops made a clean sweep of the park to round up suspects, so Godfather and I ditched the crowd and headed in the opposite direction. A gang of cops met us at the far end of the park, and when I backtracked, I was met by yet another squad coming up from behind us. Sensing a showdown between me and the LAPD, I took out my long earring in preparation.

One tall cop nicknamed Red barked, "So, Tookie, you're a big and bad Crip, do you think you can fight all of us?"

I looked at this cop, who seemed to be growing horns and

spewing hatred, smiled and said, "I can whip all of you idiots if you put your guns in the trunk of the car."

I heard guns and shotguns being cocked, then Red said, "Raise your hands, Tookie, you're under arrest for assault on a peace officer."

I actually had to bail out, hiring Johnny Cochran once again to defend me.

When I arrived at the Palm House, Godfather told me that Tam, one of the most respected Pirus, had been murdered (may he rest in peace). It was time to be on extra guard because Puddin – one of the more lethal Pirus – and his crew would now be on the warpath. The apartments Godfather managed were being fire-bombed in the front and there were constant drive-bys. But the Carver Park Crips – R. Tucker, U.T., Terrible Tee, Trouble Man, Willie Herb, Big Chuck, Felton, and plenty of others who frequented the apartments – were eager to assist. In systematic fashion, the Pirus were hitting Compton Crip hangouts like they had a licence to do so. This was the dawn of a Compton war between the Crips and Pirus. Drive-bys took a nosedive; instead Buddha-like walk-up shootings escalated on both sides.

Living and working in Compton, the most devastating year for me was 1976. My grandmother, Momma, was on her deathbed, and from what I gathered, was a little delirious. But when I spoke to her, her voice was clear. My mother told me that the day before Momma died, she had a premonition, saying, "You have to get Tookie out of California because something terrible is going to happen to him. Please get him out of there." I brushed it off as paranoia. I was Tookie; I was invincible.

Ever since I'd known Momma, she'd been elderly. It seemed as if a grandmother would live forever, so her death devastated me. I was supposed to have a stony heart wrapped in machismo, but Momma's death was like a powerful electric jolt. To divert the pain, I immersed myself even deeper into the abyss of crippin'. I was never known for packing a gun, even though I kept my pump shotgun in the trunk. I started toting a chrome two-shot .38 Derringer for protection. I sought solace in night raids against my rivals to release my frustration, pain, and rage. I was still arrogant and foolish, with a drug addiction that rendered me lax and vulnerable to my opposition.

I often attended social gatherings packing heat as at an adult night school graduation at Crenshaw High. My stepsister Vicky was to receive her diploma. I arrived when the graduation was underway, with the auditorium filled to capacity. Always the performer, I grabbed a folding chair, sat it down in the middle of the aisle, then took off my coat. I was dressed in all black with my Derringer's white pearl handle exposed in my vest pocket; people couldn't believe their eyes. Security guards watched me from the other side of the auditorium. Sitting with my head shining and muscles bulging through my long-sleeved shirt, I was a monstrous size and more hostile than I ever had been.

Later that night, Killer Carl got out. We were in my car headed toward Shaw's home when he nudged me and said, "Look out for those fools, cuz." I turned my head to the left; car had pulled up parallel with us. I stared into the barrel of a gun. Pointing it was Little Vince, one of the Pirus' most deadly gunslingers. He had a demonic smile, knowing he had caught me dead bang. I was furious at being in that position. But instead of shooting, he chuckled, then the car sped off.

"I hate it when they do that," said Killer Carl.

That wasn't the first time I was caught under the sights of an enemy gun. The same deadly dance occurred between me and other Pirus: you pull up alongside an enemy, point or flash your gun, and then spare his life as if you are God.

I gave barbecues at the Palm House and some Crips – like Bitterdog Bruno and Pretty Skip – had a knack for showing up exactly when it was time to eat. This was an era when Crips, Criplettes and others would arrive with money-making schemes, mostly absurd, though some of their schemes had potential. But there were three things in life that I stayed away from because they unnerved me: rape, dealing drugs, and burglary. Odd that I would use drugs all day but refuse to deal them. Though I lacked ethics, I drew the line when it came to rape, while burglary I avoided because I pictured myself entering a window in a home and getting blasted back out with a shotgun.

A Criplette named Cleo used to show up often with money-making ideas. One that got Godfather's interest was the street trade, pandering female flesh. I never saw myself as a pimp, though I grew up around quite a few. When I was a youngster, I noticed that tough thugs used to rob pimps, beat them down, and treat them like punks. A thug named Big Rock used to say that any man who made a living off pimping women was the lowest of scum. He said pimps weren't respected on the streets or in prison. That's the main reason I shied away from pimping no matter how often I was approached with tempting propositions. I did know some homeboys who had turned pimp, like Crazy Crip, Undertaker, and Que, but it didn't interest me.

I sat in the living room at the Palm House with Godfather, a roomful of Criplettes and a number of other females interested in selling flesh. Cleo and Godfather hoped to school me on the fundamentals of pimping, but I wasn't motivated – and I stayed too high to really focus on their schemes. Godfather's pretext was simple: he was greedy. Cleo's objective was to have me sexually. Though she was a fine woman, she looked like a thinner version of Bonnie, so I treated her like a sister, which she hated. Her get-back strategy was to make me jealous. Whenever I visited her at her grandmother's house on the east side, she would break out letters from Raymond. Her attempts to make me jealous didn't work, but reading Raymond's letters it was obvious he felt something for Cleo – or told her what she wanted to hear. It appeared Cleo had exaggerated our relationship in a letter to him, and Raymond blew a gasket. Then someone, probably somebody close to Raymond, whispered lies to him about me trying to encroach on his territory, similar to what he did to Mac Thomas in Compton. This was preposterous. I had done all that was humanly possible to expand the West Side Crips so that it could multiply on its own. In a bastardized version of Shaka Zulu's brilliant strategy of absorbing other tribes to make them Zulus, I did the same with the West Side Crips, though I didn't know that my strategy paralleled Shaka Zulu's until many years later. I had no desire for more territory. I had pushed the West Side Crips so far west that only the Pacific Ocean could halt further expansion.

As for the pimping scheme, well, there were close to thirty females willing to hook up with me, and promises of many more to come. It was a pimp's fantasy to be handed a flock of women without having to catch them or turn them out, but for me crippin' meant more than pimping, money or the women themselves. Had I not been intoxicated most of the time, I probably would've designated Godfather as Mack Daddy and received my cut off the top, like Black Johnny, who always kept his palms fed. But any Machiavellian skills I may have possessed were waning with every tab of acid and every puff of angel dust.

What really prevented me from being involved in the criminal rat race was my counsellor's wage, and not having to buy food or pay the bills out of my pocket. Since I was able to splurge, I bought two cars, a 1963 lime-green Chevy in mint condition and a 1953 cocoa-brown two-door Oldsmobile that needed engine work but was gangster down. I decided to give the Chevy to Godfather so that he and Mad Bull could get to wherever I was quickly, in case of emergency. Numerous rumours were floating around about a Piru plan to ambush me. A Criplette named Sally warned me about this but I was too hard-headed to listen. The thought of the Pirus bringing it to me was unbelievable. I was Tookie, King Crip. They wouldn't dare try something like that. Didn't they know the potential repercussions? The idea angered me so much that I initiated a couple more night raids for good measure.

Sally was another gorgeous femme, able to manoeuvre among the Piru circle and among other rival gangs. She was gifted with the looks, the shape, and the ears to listen to the braggadocio of certain Pirus, but the more Sally told me about what she heard, the less I took it seriously – though just in case, Godfather and others held down security from the rooftop for back-to-back nights. I didn't change my itinerary; it was business as usual.

One night while in bed with Sally watching TV, I decided to take my pit bull puppy for a walk around the block and puff on some ty-stick. In my long tweed coat was my .38 Derringer and a pocket full of loose bullets. I rounded the corner to see a car slowly drive by with a bunch of hard heads inside staring at me. I continued to walk with my hand in the coat pocket and they drove off. Whoever they were, I had been recognized, so I headed back to the house, where I had several weapons more powerful than my Derringer. I made sure everything was all right, then placed my pump shotgun on the floor and closed the door.

Earlier that night I had told Godfather, Madbull, and Terrible Tee that I could handle things and had sent them off. Before they left, Godfather asked several times if I thought it was cool? I simply patted the pump shotgun and said, "Yes, it's cool." Now, sitting on the porch watching my dog run around the front yard, it seemed darker than usual and there was an unnatural peacefulness. As I drew on the ty-stick I thought about my homeboy Pretty Skip, a Long Beach Crip killed a couple of nights before on the west side, deep in the Brim territory. He was caught in bed by this woman's boyfriend and beat the guy down but returned to the scene later that night and was shot to death by the boyfriend and his homeboys. It puzzled me as how could someone catch Pretty Skip off guard when he was always packing. I wondered if he was high.

I snapped to alert when I heard my dog barking and growling and looked in the direction he was standing but it was too dark to see anything. When I looked the other way, the darkness lit up with reddish-gold flashes and the crackling sounds of fireworks. The ty-stick had me toasted, and I thought for a moment I was hallucinating – then realized I was being shot at. I dove off the porch and crawled to the side of the house. By the time I pulled out my Derringer and took aim, the shooters had vanished.

In the sudden silence, the stench of gunpowder filled the night air. A couple of times I tried to stand but my legs wobbled and I fell back down. Fiery pain burned through my legs and feet. Gritting my teeth, I used a water hose to cool them down, but I was in agony. What was wrong with me? By faint light I saw blood streaming onto the grass and into the earth.

TWENTY

The Big Comeback

Word travels at Mach speed when you're doing bad. I wasn't at Martin Luther King Hospital for ten minutes before people I knew started showing up. That hospital had never received so much attention for a patient. Countless calls tied up the phone lines and numerous visitors, mainly Crips and Criplettes packing visible weapons, demanded tight security. Drifting in and out of consciousness, I saw Bessie standing beside the gurney with tears in her eyes. Sally, between sniffles, kept repeating, "Tookie, I asked you to be careful. Why didn't you listen?" I remember being annoyed and telling her to shut up before I passed out.

The following day, I woke with a serious headache, excruciating pain, and a cast on each leg. Seated in a chair across from the bed was Godfather, grinning and eating from the hospital food tray, while Criplette Debra stood with her hands on her hips, dressed in super-tight khaki pants. Godfather launched into a retaliation strategy but I waved him off and told him to save that for later on.

"All right, just kick back, cuz," he said. "Here's your Derringer and box of shells." Indicating Debra, he added, "By the way, I also brought you some stank."

Debra fired a few expletives ending with ". . . and your mammy too!"

Godfather mentioned something about going to quiet the crowd before the cops showed up, and suggested that Debra and I could use some privacy, quipping, "If pussy can't soothe the pain, nothing will."

Debra rolled her eyes, gave him the finger, then smiled wantonly at me. I had no intentions of doing anything, but in the end I could not resist her entreaties.

Later that afternoon when the nurse re-entered, she was shocked to see Debra lying beside me partly nude. She politely scolded me: "Mr Williams, you're not allowed to have a woman in bed with you. This is a hospital, not a motel."

It didn't matter what the nurse said. My concern was the painkiller medication. I looked forward to the next shot like a junkie does a fix. My pain could not be alleviated by sex, banter or getting loaded. I needed the powerful sedative to knock me out.

Early the next morning, I felt someone rubbing my bald head and heard people laughing. Jackie was peering down at me. "He's alive, folks," he said.

Raymond was there too, and interrupted, "I see the man, but what are we going to *do* about this?" Both of them wanted to know who shot me, but I didn't know.

"It was probably the Pirus trying to make a name for themselves," speculated Godfather.

"Well, it doesn't matter who the idiots were, they have to pay," said Raymond.

At that moment, my least concern was payback, but it sure felt good to see the camaraderie and hear them fussing over the next course of action.

Being debilitated didn't tarnish who I was. The supreme sacrifices one could make for Cripism were martyrdom, retaliation or shedding one's blood. Even from the gutter level of existence, I sought approval and respect from my peers – no differently to anyone else. But being bedridden and aching, there wasn't too much I sought other than relief. Jackie tried to cheer me up, but I wasn't in the mood. Raymond started going down memory lane, reminding me about the time he tried to shoot a double-barrelled shotgun with one hand and it almost knocked his shoulder out of the

Tookie at four years old in Shreveport, Lousiana, before his family moved to Los Angeles.

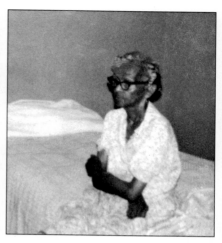

"Momma," Tookie's grandmother, in Shreveport in the 1950s.

A dapper-looking Tookie, aged fourteen.

Tookie with his stepfather Fred Holliwell.

Tookie at fifteen. Leather jackets were a fashion item and the frequent target of jackings (street robberies).

Tookie at sixteen, in a whole different look.

Tookie developing his trademark physique at nineteen years old.

OBSEQUIES

of

Raymond Lee Washington

August 14, 1953 - August 9, 1979

Thursday, August 16, 1979 - 11:00 A.M.

HOUSTON'S GOLDEN CHAPEL
9201 South Vermont Avenue
Los Angeles, California 90044

Funeral programme for Raymond Lee Washington, the charismatic Crips co-founder who was shot and killed in 1979.

On the exercise yard at San Quentin, Tookie in his late twenties.

At San Quentin in his early thirties.

At San Quentin, posing with his blue Crip rag on his head.

In the mid-1980s. Driving iron has been a lifelong passion.

Ghetto, Tookie's friend in San Quentin.

Denis Brewer, known as Herc, another of Tookie's friends inside.

Steve Campion, formerly called Treach and now known as Adisa.

Craig Ross, whose streetname was Evil but who is now known as Ajani.

With Barbara Becnel, long-time friend and supporter.

Tookie at age forty-one. Having renounced his gang past, he spends his time studying and reflecting on his life, race and culture.

With Franziska Greber, who introduced Tookie's work to Mario Fehr, the Swiss legislator who first nominated him for the Nobel Peace Prize.

With actor Jamie Foxx – who played the role of Tookie in the movie *Redemption: The Stan Tookie Williams Story* – together with Foxx's manager Marcus King and Barbara Becnel in 2003

Tookie today at fifty, in San Quentin's visiting cage, referred to as a "module" by prison authorities.

socket. Though it had been a hilarious moment, I hurt too much to laugh, so I just nodded. He then launched into a tirade about Crip factions springing up with self-appointed leaders who were giving Crip a bad name. I agreed with him, but it was too late to change the course of history.

Raymond and I were more alike than we cared to admit: defiant, aggressive, tactful, quick-tempered and egotistic. To hear him rail against the attack on me and advocate payback really felt good, especially since we were at odds on the touchy subject of shared rule. The slight discord was based on my self-promotion and the assumption that I wanted to be *numero uno* of the West Side Crips, the East Side Crips and the Compton Crips. Still, it didn't matter what the incompatibility was. The Crip agenda outweighed our trivial differences. Though there were rumours about Raymond plotting to smoke me, abandon Crip, and start a rival gang, I didn't believe it. Our behaviour in the hospital room showed our willingness to rise above such foolishness, and above Cleo's attempt to manipulate a rift.

Being cooped up in the hospital, I couldn't escape its sanitized odour, though it failed to camouflage the presence of sickness, disease, bloody wounds, and death. I didn't reflect upon my own mortality but thought about Buddha, Robin, Craig, DeeDee, Odie, Diver Dan, Pretty Skip, Bebo, Big Boo, Kane, and the other Crips who had been killed. I remembered Mr X telling me about Salty, a Compton Crip who was ambushed and killed. His last words were, "Don't let them forget me, Salty, a do-or-die Compton Crip." I pondered whether crippin' was worth all the deaths, suffering, or the tears.

The trauma of being shot was not a defining moment for me, though it did show I could take a bullet and keep on stepping. The problem was that I wasn't up and walking. When a group of doctors entered the room with medical charts, they exchanged ideas and opinions about my situation as if I wasn't present. I gathered from their medical jargon that the bones in both feet and ankles were shattered, and a calf bone was fractured, all by .45-calibre bullets. The consensus was that I would never walk again. That thought was terrifying, equal to being dead. I pleaded with God not to let this be my cross to bear. I didn't want to be like Koolaid or Toosweet, trying to Crip from a wheelchair.

I snapped out of my self-pity when my mother entered the room with an expression of grief and horror. There is nothing like a mother's comforting presence in a time of need. She sat there in a dignified fashion while I tried awkwardly to explain what had happened. As she prayed over me, I dozed off – that way I didn't have to explain myself. When I awoke, she was gone, and a new nurse was in the room cleaning up. She opened the drawer and spotted a gun and a box of bullets. She closed the drawer, played it off as if nothing had happened, continued to clean the room and then left.

Not taking any chances, I placed the tiny arsenal under the pillow. I was about to enter Lalaland when security guards burst in the room demanding to know where the gun was. Two of them searched the room while one looked inside the table drawer, then underneath the pillow. They found the gun, then stood around the bed giving me the third degree:

"What do you need the gun for?"

"Who are you?"

"Are you a Black Panther or something?"

"Why are there so many people concerned about you?"

Next some cops came in with questions of their own:

"Who shot you, Tookie?"

"How many shooters were there?"

Even if I'd known their names, height, weight, and phone numbers, I would not have uttered a word to identify the shooters. That was the ganghood code.

Later, a nurse told me that for the safety of staff and other patients I was to be moved from the hospital in the morning. She said this was the first time a patient had ever been kicked out. "Mr Williams, are you some kind of gangster?" she asked. I told her I was too broke to be a gangster.

The next day, Fred Shaw's son and another counsellor

picked me up in a van. While being wheeled out, I tried to retrieve my gun, but a sheriff informed me if I wanted it back I'd have to come down to the station – if I wanted it bad enough. I cursed as I was wheeled past a crowd of Crips and Criplettes and into a waiting van.

"We got your gun, Tookie, come and get it," the cop yelled.

The van pulled up in front of Shaw's office across the street from the Red House, and I was carried in and placed on the couch. While I rested, Bonnie appeared, staring down at me with tears in her eyes. She asked what had happened and where Shaw was planning to take me. I was too tired to answer, so I waved her off. It was Shaw's intent to find me a Shangri-La type setting where I could fade into anonymity. This house turned out to be in Pasadena. Two sisters planned to look after me there. I was placed in a bedroom with a well-lit bathroom. Next to the bed was a walker and a small table with a bowl of fruit, cups, and a pitcher of orange juice. It became evident that if I wanted to use the bathroom I'd have to travel back and forth on my own. There were no bedpans and no one around strong enough to assist me.

Somehow I'd have to call forth whatever strength wasn't drained from my body to make the bathroom trip. It was less than ten feet away, but it was like walking a mile. The question wasn't just whether or not I had the strength but could I bear the pain. Due to soreness, I had lain in bed for days unable to get up and relieve myself. Finally when I couldn't take it any longer, I managed to manoeuvre my legs to the side of the bed. It was physically impossible for me to stand up, so the only option was to crawl, and crawl I did. The entire process took from thirty minutes to an hour depending upon how many rest periods I needed. With each gruelling step I cursed the maggots who put me in this condition. It burned me up knowing that I'd probably never get my hands on them, especially since no one was eager to lay claim. If I was serious about a comeback, I'd have to do it on my own.

After several weeks I was able to use the walker, though it

felt like hundreds of daggers were poking my legs and feet. Going back and forth to the bathroom left me weak and drenched with sweat. During my hospital stay I had not eaten, but I did drink a concoction of powdered protein, ice cream, Baby Similac, cherries, and condensed milk mixed in a blender. Drinking two to three glasses of this each day, I could feel my strength slowly returning.

When the two sisters got wind of who I was, they were scared to death and wanted me to leave. I was booted back to the Slater Boys Home in Compton, where Jimel had been fired as the counsellor. From what the elder Shaw, the director of all the boys' homes, told me, a young Crip from the Red House had shot at Jimel, who had got into scrapes with other Crips, usually over women. Either they took potshots at him, or they wanted to go one-on-one. Jimel was all right. He was becoming a close homeboy of mine, but he was misunderstood by most Crips. There were times when I had to step in to prevent a serious casualty, like when Godfather, Madbull, and Terrible Tee plotted to kill Jimel. Ambushing was their specialty, and they were more than eager to follow through.

I wasn't interested in any madness. All I wanted was rest, and the Slater Home provided a peaceful habitat where I could convalesce. I was allowed to return to Martin Luther King Hospital for physical rehabilitation provided I agreed to enter from the back door with just one person, no guns, and leave immediately after each session. The doctors had said I'd never walk again, but I was already walking in casts, without the walker. I figured if I was unable to walk with the casts removed, then I'd need a set of customized leg supports made. Eventually the casts came off. My legs were skinny as toothpicks and very weak, but they were able to hold up my weight. I used the walker for a while, then graduated to a wooden cane like the ones we used to crack people over the head with. Talk about karma.

The doctor decided to leave the bullets in my feet, as to remove them would cause more damage. He told me that, over the years, each bullet would make its way back to the surface, to the entry point. On the final day of rehabilitation, he warned me that I'd have a permanent limp. I refused to believe him. Doctors have been wrong before. Amid all the prognostications, no one bothered to address the lingering trauma of being shot. The realization that I was not invincible, knowing I was vulnerable, was a rude awakening. Paranoia gripped me. I didn't feel comfortable unless Godfather, Jackie, L.C. or others were around for security.

For the time being, my flamboyance and boldness had shattered like glass. I was leery about strange noises and tentative about my movements outside the house. Everywhere I went, Godfather or Jackie was there to drive me. We armed as if we were going to war. Godfather's constant bragging about the retaliations that had taken place in my absence and future paybacks didn't restore my confidence the least bit. My nerves were so rattled that, just hearing the sound of a gunshot, I'd almost jump out of my skin. There was a moment at Bonnie's mother's house while I was visiting my son Travon when I heard a volley of gunshots. Though still in casts, I managed to dive to the floor with a speed that stunned even Bonnie. Somehow, I had to regroup and learn again how to cope with the madness out in the ganghood.

There was no time for self-pity. My rivals would have no problems trying to finish their bungled job, especially since I was immobilized. I needed my size, strength, and ability to walk if I wanted to confront the opposition. With the discipline of an African distance runner, I underwent a strict regimen of workouts and grew massive with muscle and rage. Never before had I possessed such single-mindedness. I was motivated, dedicated, and more than enthused to retaliate.

During my recovery, Criplettes like Crip Connie, Tasha, Tina, Goldie, Shelly from Long Beach, and the east side's Li'l Pamm were in and out of the Slater House. The most consistent was Li'l Pamm. She was one of many very attractive Criplettes: Crips chased after her like hounds in heat. Pamm had no qualms about packing a gun or using it.

She reminded me of Bad Bessie. I knew my back was covered
with her around. She was more than a pretty face. We would
stay in one another's life for a while, drift apart, then from
time to time hook back up for a day or two. It felt good to
have Pamm and the other Criplettes around. But in spite of
their feminine tenderness and attempts to be Florence
Nightingale, they were just as calculating and cold-blooded
as we were. Had they been born male, they would have
gained street reps equal to or greater than some Crips. I
respected the Criplettes to the best of my limited male Crip
nature, but they were an enigma to me, as were all women.

As the months passed, my legs became stronger but I still
limped badly and wasn't able to run or walk fast. What I
lacked in foot-speed and agility, I made up for in physical
strength. From time to time I would drive iron with close
homeboy Marcellis, one of the spearheads of the Lantana
Crips. We found common ground on the weight pile and in
knocking opponents senseless at parties. Other than crippin',
driving iron was the pinnacle of Crip-dom. It was rare to
find a Crip who wasn't into weights or didn't try to become
yoked. Working out seemed to get my life back on track, but
I felt that time was running out for me.

Bob Simmons knew several people who tried in vain to
convince me to participate in their youth programmes. A
black man named Fred Horn had an idea about creating a
programme for individuals in gangs to promote peace. This
eventually became known as the "Round Table." I didn't
participate because I wasn't interested, not to mention Bob
felt the guy was questionable. The director of the Uhuru
Center on the west side had an idea for a programme too,
but I waved it off too. Then Bessie, who warned me about
the Alpha List, wanted to introduce me to another man
interested in establishing a youth programme. Godfather
and I arrived at her apartment in the Avalon Gardens, where
I shook hands with a tall, burly figure I didn't recognize. His
name was Rosie Grier and he was an ex-football player. I'd
never heard of him. I sat in silence listening to his plans to
make the community better and safer, but it didn't chime

with me. I wondered what was this guy's angle? He appeared from nowhere with this grand idea in his mind that missed my interest by a thousand miles.

Whatever Rosie's intent, his agenda clashed with my ideas of revolting against other street gangs and against the status quo – of which he obviously was a member. My rejection of outside help was indicative of the juices of fury flowing through my veins. There was nothing Rosie could have said to make me alter the only life style I knew. Crip defined who I was. I didn't need a cane, blue rag, or tattoo to confirm it. My name spoke for itself, and everybody knew what I represented. I was the Crips' figurehead and politician rolled into one. And I was recuperating in record time.

TWENTY-ONE

The Old
Stomping Ground

Since my rivals failed to lay me to rest in Crip martyrdom, I knew I'd be back in commission sooner or later. For a while I travelled back and forth to Compton, feeding my ego with night raids that felt ridiculous as I limped away after each dirty deed. Terrible Tee and Godfather enjoyed the action, but for me the thrill was gone. I was the walking wounded, unable to perform the simplest of movements with my crippled legs. I was tormented by thoughts of never being able to smash the so-called death squad, haunted by feelings of inadequacy. I needed to return the favour, *lex talionis* style.

This was 1977. I was comfortable enough to be out driving alone though I packed heat for potential trouble. I drove a souped-up 440, a green Charger with thick racing tyres and phenomenal speed. I wasn't the speed-racer type, but to compensate for limited movement, a muscle car wasn't bad. I could often be seen flying down the block with some undercover cop car trailing in the distance. I'm sure they followed us when Jimel and I tried our hand at becoming professional bodybuilders with the Weider establishment (the Weider brothers created the Mr Olympia contest). A photographer arranged to take some photos of us at Santa Monica beach. I don't know about Jimel but I was embarrassed to be posing in a pair of tiny trunks I called bikini panties. I wore my robe for dear life up until the very second it was time for me to pose. After the photographer had finished, he assured me that I was a shoo-in to become a bodybuilder and that I resembled the former Mr Olympia Sergio Olivia. But who's to say he didn't tell Jimel that *he* resembled Dave Draper or somebody?

A few days later the photographer said they were impressed with my physique, but I couldn't be accepted because of the rumour that I was the leader of the biggest gang in Los Angeles and would bring bad press. Though I couldn't prove it, I suspected they had seen cops trailing me and been spooked. I was disappointed but accustomed to calamity. Next!

Back at the Slater house I was confronted by a problem involving a fourteen-year-old named Creeper who claimed he was a Bounty Hunter, a Bloods faction. He had been arrested for armed robbery. At the police station, he allegedly told the detectives he had been pulling robberies then bringing half the loot to me. Later I was told the cops had coerced Creeper into fabricating the story. The lie stunned me, but the cold part was that Shaw believed it. Years of service meant nothing, and I was fired. In truth it was a relief. I was freed from having to live a double life. Crippin' night and day could now be the only way.

I packed my weights and other belongings, left Compton and headed for the west side, my old stomping ground. I went straight to my stepfather's house on 69th. Across the street in a duplex lived my stepsister Vicky and her children, Bacbab and Kameshi. They were planning to move to San Pedro. Although I had no idea what I would do for income, I agreed to take over the rent after they moved. But instead of looking for a job, I was out in the street re-establishing old ties with homeboys I hadn't seen in years. Much had changed on the west side. Quite a few Crips had been killed and imprisoned, and there was a new breed of young Crips anxious to make names for themselves. They were also dying fast.

The ultimate platform then for attention was Centinela, the park of all parks, in Inglewood. It used to be the favourite hangout for the Inglewood Family gang (a Blood set), but the mass migration of Crips from all over the city changed the tenor of that park without a single battle. For Crips, local families, and children, Centinela was probably the safest park in America. Other than me or some other Crip knocking out an unfriendly guest here and there, the park was peaceful. Jimel and I used to stroll throughout the spacious park in overalls, shirtless, wearing power-lifting belts. Under the sun, our muscles sparkled with baby oil. Fascinated women and wide-eyed children would ask for our autographs on paper or paper plates; local people and street celebrities mingling on the same playing field.

The stage was set no matter where Jimel or I took off our shirts. Prior to "breaking out," Jimel would perform a round of push-ups to feel pumped. One evening we were planning to attend a concert at the Forum. Jimel and I had driven iron for two hours at the Slater Boys Home, so I offered him the shower in the back bedroom. To my surprise he declined, stating that "the water will take away my tight." As a substitute, Jimel loaded up heavily on my Old Spice cologne, slipped into his white tailored suit and was raring to go. Then, at the concert into the men's restroom, he still did close to two hundred push-ups.

Though the Forum was a highlight performance where we would flex for the entire audience and receive a standing ovation, nothing could beat being at Centinela Park on a bright Sunday afternoon: family picnics, children playing, women galore and the sweet aromas of barbecue chicken and ribs. On Sundays, the park swarmed with Crips strolling with their pit bulls, playing football, gambling, getting loaded, hawking females, breaking out, or just kicking back and snacking on barbecue.

On one particular Sunday, I was listening to Godfather's not-too-subtle comments about Jimel being a joke and how nobody could stand him. "Let's just blow him away and get it over with," he said. Before I could respond, somebody hollered, "Fight," and a crowd ran up the hill toward the parking lot. At the top of the knoll, Godfather, smirking, blurted out, "It's your doofus buddy Jimel about to get beat up." I headed towards the giant circle of fifty or more Crips with two combatants in the middle – Crazy Ed from Hoover and Jimel, with Raymond acting as referee. Bare-knuckled street fighting had its own mystique. Being trained in boxing, karate, or jujitsu could be a liability if you expected to win. I've seen plenty of cocky boxers and karate enthusiasts get mopped up quickly There were no rounds, no cut man, no water and no ringing of a bell for a hiatus. When you fought, you fought for however long it took. Inside that gladiator circle of testosterone anything goes: punching, kicking, biting, cheating, spitting, kneeing, eye gouging, arm- or leg-breaking, cursing, and any other weaponless tactic. Though I didn't approve of Crips fighting one another, it was by far better than their killing each other.

Crazy Ed was looking stylish, throwing jabs and combinations, but made the mistake of getting too close. Jimel grabbed him and the tables quickly turned. Crazy Ed was soon sitting on the ground with his legs stretched out and Jimel kneeling behind him, holding him in a choke. Everybody stood in a trance while an infuriated Jimel tried to choke Crazy Ed out, but Raymond and I stepped in to stop it. Though the fight had ended, a feud was brewing. Some Hoover Crips flashed their weapons, ready to blast Jimel on the spot. Raymond and I talked them out of it.

Later, East Side Crip Bulldog, one of the spearheads of the Hoover Crips, told me that Jimel was very lucky. Violence was the primary Crip negotiation technique as well as an attention-getting device. My own need for attention had increased, as it helped to blot out the unhealed scar of being shot down like a mangy animal in the street. In truth I was still trying to piece together my shattered ego. Flamboyance, rage, self-hate, drugs and Crip aggression had become my pillars of support. I didn't have to peruse Frantz Fanon's literary works to perceive violence as a means to an end. Urban street violence had long since mutated into a common ganghood. I was so permeated with self-hate that Caucasians were safe from my wrath. But black humanity beware! I was death in a tinderbox, ready to explode.

The same enemies I had repelled for years were now watching me and Jimel strolling in their territory with our shirts off. It was lunacy to be out there flexing our muscles in the midst of gang warfare but that was the insolence of crippin', do-or-die, can't stop won't stop, this is Crip, fool! I still managed to hurl my body into the fray for any Crip. No Crip who knew me could deny that in a pinch, the words "go get Tookie" would bring me forth to redress their problem. In the 'hood where East Side Crips commander Little James lived, on 118th Street, he and his homeboys clashed with a big, stocky, armed lunatic. When James called I didn't hesitate to show up and confront the figure, who looked like a madman. I pulled the guy to the side and he quickly started nodding his head in agreement to everything I said, like a doll attached to a car dash. Even in his mental turmoil he understood it was in his best interests to leave Little James alone. Perhaps he had recognized a slight madness in me. Little James didn't have any more problems with that guy, nor did I ever question why they didn't smash him. I knew they could.

It was this sort of incident that made me appear bigger than life. Whether it was acting as a negotiator or as an aggressor, I always managed to quell the storm or carry the day. Crips like my stepbrother Wayne, Godfather, Sweetback, Blackie, Big Marcus, Mansion, Capone, and a long list of others would routinely seek my assistance. Though Godfather had warned me about Jimel bringing trouble to my doorstep, I didn't mind because I never discriminated against a Crip homeboy. Once, Jackie and I had finished driving iron when Jimel met us on the corner. He was huffing and puffing after running from his mother's apartment on Century Boulevard at about 100th Street, all the way to where we lived on 69th. Jimel complained about some youngster with several friends who had crowned him with a baseball bat, busted out his back car window, and appropriated his tape deck. The feud involved this high school guy's girlfriend whom Jimel tried to hit on and who rejected his advances.

When I arrived, Jimel's car, parked in back of the apartments, had been vandalized. I talked with the youngster's father, who had his son return the tape player and agreed to pay for the damages. Whether or not he followed through with the payment I don't know, but the conflict was squashed. I relished doing the dirty work because it added to my legend. I seized every angle in life to define myself as being *somebody*. It didn't matter how ruthless or despicable I had to become in the realm of ganghood, as long as I was the best. Gradually, I was morphing into a combination of Buddha and Black Johnny, becoming one highly unstable character. I was back home on the west side – this time bigger and worse.

TWENTY-TWO

Float On,
Float On, Float On

The years 1977 to 1979 were the lowest point of my life. I allowed drugs to rule my consciousness and render me an addict. I had used marijuana, angel dust, LSD, barbiturates, cocaine, Thai stick and sniffed glue, but none of these were more chronic than Sherm, a cigarette soaked in phencyclidine, better known as PCP.

The first time I tried this powerful drug it rocked me to the core. While walking towards the liquor store for some orange juice, Calhoun, an Avalon Garden Crip, and I detoured through an alley and puffed on a Sherm. It produced an immediate high that scared the hell out of me, and I told Calhoun never to offer it to me again. But a month or two later, at the Festival In Black at MacArthur Park, I smoked a Sherm with Lynn after she cornrowed my hair. This time I felt wonderful, euphoric. Later, what really caught my attention was that it didn't seem to hinder my ability to drive iron – it appeared to enhance it.

For a while, I smoked Sherm "only on the weekends and for recreational purposes" – and so from Friday to Sunday it was on. Whatever excuse I could find for frying my brain cells, I used. It made my troubled world magically disappear: puff, gone, just like that. Reality and delusions intermingled in a deadly, phantasmagorical cocktail. The longer I remained in such a state, the further I was alienated from society. I failed to notice the increase in my aggression and outlandish behaviour. It was a personal hell.

I jacked the local dope dealers for their supply of drugs or money out of need, greed, or for the hell of it. My homeboys and I viewed dealers as just another street gang with limited options for dealing with us Crips. Since they couldn't complain to the cops, they either had to fight us or pretend the jackings hadn't happened. They weren't chumps, but they were less ruthless than us, they were outgunned and they were fewer. In spite of my roguish life style and drug use, I still managed to drive iron five to six days a week.

The 69th Street duplex that Jackie and I shared became a quasi-embassy where Crips from the west side flocked to hang out or drive iron. Neighbourhood youngsters who later evolved into Crips – Kody, Frank, Aaron, Chico and others – flocked around the duplex, starry-eyed, wanting mostly to watch me while James Brown's "The Payback" played in the background. On just about any occasion they would see Big Vertice, Bogard, Jackie, Raymond, Big Bamm, Cutes, Mouse, Big Lunatic, Rusty, Godfather, and a host of others. Young Kody, who would grow up to become known as Monster (and to author a book of the same name), lived down the block. He used to show up bright and early to help stack weights, run errands, or help me wash my car. He and I would stroll to Centinela Park or long distances to some woman's house. I preferred walking because it was the best way to be seen flashing my muscles. Sometimes Kody would sit for hours on a milk crate watching us drive iron, amazed at our size and strength. I regretted our smoking Sherm around Kody because we made it appear to be cool. Sometimes he joined right in and ended up zombie-like, as most of us did.

Smoking Sherm, a person's behaviour can range from moving in slow motion to streaking naked, being hyped up or feeling immune to pain, being amnesiac or becoming violent with enormous physical strength. When my step-brother Wayne was floating on Sherm, he sometimes moved in super-slow motion as if he was in another dimension. Once while I was getting my hair braided by my stepsister

Demetri, Wayne was high on Sherm and got up in super-slow motion to creep over to where Demetri's friend's purse was. He took out the wallet and placed it under his jacket, then returned to his seat as if nothing had ever happened. I shook him out of his trance, and he wasn't even aware of what he had done. Though we all laughed, it was one of the most bizarre things I had ever seen. In time I would do stranger things.

Sherm was cheap, and if it was from a strong batch, a few puffs could keep you high for hours. It enhanced my mood swings, making me far less tolerable of petty things I'd normally let slide by. At the height of my aggression I developed a terrible habit of "jap-slapping" – spitting in somebody's face to provoke a fight. I'd even launch into a debasing monologue about a guy's mother, and if that failed, I'd simply knock him out. But I was never hostile toward women, and no matter how high I flew on Sherm, I didn't let it interfere with my womanizing.

It wasn't long before I accepted employment, along with Godfather, Madbull, Big Curtis and about twenty other Crips, working for Wayne's mother, whose company was the C-and-C Dog Academy. She had no idea that her son and her new employees were Crips. The job was simple enough. All I had to do was keep an eye on a German shepherd or Dobermann pinscher guard dog while it patrolled a particular work site. I reported to work at a beer distribution plant in Compton. The dog handler was nowhere in sight, but outside the building stood a large crowd of angry strikers who were vandalizing cars and beer delivery trucks and threatening employees. They had already chased off several people standing guard.

I didn't realize that the plant's boss was viewing the entire scene from a car in a nearby parking lot. For at least thirty minutes I sat underneath the sun with my arms crossed and watched the crowd whisper and point in my direction. A small group of ten Caucasians, Mexicans, and blacks finally swaggered towards the left side of the lot. I got up and matched them stride for stride, sliding out of my shirt ready for a fight. We met in the middle of the parking lot, where they stopped and stared at me. A short pudgy black fellow and a tall and husky white guy took turns running off at the mouth about what they planned to do to the building and me if I tried to stop them. The black guy asked what was I going to do when all of them rushed straight at me.

"I'll knock you and your hillbilly friend out first, if you're stupid enough to try me," I responded.

They had an opportunity to rush me, but none of them was willing to be the first. I gladly would have fought them all. I knew that had I been defeated, a Crip force would have retaliated. My confidence was higher than the moon, heightened by intoxication.

The following morning, the plant boss greeted me at the gate with high kudos for doing what I often did, "standing up against the odds." He pumped my hand for about two minutes while stating he had watched the entire scene from the next-door parking lot. After thanking me fifty times he vowed to always be there for me if need be, but I knew he was caught up in the moment and didn't really mean it.

For several nights it was quiet, till I heard several gunshots in the back of the building. Being drug-inspired I no longer feared gunshots, so I scanned the back area, finding nothing. I knew right then, however, that I'd arm myself for work. The next evening I had my pump shotgun resting on my shoulder when I told the crowd somebody had shot several times and almost hit me. I warned them if it happened again, I'd be forced to hunt them down like dogs. I ended with a parting remark, "Remember this, fools, I'm not alone. There's more of me around." My words may have been ignored, but the shotgun was respected.

The following night, the strikers watched as a ten-car caravan of my homeboys and some homegirls pulled into the driveway flashing rifles and guns out of the windows. The music blasting from car speakers was "The Big Payback." Big Curtis and Godfather stepped out Crip-walking, and immediately after, a group of Crips and Criplettes Crip-walked with their weapons gleaming from the car lights, hollering "Crip here! Crip here!" The strikers seemed to disappear. The party was on. Some of the empty beer trucks served as mini-motels, the parking lot became the dance floor, and there was a buffet table inside the building replete with cookies, doughnuts, cake, candy, chips, coffee, tea, and sodas. Coming to work each evening became nothing but a party, or a workout session, since Jackie would show up with his car trunk filled with weights, and we'd work out in the parking lot. My job literally consisted of getting loaded, lounging, partying, working out, and using the trucks as motel rooms.

Sometimes when I was supposed to be at work, Jackie and I socialized in Marina Del Rey at two of the most popular clubs, the Bahama Mamas and the Juke Box Jury. Neither of us were there to dance, but to catch a different female to take home or at least get her phone number for future conquest. The area was really squaresville. Fortunately for them, most Crips felt it was too far to drive to a club. I entered these clubs with an unmistakable air of malice. If I wasn't mellow on Sherm, I was sky-high loaded, but either way it didn't take much to piss me off. Crip rage was my response to just about everything, so it was no surprise that I collared a few people there, especially for accidentally stepping on my biscuit shoes, a cardinal sin. After leaving the club, I'd return to the workplace, where I kicked back until my shift was over.

Though I worked twelve-hour shifts, there was no way I'd stay there the entire time. When I wasn't partying on the company lot, I'd simply unmuzzle the dog and let him run loose, then vacate the premises and return a few hours before I clocked out. There was nobody there to hassle me or to report to, so I had free rein. Once while on my way to work, I saw a bunch of cop cars parked around the building, so I made a U-turn to drop off my rifle at my friend Janice's house and then returned to work. The strikers had discovered who I was and snitched to the cops about us packing weapons. Earlier that day, the cops had mistakenly arrested this guy Bear (years later he would end up on San Quentin's death row) who didn't remotely resemble me. But after that episode there were no more run-ins with the strikers. They never crossed their side of the picket line. It was reminiscent of the 1920s when big companies hired the Mafia or other thugs to guard their property against strikers – who seemed quite tame to us. Crips were hired to work because no one else wanted to deal with the hostile strikers. For us it was easy money.

Within a matter of weeks I purchased a clean gold 1970 Cadillac with spoke rims. Cruising around Compton with a nice-sized afro, I was unrecognizable, but I still travelled with a weapon for security. Ever since I had become a counsellor, I had bought all of my weapons legally and kept the ownership documents in my wallet to avoid going to jail – I hoped. The law stated that a legal gun owner could carry a gun in the vehicle as long as it was not loaded and the bullets were carried separately – the gun or the bullets had to be in the trunk or somewhere inside the car but never together. To some cops the documents didn't make any difference. They'd take me to jail on general principles just to have the papers authenticated. In South Central the simplest of civil rights are lost at the moment of birth for blacks, even when you are confronted by an authority figure of even the lowest status.

Working at the beer distribution plant was easier than being a counsellor. I didn't expect to hold the job for long. Somehow I would deny myself prosperity, or fate would do the same. There was an incident where one of Wayne's mother's female friends argued with me over a paycheck I had received from her. I was told later that the dispute had more to do with her affinity for me (which I didn't reciprocate) than the payroll check. While I was kicking back at work, the woman showed up with her husband and several cop cars and escorted me off the premises. So I packed up the few scattered weights and drove away, not knowing that I'd never return to Compton.

Back at the duplex, my morning routine began with puffing on a Sherm, then I'd prepare for whatever the day would bring. I lived in three worlds. There was the real world that I didn't fathom, the violent gang world, and the illusory world of intoxication where past vulnerabilities were suppressed, where I was the man of steel living in a fool's paradise. I spent all that time indulging in the frivolity of drugs and becoming a Sherm addict. During my mind-altering experiences, I slapped long-time friends Bimbo and Mansion, broke a broom handle over Eddy's head, and was said to have attacked many others for no apparent reason. Not too many people wanted to be around me because I had become too unpredictable. There were episodes when I waddled in dirt, got down on all fours and challenged a vicious dog bark for bark and growl for growl through a fence. I was on the brink of insanity.

When I wasn't tripping out, I was chasing after women like a dog in heat. Calhoun used to show up bright and early, all excited about us going out to scour the west side for available women. One sunny morning he showed up talking about how we had to go to South West College where the campus was full of beautiful black women. After we puffed on some Sherm, I was raring to go. I went through my usual ritual of oiling up my yokes in case I needed to break out in front of women. When we arrived the college looked deserted, and I asked Calhoun what was up with this madness. He assured me everybody was in class and at lunch I'd get an eyeful. In the meantime we strolled down the hill towards a tiny gym. For kicks I worked out alongside some of the football players, who asked was I planning to go out for football practice. I responded, "And what, mess up this beautiful body?" Calhoun almost fell to the floor laughing.

Before I left the gym, I gave a few of them some pointers on how to build up their arms, then we were out of there. As we were walking up the hill I saw a small crowd of women walk by and all of them were thick and shapely. A black man sometimes chooses a woman in the image of his mother in hue and stature. Perhaps that's why the beauty of this female caught my eye. As we passed, I turned and smiled, then complimented all of them on how well they looked that afternoon. They smiled and giggled.

We reached a grassy area in front of the college. It was packed. A music box was blaring out Marvin Gaye's "Got To Give It Up." I didn't need to scan the crowd; I had already chosen the voluptuous beauty I wanted. Calhoun, knowing the catch action was good, urged me to "break out," but I told him it was all about timing, to be patient. Minutes later, with the sun beaming, I sauntered over to an area where I couldn't be missed. I slid out my shirt and started flexing my muscles. The moment I started making my chest jump to the beat of Marvin Gaye's song, women started ululating and clapping like they were at a Teddy Pendergrass concert. After flexing, I made a beeline to my female of choice, who had been ogling me.

"Hello, my name is Stanley Williams, but my mother, relatives and close friends call me Tookie."

Her eyes widened. "You're Tookie?"

"I sure am."

Her name was Michelle. She told me her brother Michael was known as a hustler and was in a wheelchair, paralysed, having been shot for gambling with loaded dice, according to the story. It was awkward when she talked about all the horrid stories she'd heard about me, especially when she asked if I remembered when some of my crazy Crip homeboys and I trashed her mother's apartment during a late-night party across the street from the golf course on Western. I remembered that party all too well. I told her things had gotten out of hand that night, and I apologized. She talked about how different dudes she knew described me as being bald-headed and muscle-bound, with scars all over my face. They told her I was mean, ugly, and always jumping on people. She said, "You don't look anything like they said, and you don't appear to be mean." After a long, pleasant chat, we exchanged phone numbers and I promised to call her later that day. Calhoun and I left.

When I called Michelle that evening, she sounded down-hearted. Her mother disapproved of her having anything to do with me and didn't want me calling the house, because she knew exactly who I was. Michelle told me she cried for hours, pleading with her mother to allow me to call the house, and she claimed her brother Michael cried alongside her in an attempt to change their mother's mind. Her mother finally approved of my calling.

Floating on Sherm, Calhoun and I arrived at Michelle's mother's home in Gardena. It looked like a family tribunal. Michelle's mother was beautiful and gracious, and not once did she bring up the madness of my past. I met Michelle's stepfather, her sister Nunu, and one of her four brothers, Michael. I had met another one of her brothers, Lewis, at Washington High. I'd been surrounded by him and some of his homeboys. He had stood with a blackjack in his hand trying to question me about a run-in his brother had with my homeboy, Bimbo. Whatever Lewis and his cronies' intent, it dissolved when they realised Buddha and twenty of my homeboys were observing. The misunderstanding immediately disappeared. Lewis eventually began hanging out with Melvin and his crew. A decade later, Lewis's younger brother Michael would claim untruthfully to be a founder of the Crips. Odd that Michael would make such a bogus claim; his brother Lewis became a Crip before he did.

The chequered history between her family members and me didn't stop Michelle and me from hooking up. Though I was able to hide my addiction from her for many months, she heard vivid accounts from others of my drug escapades. Like the time Blackie and I visited the "Coolie Cools", the notorious Inglewood apartments, nicknamed "Sherm Alley," with its two giant stone statues of African heads in front. Blackie's car was parked in the middle of the street with the motor running while I jumped out, mobbed a drug dealer, and pummelled him to a bloody pulp. Before a cheering crowd, I held a shopping cart overhead and slammed it down on the guy several times. The cops later had a warrant for my arrest, but the guy regained consciousness after his coma and refused to press charges. Michelle didn't believe the story, while for me it was concealed in amnesia.

My life was a maze of contradictions. I was a hypocrite of the highest order. Absurdly, I believed that I could maintain a job and smoke Sherm simultaneously. I began working again as a counsellor for a boys' home near West Hollywood on Normandie Avenue. The two-storey home was an ideal place for youngsters to try to get their lives on track, far removed from the urban tapestry of gang propaganda. Though the boys came from diverse racial backgrounds, the only conflicts were minor, which made the job less hectic.

Still, serving as a live-in youth counsellor had its challenges. Sometimes, when I was too high to drive home, Michelle would stay, keep me company, and then leave early in the morning. Other times, Calhoun showed up and we'd drive iron, then puff away on some "love leaf" (marijuana dipped in PCP). Love leaf caused more blackouts – amnesiac incidents – than Sherm. One evening before taking a shower, I entered the living room where counsellors and youths were watching TV. Wearing only boxer shorts, stoned out of my mind, I demanded that they "look at me, I'm beautiful." I then pounded my fist on the big wooden dining room table, splitting it in half, causing everyone to run out of the house. Then I went out in the middle of the street and tried to pull people out of their cars, ranting and raving like a madman. I remember none of this.

When I snapped back to reality, I found myself standing in the shower. After I dried off, I heard cops calling my name on a bullhorn. I opened the door to see cops everywhere, pointing guns and ordering me to walk towards them. I was handcuffed and placed in the back seat of the patrol car. On the freeway, I asked the cops what was the problem, and one of them told me, "Just relax, Tookie, the doctors are going to take good care of you." Drifting in and out, the next thing I knew I was in Metropolitan Hospital strapped to a gurney and being injected with some kind of drug.

I came to the next day. I was sitting in a day-room chair wearing a quasi-straitjacket. To make matters worse, I was sandwiched between a white guy in a hospital gown, who rapidly recited, "Do you remember me, do you remember me?" and a Latino woman gently stroking my face, saying, "Pretty, pretty, pretty." I figured I was still high on love leaf and that this nightmare would end any minute.

Nearby, a female was singing a country western song, and some guy was swatting at imaginary objects. A black fellow was tap dancing, and other people were walking around like zombies. It was a scene right out of *One Flew Over The Cuckoo's Nest*. Another black guy hollered out "Tookie!" and declared he knew who I was and knew Raymond Washington too. He said, "Tookie, you've been living a wicked life. It's time for you to stop and repent. Bow your head and pray with me, my brother." He babbled on for several minutes about revelations, fire and brimstone, then digressed into pleading that I allow him join the Crips so he could help purge the world of the Brims. This had to be hell.

I believe it was two days later when I sat in the day room waiting to see the resident psychiatrist. Then reappearing like incubi were the same three figures I had thought were part of the earlier hallucination. Though no longer in a straitjacket, I still felt disoriented. I headed to the restroom, moving with great difficulty, but was escorted by the three irritants. Even as I stood relieving myself, the self-professed black preacher stood off to the side preaching. The white guy kept restating the phrase, "Do you remember me?" The long-haired female stroked my face repeating, "Pretty."

I was eventually escorted into a psychiatrist's office, where he asked questions about my drug use. I denied ever using drugs and said someone must have spiked my protein drink with LSD or something. I told him I was a bodybuilder and that getting high would destroy my chances of becoming a professional. Then he started asking me weird questions about whether I'd ever had sexual relations with my mother, sister, and aunts. I almost exploded.

"Have you ever gotten a blow job from your mother?" I countered.

Fortunately for him I was physically incapable of reaching across the table and slapping the taste out of his mouth.

Perhaps my scorn and silence convinced him to change the subject. He asked if there was anyone who could pick me up if I was released. He didn't see why I should be kept there any longer. When I said "yes", he gave me the phone and left the office. I contacted Michelle and Jackie and they picked me up. Having floated into the Metropolitan Hospital, I just as easily floated out, untransformed.

TWENTY-THREE

Schemes and Things

Somehow I continued to avoid the traps of the law. In a Los Angeles court room, Johnnie Cochran, my attorney, persuaded me to accept a $100 fine and six months probation for the charge of "assaulting a peace officer." As long as I wasn't doing time, I didn't trip. After shaking my attorney's hand, we parted ways. Other troubles found me, however. A bookie called Chunky was owed five grand by a white guy. Chunky gave me the guy's address and description and said, "My brother, if you can collect the money, half is yours." Now, though his offer was gracious, I planned to pocket everything. Nothing personal, just a Crip thing.

While I knocked on the white guy's door in Gardena, Wayne stood off to the side. In these situations I felt I had the upper hand. The guy was living foul, and for him to call the cops would be a joke, because he was considered white scum. The moment the guy opened the door I grabbed him by the collar and demanded Chunky's money.

"I only have two hundred dollars in my wallet," he stammered. He handed it over and I asked what else he had that was worth the debt? The guy blurted out, "Take my car, it's a 1975 Monte Carlo that should settle the debt, and I can sign over the pink slip right now."

I smiled. "Okay, but we'll go to the DMV and have it put in my name."

At the Inglewood motor vehicle department I paid for the

registration, then we left to get a smog device. The car was legally mine. Throughout the day I spread the word that I won a car in a big dice game. However, the next morning some southwest cops showed up to inform me that the owner of the Monte Carlo claimed I took his car and forced him to sign over the pink slip. If I wanted to keep the car I'd have to submit to a lie detector test to prove I didn't coerce him. Once again, I found myself at the Glass House police station. Though I was innocent, I failed the test. When they completed testing me and the white guy, I heard a detective say the test showed both of us were lying.

Before I was released, a detective said that if either of us wanted to own that car, we'd have to go to small claims court. For days I toyed with different schemes to get the car back, but decided the hassle wasn't worth it. If nothing else, the ordeal confirmed my suspicion that I was being followed, that it wasn't paranoia or my imagination. I was painted as a villain, and this was the type of cop harassment that can lead to a frame-up or extermination. Being harassed was business as usual. This became evident one early morning around 3 a.m. when Michelle and I were asleep, and there was a loud knock at the front door. Moments later, an excited Jackie banged on the bedroom door alerting me that a battalion of cops were outside and for me to be careful when I came out. In a gallant gesture I told her I'd go out first in case they started shooting.

It was pitch dark as I eased down the narrow hallway into the living room where I had to weave past a maze of weights and benches. Through the opened front door, I could see Jackie spread-eagled on the wet grass surrounded by cops and a helicopter overhead. The door opened and an armed cop barked out, "That's right, Tookie, just keep walking with your hands up and don't try any Crip heroics."

Outside, I was ordered to lie down next to Jackie. Moments later, Michelle was lying beside me. An elderly lady named Opa, who lived two houses down from me, stood several yards away. I'd known Opa ever since my family started living on 69th. She was mother to five sons and a daughter. Her two youngest sons, Frank and Aaron, would as teenagers become Crips. Opa stood there demanding to know what the problem was. A cop told her there was information received that gunshots had come from inside my apartment. "Gunshots?" Opa shot back. "That's odd, because I've been awake all this morning, and I haven't heard anything until you guys and the helicopters arrived." Although she continued to protest their harassment, it was to no avail.

A cop came out with a huge grin holding up my AR-15 and a pump shotgun. He asked if I had ownership papers for the weapons. It seemed to piss him off when I produced the documents. As soon as the cops finished searching the apartment, one of them warned me to watch my back.

"Tookie, why are they always harassing you?" asked Opa when the cops had gone. "And what in the world have you been doing?"

I smiled and said, "Miss Opa, your guess is as good as mine."

Who can you turn to when you're under surveillance and can't do anything about it? Though I wasn't Los Angeles's favourite inhabitant, I didn't think my behaviour warranted the constant attention.

It was Yea Yea who approached me with a harebrained scheme to rob a particular church of its monetary offerings. I looked at Yea Yea as if he were Mephistopheles himself, then said, "Hell, no, are you crazy?" Even after he told me it was an inside job, and that there was nothing there to stop us, I couldn't do it. I may have been immoral to the bone, but I was never crazy or sick enough to desecrate, vandalize, or stick up a church. But mobbing other criminals wasn't a crime. In fact, it was open season on them. Whenever my homeboys and I heard about a dope dealer, street jacker, bookie, hustler, thief, or non-Crip who had come across some money, he was in trouble. Like myself, most of my homeboys didn't put much stock in their lives. We were willing to risk everything for the almighty dollar, or for drugs.

Case in point: an East Side Crip called Syles was daring enough to rob an east side gambling shack. He knew there was a strong possibility of losing his life, but the potential for financial gain outweighed the consequences. Syles probably would have escaped with the loot, but the back door and windows were nailed shut. He was shot dead on the street. Another youngster's death for a worthless cause. May he rest in peace.

Then there was Mac Thomas, the Compton Crip leader turned full-time hustler. It was said that his adopted running buddies were the shadiest of characters, but he insisted on being with them. I remember when Mac was released from Youth Authority; he told me that he was no longer interested in crippin', and his conversation only revolved around hustling. He tried in vain to convince me to hook up with his crew, but I declined. Later on, from what I gathered, Mac's life was snuffed out by some of his hustler cronies who wanted his share of a heist. I didn't know too much about Mac's last days, but he was another companion from the early days of the Crips who became another black statistic, dying from a thug lifestyle. May he too rest in peace.

I have known hundreds of Crips exterminated while travelling down the path of drugs, gang-banging, pursuing money, whatever. But I wasn't intimidated by the possibility of death, and continued to sift through the schemes coming at me from all directions. Sweetback approached me with sketchy details about a score that involved mobsters needing some outside help to pull a big heist. There were tens of thousands of dollars to be made by each of us. Though Sweetback didn't know the mobsters personally, his friend James Garrett knew them. I thought, why not? If we were being hoodwinked, hell, mobsters could bleed just as quick as any Crip or Blood.

The plan was for us to meet the following day at the Marriott Hotel, not far from the Fox Hills Mall, to discuss the heist. When we arrived at James's home, in the living room were Juice and Hillbilly, two 83rd Street Gangster

Crips I had known since their childhood. After a brief chat, we caravanned and parked down the street from the hotel. I noticed I wasn't the only one packing. A few weapons were flashed in a show of confidence and readiness. Inside the hotel we waited in the bar until a short, stocky Italian guy wearing a suit and tie appeared. He briefly talked with James and his hefty wife Esther, then picked up the big duffel bag James had been carrying. Before they left, the Italian told us that someone would be down to get us, but until then the drinks were on the house. As I sat there looking uneasy about the entire setup, two other mobster-looking guys in suits appeared and motioned for us to follow. Once upstairs, one of them turned around and said with an Italian drawl, "Okay, the boss doesn't want anyone there packing heat, it's for security. So if you're holding something, leave your gun with my partner here and you'll get it back on the way out." I failed to comply.

When we entered the room, two scantily clothed white women were holding silver trays of *hors d'oeuvres*. On the table were more refreshments and an opened black duffel bag on the floor exposed numerous handguns. I sat in a chair next to the slightly opened window in case I needed to jump down several stories. Minutes later, two figures, one black, the other Italian and both in suits, entered the room. The tall black guy began talking about jacking a train that supposedly carried a shipment of high-tech weaponry and hundreds of thousands of dollars in UPS bags. While he continued to talk, another Italian guy entered the room with a huge suitcase and pulled out a replica of the type of rifle that would be on the train. The weapon was impressive, twice the size of my AR-15 rifle. It resembled a James Bond rifle with a long clip and silencer. But I was still suspicious, and the black dude just didn't fit in with the Italians.

Maybe this was how the Italian mobsters did business, but before I left, I wanted to hear more. To my surprise, the black guy said each of us had to be questioned to determine if we had what it took to pull off the heist. One by one we had to enter a separate room to be quizzed. I was the last one.

"So, Tookie, how many people have you killed?"

The query caught me off-guard. I almost stammered when I told the guy, "Hey, dude, I never killed anybody before."

The guy said, "Look, Tookie, everybody in town knows you're a dangerous dude and that you have a reputation for killing people."

I stared the dummy in the eyes and said, "Whoever told you that is a liar."

He tried to laugh it off to ease the tension and said, "We need someone like you who has the guts to kill."

Infuriated, I told him, "I'm not a killer. I'm a fighter."

Back in the living room I told Sweetback I didn't like the setup and was ready to leave. Seconds later the door burst open and in rushed plainclothes cops hollering, "Lennox Police, FBI!" A quick glance outside the window revealed cops down there pointing their guns up at the window. There was no escape, but I managed to slip the gun under the couch during the chaos.

All of us were handcuffed and driven down to the Lennox Police Station, then transferred later to the Los Angeles County Jail. At the court arraignment, James, Esther and Sweetback were released, but I had to reappear in court the following day. Both Juice and Hillbilly had pending charges of allegedly robbing a Big 5 Sporting Goods store for its guns, and I was charged with possession of a loaded weapon. Unknown to any of us, James and Esther had conspired with law enforcement to set up a sting operation. For many years, James had been an agent provocateur working undercover for the FBI, ATF (Bureau of Alcohol, Tobacco and Firearms), and other law enforcement agencies. He was a paid snitch, ready to lie, frame, fabricate and commit whatever duplicitous act his masters commanded of him. Needless to say, James was playing a deadly game. In Africa a snitch would undergo a "necktie" – a car tyre placed around the neck, doused with gasoline and set afire before a jubilant crowd.

In Los Angeles Court, the judge dismissed the charges against me for lack of evidence, but years later I'd be recharged for the same offence and much more. I was used to it. Happiness was something I'd never experienced.

TWENTY-FOUR

Living the Funk

South Central Los Angeles was an environment that made it difficult to dream. Hope was absent. I lived in a mental funk that raved for salvation, but the Crip god denied me reprieve from my hell. I was dying a slow death with no purpose or legitimate cause worthy of such a sacrifice. Though I'd boldly challenge any gang rival, I shied away from revolting against the conditions I allowed to dominate my past, present, and future. I was a total mess.

My life's soundtrack was P-funk, music notable for the funkedelic phase of musical madness, drugs, sex, and urban violence. Popular funk artists like Bootsy Collins, Ohio Players, Rick James, Barkays, and the greatest of all funksters, Parliament, reigned supreme in South Central. So when Parliament were scheduled to appear at the Inglewood Forum, most Crips I knew were pumped up for the concert. Prior to their performance, Parliament drove through South Central in a green limousine, amazing the residents. But while everybody else was looking forward to being entertained, I was preparing to be seen.

The evening concert was so packed that Jackie and I had to park several blocks away from the Forum. Some of us had our own methods of gaining admission. If we were unable to rip the door off its hinges, then somebody would jimmy the door or, in this instance, would pay to get in, then open a side door for the rest. Inside were wall-to-wall women, while speakers blasted Marvin Gaye's "Got To Give It Up." When the time was right, Jimel and I started strolling around the Forum with our shirts off before crowds of people shouting, "Tookie! Jimel!" During our posing routine the crowd began to chant, "Go to the stage, go to the stage." We descended parallel stairways towards centre stage. Abruptly, the lights were cut off, the music stopped, and Parliament's mothership – a replica spaceship – lowered onto the stage. Though our unscheduled performance rocked the house, we were up-staged as Parliament tore the roof off the sucker.

From musical funk to a funked-up situation: Jackie and I were evicted from the duplex for refusing to pay rent because of a serious roof problem. Jackie moved in with his sister Gloria and brother Joey, and I drifted like a nomad. I kept a razor, toiletries and a few clothes in the trunk of my car and left the bulk of my clothing at my mother's apartment or at some female's house. As for the weights, Sweetback suggested I talk to James and Esther Garrett about storing them in their garage. They agreed, and I unloaded more than 3,000 lbs of weights, dumbbells, squat racks, and five different heavy-duty weight benches.

The Garretts told me I had access to their garage any time and if need be their home was open to me. They were seemingly friendly people, willing to help. None of us suspected that they were agents provocateurs, snitches. Being smoked out, I had long since lost my edge to detect a snitch when no one else could. The Garretts managed to snake their way around without exposure, plotting nefarious schemes with anyone seeking to make a buck, then turning them in to the cops.

Loaded or not, I managed to drive iron with consistency. Between workouts I Crip-walked around with my chest stuck out, playing a man of indomitable posture, along with my trusted stepbrother and sidekick Wayne, sometimes known as Li'l Tookie. Wayne was shorter than Napoleon Bonaparte but his madcap exploits elevated his stature. When we were there, we made the Coolie Cools apartments a terrible place to be. Only women, children and other Crips were exempt from our hostile greed. With sick insolence we caught a lone dealer before he could hide several jars of wet sherms. Wayne was supposed to search the dude for a weapon but being loaded he did a sloppy job. When we turned to walk away with the loot, the guy whipped out a gun and I heard it click several times. It misfired, unfortunately for him. He became a human punching bag at our hands.

That was the incautious me, always trying to tempt death's embrace. I lived my life looking through the lens of a movie camera, seeing a caricature of myself going through the motions of an impersonal existence. I can't recall why, but one day Yea Yea – former Compton Crip turned West Side Crip – broached the subject. He asked, "If you had to pick between death row or life in prison, which one would you choose?" Without thinking, I nonchalantly said, "Death row." Looking bemused he asked, "Why death row, big homie?" I told him we were already living on death row, biding our time, so to me there was no difference. Oddly enough I forgot to mention having envisioned myself being in a death row cell sitting in a Rodin's thinking man position. Yea Yea's eyes lit up as he said, "That's deep, cuz, but this (he pulled out a wet Sherm wrapped in aluminum foil) is deeper."

Although there were other dreams and omens, warning of a ruined future, what other than death could possibly be worse? I was already living the funk. By no stretch of the imagination could I conceive any Crip or acquaintance conspiring with the cops against me. Such Shakespearean intrigue only happened in the movies. Such trust laid me open to being blindsided, and would be my undoing.

In 1979 I met Capone at the Workshop club on Western. Jimel and I were semi-bouncers there and were given a free pass inside provided my homeboys maintained their composure. On a particular evening Capone and a handful of his cronies tried to bully their way through the side door of the club, something I stopped immediately. Capone's expression told me he was shocked. Under the streetlight I could see him for the first time. If looks could kill, he would have murdered an entire army. Dressed all in black with gloves and dark shades to match, he looked like the movie character Shaft. Capone was of medium height, dark-skinned and muscular, with a manicured afro. He had unique features, resembling a swarthy monitor lizard with a fierce grimace that probably alone won many battles. He had an unforgettable mug.

I stepped from the club onto the sidewalk. Capone's posture was begging for a right jab, and I was positioning myself to do just that. Stepping into full view under the light I heard a few of his homeboys acknowledge loudly, "Hey, wait a minute, cuz, that's big Took." Immediately there were smiles and "C" handshakes (thumb and forefinger made to form a "C" then connecting with someone else's forefinger) and even Capone had a toothy grin. While introducing themselves as Harlem's Crips, somebody from behind us hollered out, "What's the problem, cuz?" A small crowd of West Side Crips approached, with Yea Yea out front doing the Crip walk. Being a showman, he said, "I hope I don't have to get physical here." It was hilarious because Yea Yea weighed no more than a buck-fifty.

After introductions, a few of us caravanned to other parties in the jungle then to the Show Case, an after-hours club off Crenshaw on Adams. When we arrived, there were cars and people all over the place. I bumped into my stepfather Fred, a professional photographer who worked concerts, fashion shows, professional fights, weddings, clubs, and premieres, among other events. I was trying my best to stay out of his view because my homeboys and I were acting like complete fools.

Back then the Show Case was a Crip predator's paradise, with an abundance of women, drug users and suppliers. Capone and I started hanging out more, getting high like there was no tomorrow. We clicked like junkies sharing a needle, but in our case it was sherms. Sometimes, sitting in Capone's black Chrysler townhouse car blowing our minds off on Sherm, he'd complain about not getting the respect he deserved while crocodile tears flowed down his face. I thought the most ugly thing was a man bawling like a baby. I'd humour Capone by telling him, "Cuz, you have to start acting mean and crazy like the real Al Capone." Other times I'd say, "Capone, look at me, I'm Tookie, I attack first then ask questions later. You're Capone, so be Capone, and stop all this boo-hooing." Sherm seemed to affect each person differently; for me aggression was always up front.

One sunshiney afternoon, while driving down Adams and getting high, Capone spotted two dudes he'd had a run-in with a few days before. I told him to pull over and then I bailed out of the car. One of them ran off, but the chubbier of the two was too slow. He received the brunt of my rage. With a beaming grin and no remorse, I Crip-walked away and got back into the car. Capone sped off shaking his head, stammering, "Man, I didn't expect that, Tookie...you are crazy." That was music to my ears. Being viewed as maniacal or whacked out fed my ego.

For over a decade, self-hate had been eating me up like a streptococcus consuming an inch of human flesh a minute. Had I run into someone who acted like me, I would have peeled his cap without hesitation. My blue rage was now mimicking Buddha's. I craved money and drugs but failed to realize my poverty transcended the physical. I was mentally shackled and incapable of emancipating myself. Darn near everybody I knew was a psychological captive to poverty.

Further, I was unable to evacuate these ugly premises – where could I go? During the worst moments I'd drive to Santa Monica beach to sit with my bare feet under the sand and stare out into the distance. Under a starry sky and with the comfort of a cool breeze, the demon of anxiety was held at bay. There were no deep thoughts during those moments. It was a high of a different kind, inhaling the pure oxygen of relief before I had to return to the toxic world called home.

I sensed a finale of some kind coming. Like a madman I was on the move, crisscrossing throughout the west to the east side 'hood of the Q-102 Street Crips. I hung out there with Frog and company or with D-Dog in the JDs. Other times I'd show up at the PJs in the wee hours of the morning to visit Beverly and our son Stan. Though she welcomed me with open arms, I wouldn't blame her or Bonnie if they resented me for being absent, for drifting in and out of their lives. Watching my son Stan playing on the carpet, I knew that any effort to reconcile would be too late. It felt the same way when I was with my other son Travon, whom I drove to school occasionally in a pitiful attempt to play father. The world was closing in on me. In a moronic haze of drugs I sought redemption for abandoning my children.

Cruising in a recently purchased gold two-door 1974 Fiat, I was game for anything. Driving down Hoover Street I spotted Bulldog with a voluptuous female. He was limping badly, having been shot in the leg, and was using a walking cane. Bulldog introduced the Criplette as a relative called Koko and said they were headed to a Crip house to get high. Inside my car I whipped out aluminium foil with a Sherm inside, and Koko's face lit up as she made a wink-wink gesture. I had high expectations about what was going to happen between Koko and me that afternoon.

In front of the shabby house off Broadway, Hoover Crips drove iron or stood around getting high. We entered the house and I sat at the kitchen table, kicking it with Devil. I heard Koko call me, then motion for me to follow. Inside a bedroom we sat on the end of the bed and talked for a few minutes, then started kissing. After I pulled out a Sherm and took a few puffs, I handed it to Koko, who had already slipped out of her khaki suit to reveal a leopard ensemble. Maybe it was because I was loaded, but she looked like the poster on the wall, an African warriorette kneeling beside her man. I watched as Koko took long drags on the Sherm then asked was I going to undress. As I took off my khaki shirt Koko's eyes looked as if they were about to pop out of their sockets. She started screaming, "Ah! Ah! Ah!" I almost panicked, thinking that my yokes had melted or something, but when I looked in the mirror I saw nothing amiss. This chick had to be crazy!

Seconds later Bulldog burst into the room asking Koko

what was wrong. Cowering under a bedspread, she continued trembling and screaming as if she had seen a ghost or monster. I left in a fury and went outside to sit on the porch. Minutes later Bulldog came out and sat beside me. He mentioned how Koko had a tendency to trip out when she smoked Sherm.

"That's an understatement," I said.

"You won't believe it, Tookie," said Bulldog. "She hallucinated that your veins had turned into snakes, and your yokes were about to explode."

Every Crip standing outside burst into laughter except me. Several hours later when Koko asked if I could drive her home and spend time with her, I angrily declined.

I left the house, only to return that evening with Dianne and Opa's young son Frank, who kept pestering me to let him ride with us. At the Crip house I kicked it for a while with Hoover Crip commander T.S. and drove a little iron. I came back to jack a drug dealer in the area along with a couple other Hoovers. The guy's stash turned out to be quite low, and disappointed I returned to the house and snatched up the dude who gave us the bunk info. I dragged him by the collar outside to the back of my car and positioned him on his knees. I popped the trunk, pulled out my pump, jammed it in his mouth and told him not to move. I launched into a holier-than-thou lecture about the perils of lying to us, and especially to me. I was flying high as a rocket, but my intent was to put the fear of the Crip god in him.

A large crowd of Crips had gathered outside to observe the bizarre spectacle. A smiling T.S. advanced to the front and appealed to me to spare the guy further humiliation or worse. Removing my weapon, I kicked him to the ground. Nodding to T.S. and the other Crips, I got in my car, threw up the Crip sign and then sped off. It would be over a decade before I'd see T.S. again.

I continued to be called upon as a protector. My stepsister and her man Allen were having problems with some fools who mistook their apartment for a dope house. Although they were told differently, the troublemakers continued to harass them and threaten bodily harm. For two evenings straight I camped outside from dusk till dawn waiting to ambush the culprits, who wisely didn't come back. That same evening, the Garretts experienced drive-by shootings into their home. Frightened to death, young James contacted me, and I rushed over to protect them and their visiting nieces and nephews. During the entire week I hung around watching over them, and the drive-bys ended as quickly as they had started. When I told James that I had to leave, he begged me to leave my twelve-gauge shotgun with him for safekeeping. I agreed and told him I'd check in periodically. I didn't know that the drive-bys were a retaliation for James having set up Juice and Hillbilly.

TWENTY-FIVE

The Longest Day

March 15, 1979, was a day of chaos. At 8 a.m., Jackie and I were driving iron over at the Garretts' while Yea Yea huffed and puffed with a set of dumbbells too heavy for him. I went to my car to retrieve my "Paycheck" tape. Returning, I saw James pointing a .38 calibre pistol at Jackie's head warning him to leave or he'd shoot. I hollered at James to put the gun down, that he better not shoot Jackie. Whether James knew it or not, he had severed the ties between him and us. As I drove away I assured Jackie that tomorrow I'd be moving all the weights over to his sister Gloria's house and that payback was imminent.

That afternoon at McDonald's on Century and Avalon, I ran into an irate Calhoun. He accused Wayne of ripping off a large container of PCP. Though Calhoun was a good homeboy of mine, I warned him not to retaliate against Wayne or I'd come looking for him.

Shortly after the encounter with Calhoun I visited my stepsister Bridget, who told me about several dudes barging into her apartment looking to kill her boyfriend JoeJoe. With Godfather, Bear, Creeper, Diamond and Crusher, I went over to one of the guys' houses. His parents were there but he had left. I assured Bridget I'd be back to iron out the problem.

En route to see Lynn I stopped off at the apartments where some of the Q-102 Crips lived and hung out. As we sat around smoking Sherm, a guy showed up wanting to purchase a Sherm stick and started haggling loudly over the price. I had him kissing the cement quickly, compliments of my wrath.

Finally I arrived at Lynn's apartment, exhausted, hungry, and in need of washing off the day's filth. Lynn was lying on the couch crying. Someone had broken in and stolen her brand new entertainment centre. "Baby," she said, "I know who and where they live, too." Though my slate was full, I told her I'd handle it later; first I wanted something to eat, to bathe, then to sleep. On the stove was a huge pot of seafood gumbo, rice, corn bread, and for dessert, German chocolate cake and vanilla ice cream. After eating I stretched out in the bathtub trying unsuccessfully to free my mind of the tasks at hand. Kneeling beside the tub Lynn washed my back while whispering sweet nothings in my ear. Soon both of us were in the tub. When I finally did lie down to rest, it was lights out.

Hours later I woke with Lynn lying next to me, grinning and rubbing olive oil on my chest and arms. I perceived her oiling me down as a ritualistic anointment prior to my going out to face the unpredictable night. What would be the toll, would I return unscathed? There was the pungent smell of a recently lit Sherm drifting with a beckoning aroma. I reached over, pulled the Sherm from her lips and inhaled it like my life depended upon it. The septic smoke shot up to my brain and exploded with the force of a grenade, charging my mind and body up like an energized Frankenstein. I was ready to roll.

A strange thing happened after I embraced Lynn and kissed her before leaving. It felt like farewell. Needing more clothes, I headed toward Fred and my mother's apartment where I stayed off and on. I felt I was going away – but where? I put more clothes in the trunk and planned to return later to get my car. Capone then picked me up, and we drove out to Jackie's pool hall on Avalon. He was still vexed about that morning's conflict with James. We shot some pool, then I told Jackie I was headed out to PeePee's spot. He said

PeePee was at the car shop several blocks away. We jumped into Capone's car, and Jackie gave him directions to the place.

We parked down the street and walked through a short alley to the entrance of the repair shop. The garage was well lit inside, with people working on cars. I heard PeePee in the back of his low-rider car arguing with his woman. I had known him for about six years and we had become tight. He enjoyed driving iron and was yoked up. As I approached he smiled and said, "Big cuz," then went back to arguing. I stuck my head through the window and said, "When you finish, cuz, I need to holler at you." Our plan that night was to jack a known dope dealer. The last jack had been a fiasco because bottles of PCP had exploded in Crip Coco's car trunk. No one had seen Coco since.

I could tell PeePee was whacked out on Sherm when he jumped out of his car screaming, "Tookie, I love you like a brother, but don't you tell me how to treat my woman!" He became incoherent, saying that if I didn't stop interfering he would have to fight me. "I know who you are, Tookie, but I'll still fight you."

"Are you sure, cuz?"

"Hell yes, let's fight right now."

As we walked outside I planned to grab PeePee and put him in a headlock until he lost consciousness, but the moment I turned around, PeePee whipped out a .45 calibre pistol bigger than his hand and pointed at me. Tears streamed down his face and his expression was maniacal.

Jackie walked over, stood beside me and then told PeePee, "Don't shoot my homeboy. You'll have to shoot me too!"

"No problem, my cousin, that can be arranged too."

Capone had vanished. I stood there with my arms folded defiantly. PeePee was still crying when a truck pulled up and people jumped out with rifles and ran towards us. When they got closer, someone said, "PeePee, are you crazy, that's Tookie." His brother tried to take the gun away, PeePee told him to stay back.

Pissed off and growling, I said, "Look here, I'm tired of

this madness, I don't have time for this. So if you guys are going to shoot me, then shoot, I'm out of here." I stormed away with Jackie trailing me. I didn't care if they shot or not.

At the end of the alley Jackie caught up with me. There we were confronted by DeeDee, whose hustler brother I had slapped several nights before outside Jackie's pool hall. I brushed past him saying, "Buster, if you're going to shoot, shoot." Jackie tried to reason with me, but I wasn't hearing it. Back at his pool hall I decided to hang out and went outside to get toasted. I vowed to return and make examples of everybody. As I puffed on a Sherm, Capone drove up, jumped out the car with his double-barrelled shotgun, and said, "Where are they, cuz? I'm ready!" I continued to hit the Sherm and ignored Capone's comedy act. I shook hands with Jackie, told him I'd be back later, then motioned to Capone, "Let's go."

I went to the Garretts' house to retrieve my shotgun. The ambience felt weird. Several suspicious white vans were parked out front. When Capone and I reached the front door, it was ajar. I could hear the TV playing. I rang the doorbell a few times, but there was no response. I chose not to enter though the door – a good thing, too. I found out later that cops were inside waiting to arrest me and that they had been told to shoot if I resisted – which I would have.

We returned to the pool hall, where Jackie and I had a brief chat. I agreed to meet with PeePee's brother the next day to iron things out and to follow through with jacking that dope dealer. But there was no hope for DeeDee when I caught up with him. We then drove on down Central Boulevard on our way to see Bob Simmons – but we never made it. Two sheriff cars from Firestone pulled us over. Their bullhorn blared warning us to exit the car with arms raised above our heads. Four sheriffs, guns drawn, approached us cautiously. After they searched us, we were handcuffed and ordered to sit on the curb. Two sheriffs guarded us while the other two started tearing apart Capone's car. Within minutes, at least five more Firestone patrol cars appeared. There were so many white sheriffs around, it looked like a Ku Klux Klan meeting. The air stank of racial slurs and hate.

Capone fell out in the street on his back, behaving as if he were having a heart attack and asked the sheriff to contact his wife to bring him his medication. His health problem was news to me. "Nigger, get up," one of the sheriffs said, but Capone persisted until the sheriff pointed his gun at him, fingered the trigger and threatened to blow his head off. Then Capone, with the agility of a gymnast, jumped and landed upright on the kerb. His antics caused the sheriffs to laugh for several minutes. "You believe that coon could move so fast?" asked one, between gales of laughter.

The merriment of the sheriffs quickly vanished with the announcement that a double-barrelled shotgun had been found in the trunk of Capone's car. Capone produced a licence for the weapon but they refused to accept it as valid. As we were being pushed into the back seat of the patrol car, I heard a voice say, "I know who that big dude is, that's Tookie."

As if on cue, every sheriff said, "Who?"

"You know, Tookie, the big Crip leader everybody talks about," responded the first sheriff.

I then became a specimen for all of them to gawk at.

"Are you really Tookie?"

"How big are your arms?"

"Can you really bench-press over five hundred pounds?"

"Are you still leading the West Side Crips?"

The queries continued as if I were being mobbed by reporters, but I refused to answer. Capone and I were rushed into the back seat of a squad car. Inside, Capone made an absurd statement about preparing to jump through the closed window to escape, which I ignored. When we arrived at the Firestone Sheriff's station, he became even more eccentric. He paced back and forth in the holding tank with tears streaming down his face, mumbling over and over that his wife needed him.

After our one phone call, I was escorted from the holding

tank into a cell with a steel door. Several minutes later Capone was brought to the door. He braced himself in the doorway and refused to come in. He yelled out, "I don't want to be locked up, I want to go home." Two sheriffs tried to push him inside the cell, but he wouldn't budge. Finally, one sheriff snatched him by the collar and pulled him backwards from the doorway while the other slammed the door shut. I could hear Capone screaming like a woman in labour and the sheriffs hollering, "Stupid nigger." I could also hear the sickening sounds of a stick hitting flesh.

After a few hours, Capone began to cry and scream, "Let me out of here, please let me out of here." I called out to him numerous times but he didn't respond. After a while he quieted down but still refused to answer when I called his name. This was the first time I had ever seen a black man react so strangely in jail. I didn't know then that Capone had never before been arrested. I didn't know a black man about my age who had not spent time in jail, whether he was guilty or not.

Before the night ended, I heard someone yelling at Capone, "Didn't that nigger do it? Didn't he murder those people? Or was it you, nigger?" He again started to cry. His wails were punctuated by denials, that he knew nothing and had nothing to do with a murder case. After being beaten again, though, his story dramatically changed.

"Yes, yes, yes, he did it," I heard Capone scream. "He did it, I'll say whatever you want. Please, just don't beat me any more."

I had no idea who "he" was. Later, legal documents would show that Capone's ribs were broken that March night, that he was beaten unconscious by the sheriffs and left lying on a cell floor in a pool of his own blood. I did not see him again for several months, until the day he took the witness stand to testify under oath – falsely – that I had killed three people. I was ultimately charged with four murders. Falsely.

TWENTY-SIX

Rage of Another Kind

This was the beginning of phase two of my life. I was twenty-five years old.

To this point, my life had been possessed by a Crip rage, a lethal momentum hurling me into perilous situations where the odds of living were long. Playing my own version of Russian roulette, I got an adrenaline high from roaming the streets and terrorizing entire communities, as if daring someone, anyone, to fire the bullet that would stop me forever. My Crip rage was a distorted expression of my virility. I felt invincible, indifferent to societal or mundane affairs, I lumbered through life fuelled by brute strength and bent on intimidation. I held no allegiance to anything other than crippin', and I beckoned violence like a bullfighter beckons a bull with his red cape. My rage was nourished by the hate I saw and felt from mainstream society and white people, a hate based on my black skin and my historical place at the nadir of America's social system. I was filled with hate for injustice. Yet my reaction to the hate was violence directed only toward blacks.

Unlike those ashamed to admit their motivation or too blind to recognize it, I forged through life locked in hostile intimacy with America's wrongness. Conditioned and brainwashed to hate myself, and my own race, other black people became my prey and the Crips my sword. Though I cannot condone it, much of the violence I inflicted on my gang rivals and other blacks was an unconscious display of my frustration with poverty, racism, police brutality, and other systematic injustices routinely visited upon residents of urban black colonies such as South Central Los Angeles. I was frustrated because I felt trapped. I internalized the defeatist rhetoric that served as street wisdom in my 'hood and that said there were only three ways out of South Central: migration, death or incarceration. I found a fourth option: incarcerated death.

The day after Capone's beating I was moved from the Firestone station, entombed within the Los Angeles County Jail and assigned to the High Power unit. A mix-up occurred, and I was thrown in with the general population. I ended up in a cell with six other black men. They were engaged in a great debate over the black market rate of a pack of cigarettes. The parasitic merchant was a huge black trustee weighing over 300 lbs. He stood in front of the cell with a smirk and berated these men like they were children.

I interrupted the guy in mid-sentence and asked, "How much do you want for those filthy cigarettes?"

Annoyed, he spat out, "For you, twelve dollars!"

After evil-eyeing one another, I said, "Okay, it sounds fair to me." But when he handed me the pack, I told him, "You're paid."

Fuming, he threatened to beat me down and take all my money when the gates were racked open. Then he left. There was complete silence among these dudes. They were so terrified that when I offered them cigarettes, not one of them would accept. Tearing up an old tee-shirt on the floor, I used the strips to wrap my knuckles because I planned to put on a vicious display. Dressed in an over-sized shirt and pants, I guess to them I looked incapable of challenging this mammoth of a bully.

When the gates racked, I stepped out to an empty tier. The guy was standing at the end of the landing. Nothing was between him and me but funky air but as I approached him, some deputies rushed out to intervene. I was handcuffed in front of the heckling giant. One deputy reached into my front shirt pocket and snatched out the pack of cigarettes. Someone behind me said, "Don't you know you can't just go around taking other people's property?" It was obvious that this big oaf posing in the corner had snitched on me. Later I'd come to know him as Belchum, a.k.a. "Too-Sweet," a Bounty Hunter of notorious ranking from the Nickerson Garden projects.

Sitting in a small room with a large computer, a deputy told the others that with my attitude I should have been in High Power. He punched in my name. "Whoa," he exclaimed, "wait a minute, this guy shouldn't be anywhere near the main line. This fellow here is who they call Tookie, the leader of the West Side Crips, and he's charged with four capital murders." There was a chorus of "wows." I was quickly escorted to the unit called High Power. At the time I wasn't aware that High Power was a security section of the County jail designed to house individuals in high-profile cases, detainees displaying defiant behaviour, celebrities who needed to be kept apart from the main jail population, and snitches and dirty cops who required protective custody.

High Power was also used by law enforcement agencies to plant an informer in a cell near a particular prisoner, hoping that the informer could extract a damaging statement or confession that could then be used in court. Informers are notorious for faking results, pretending a confession has been secured to use as leverage to reduce the criminal charges that they themselves may face.

I was confined to High Power for several reasons. I was fighting four capital offences, my reputation as a Crip leader had preceded me, and I was labelled as too powerful a negative force in my 'hood. My enormous size from pumping iron also frightened hell out of the authorities. At that time I sported a pair of twenty-two-inch arms and a chest over fifty-five inches across. High Power had a certain reputation: black men knew that inside the unit, Klansmen found it unnecessary to wear their white linen hoods to conceal their identities. The sheriff's uniform itself symbolized racism and ruthlessness. Not all white sheriffs in High Power hated black men, but those exceptions were few. The majority needed no excuse to exhibit sadistic aggression, especially with a handcuffed black detainee. That's when sheriffs were most dangerous. Moreover, there was always a brainwashed black or non-white bootlicking sheriff around who would ingratiate himself with his fellow officers by brutally pounding on a handcuffed Black or minority prisoner, smiling all the while. Even now, more than two decades later, my experience in Los Angeles County jail still affects me. Whenever I am handcuffed, I begin to sweat profusely.

The atmosphere within High Power was no doubt established to isolate, humiliate, dominate, violate and, when convenient, eradicate. My size and seemingly anti-establishment posture quickly drew the attention of sheriffs of a Gestapo mentality. For a voyeur's pleasure, in front of the tier of cells was an enclosed walkway with walls that featured tinted glass windows, each window positioned directly across from a 9' by 7' cell. The darkened windows permitted deputies to observe prisoners, ostensibly without their knowledge. But the sheriffs' silhouettes were quite visible; we could always tell when they were watching us. As far as they were concerned, just watching me was rarely enough. During my two-year stay in High Power, it became customary for the officers to try to provoke me by yelling racial epithets through the glass. At other times they would watch me in silence. But their observations lasted much longer than normal: they would often stare for two or three hours, no matter what I was doing.

To those racist voyeurs I no doubt seemed a gargantuan black beast whose presence induced inadequacy and apprehension. In an effort to camouflage their fears, they sought to emasculate me and to destroy my sanity. They went to the extreme. I would find objects in my food: staples, thumb tacks, paper clips, clumps of hair and broken glass. I leave it to your imagination what other items were mixed in my meals, items that I overlooked and ate. They were terrorists by any definition of the word.

My response was limited to verbal warfare or to throwing

objects. Sometimes I lowered myself to primitive levels of retaliation by spitting on the officers. I was not yet familiar with the jailhouse art of weapon making, so my tormentors were exempt from the true violence they had earned and probably would have respected. They had become manipulators of my reactions by knowing how and when to aggravate me, to draw out my rage. My attempts to protest fell on apathetic ears. It was my word against the supposedly respected, infallible sheriffs. Help was nowhere to be found. Treated worse than an animal, I was expected to tolerate the abuse as many captives before me had done. But even the most debased human being has limits.

One day, after being the only one harassed by two cell searches a couple of hours apart and being bombarded with racial slurs and taunts, I was directed over the loudspeaker to prepare for a dental appointment. One sheriff was sent down the tier to handcuff me while another sheriff waited outside the all-steel-bar door at the front of the tier. Once I was handcuffed, the sheriff found it amusing to use undue force by twisting my wrist, which resulted in an exchange of threats. I was serious; I can't speak for the other guy. Afterwards he waddled away towards the front of the tier. A minute later, when the electronic door opened, I exploded and broke the handcuffs in two, then dashed toward the burly sheriff, snatching only a piece of his shirt before he escaped through the open door, which immediately closed behind him.

I could smell the stench of his relief that he had evaded my grasp. It didn't take long for a mob of sheriffs to respond to the alarm bell. I steeled myself for the inevitable onslaught, but instead over the loudspeaker I was repeatedly ordered to return to the cell. Once I calmed down and was back in the locked cell, I was puzzled that the sheriffs did not rush in on me. This was common, their opportunity to brutalize or kill me and then justify it under the law. Around dinnertime an officer appeared to serve the meal. While handing me the food tray, he offered to take off the broken handcuffs, which I refused, believing it was a ruse. Once the officer exited, I went through the ritual inspection of my food, probing for foreign materials. I ate the meal while continuing my vigil against an attack against me, which never came – at least not visibly.

That meal had been spiked with a tranquillizer that knocked me out cold.

When I regained consciousness, I found myself in the jail's medical unit. I was in excruciating pain from the neck down, harnessed to a steel bunk in "five points." The name refers to five leather straps attached to a bunk. Each strap is positioned at one of the four corners, or points, of the bed, to secure both wrists and both ankles. The longer, thicker, wider fifth strap extending from the middle point of the bunk, is wrapped around the upper torso. Since I was neither apoplectic (a stroke victim) nor narcoleptic, it was apparent the food I had eaten was spiked with a powerful sedative. Later I found out why I was in such pain when I awoke.

They really didn't know what to make of me, especially given my ability to rip off the handcuffs from behind. To them I was a powerful madman who needed psychiatric sedation. From the start it was clear they were trying to make me loony. But why? Whenever the sheriffs wanted to move me from High Power to the medical unit to be placed in five points, I was drugged. My defiance constituted a wide variety of offences in their eyes. If I refused to respond to their insults, paced the cell too much, didn't eat, looked at them disdainfully, did not follow their ridiculous commands – such as stand on one leg in a corner with one hand on top of my head – I was labelled as defiant and then drugged.

My only defence was to avoid eating the jail food, so I tried to subsist on store-bought candy to avoid the druggings. I remember devouring so many candy bars, sometimes for weeks on end, that they caused serious acne problems and made me constantly nauseated. I didn't want to wake up in five points but I couldn't survive indefinitely on a diet of sweets. Eventually, I had to take my chances and eat what was placed before me. I discussed these matters with each of the three successive attorneys who represented me during the two-year period and they all promised to check into it, without result. Nothing was ever done to stop the periodic druggings.

On several occasions, despite being drugged, through force of will I remained semi-conscious enough to witness the sheriff's ritual. Once I appeared to have passed out, they would come into the cell and handcuff me, wrists behind my back, then drag me to the medical unit. Before I was put in five points, I was thrown to the floor, then stomped and kicked in the groin and other parts of my body (though strategically they avoided head injuries). The sedatives were a fortunate anesthetic that dulled the physical abuse. I felt nothing while this was going on. It was no longer a mystery why, when I regained consciousness, I felt pain. I now understood why my groin often hurt and why I sometimes urinated blood.

The violence being done to my mind was far worse. I'm convinced there was a deliberate attempt to render me certifiably insane. Sometimes the tranquillizer was administered intravenously by medical staff while I was in five points. It would suspend me in oblivion for days. Even when I woke, there was no way to banish the experience from my mind because of the lingering after-effects: drowsiness, poor coordination, slurred speech and mental confusion. At other times the mind-altering drugs would be handed to me by a nurse, disguised as part of my hypertension (high blood pressure) medication. She would stand and watch to make sure that I put all the medication in my mouth then swallowed it. Like any person who's suffering from a physical ailment and wants to get better, I felt obliged to take the medications. And since I wasn't able to recover my drug-blown senses in between these regular druggings, it was easy to dupe me into believing that all the medication I was given was improving my health.

Most frighteningly, no one was trying to revive me from my coma-like state. My mind had to be strong enough to override the power of the sedative and burst through the horror of total darkness. I do not remember dreaming during that period; not even a nightmare. Nothingness was all that embraced me during sleep. It was a living death. Waking up, I felt bewilderment, then despair. I would think, Where is my do-or-die passion? At those moments the crazed passion that once fortified my boldness, the stimulus familiar to every Crip who defied bullets and fought foes, was absent. I felt defeated, engulfed by desolation. If there was a psychological value in their intent to demoralize me, then they succeeded one-thousand-fold.

Prior to my abduction from South Central, I had spent purposeless years under the influence of drugs such as PCP and LSD. I will never forget the weird trips I experienced nor the aggression I initiated because of my personal drug use. Nevertheless, the psychopharmacology employed against me in High Power proved far more devastating. It was like being buried alive. I felt my brain was suffocating, as if I was falling through space deep into nothingness. This was nothing like getting high off of street drugs. The Medical Unit's medication was a mind killer.

In May of 1979 I was taken to a Torrance, California, court for a pretrial hearing. I sat in the courtroom fully shackled, with bright lights beaming down on me. Physically I appeared in perfect health but my mind was in a psychotropic uproar. The presiding judge noticed something was wrong; something about me was not what it should be. He asked if I understood what was going on, but my disjointed mind would not permit me to respond. Instead of words coming out, I giggled or laughed. At other times I was completely out of it. Sometimes I understood what the judge was asking and wanted to answer properly, yet I could not.

The judge turned to my stepfather Fred and asked, "Does he get in these moods frequently, Mr Holiwell, where he won't speak?" My stepfather responded without knowing I was unlawfully drugged. "Well, he's been on PCP, and ever since then … he just hasn't been alert. He goes into strange moods." Court transcripts indicate that the judge said, "All right. Well, I'm aware that at least he's alert and looking at me and he's not choosing to respond to my words. But I can't say he's understanding what I say." Common sense would have picked up that something was wrong then and there. Had I been non-black and exhibited such behaviour in a courtroom, I'd have been analysed by the best psychologist the county had to offer.

During the preliminary hearing in April 1979, the drugging affected me differently. I couldn't laugh, but instead groggily gazed at the inside perimeter of the courtroom and saw that it was overrun with armed bailiffs and undercover detectives. Scanning the room I noticed that most of the spectators were white, were unknown to me, and wore unmistakably angry expressions. They radiated the enthusiasm of a lynch mob as they waited for proceedings to start. In sharp contrast stood my mother and stepfather, their African features marked by worry. As in all my courtroom appearances, I was shackled around the waist, wrists, and ankles. I felt like a wild animal. I'm sure to all the strangers I looked like one too.

A gasp went up from the spectators when the judge read aloud the allegations: multiple robberies and the shotgun murders of four people, three Asians and one Caucasian. Vaguely I recall the judge's grimace, which caused me to reciprocate whenever we locked eyes, neither of us hiding our mutual disdain. I wanted desperately to holler insults at this white figure who sat high on a pedestal as if he was better than me. But the nexus between my mind and voice had been severed. I possessed no defensive or offensive capabilities. All I could do was sit there and listen. Looking back, I see that those moments of laughing, giggling, and scowling were nervousness to hide the stinging feeling of being defenceless with no recourse.

During my prime I had felt as powerful and invincible as a bull elephant in its primal rutting stage. But in the courtroom I felt as weak as a lamb, physically defenceless, in chains and with no control over what was being done to me. My reasons for feeling mentally defenceless were twofold: my mind was unstable due to the "therapeutic" druggings I was enduring; and, though I would never have admitted it, the courtroom's legal language and manoeuvring were beyond my comprehension. What limited skills I possessed were of no value in this setting; neither street savvy nor intimidation produced results within this world. I was reduced to a marionette, nodding my head if and when an attorney suggested it, though I comprehended nothing.

Instinctively I expected the worst from the judicial system, since it reflected society as a whole. I never allowed the self-indulgence of false hope. Facing America's killing apparatus meant no more to me than being given a speeding ticket. The truth was, I didn't care what happened to me or to anyone else. My indifference to life or death was exacerbated by my imprisonment, the tranquillizers and the officers' brutality. But long before this most recent arrest, I had retreated into the psychological death chamber of my blue rage. I had become a castaway within my own mind. I felt no hope, saw no dreams, expected no bright future.

Death was the only reality I anticipated. I was convinced that love was unattainable and incapable of penetrating my stone-encased heart. I possessed the death-look of the wretched. I devalued life since I saw no worth in my own. No matter how many people visited me while I was in the County jail, I still felt alone and abandoned. My smile served as a theatrical means to influence a given circumstance, or as a tight, cold gesture of formality. Not even my beloved mother could reach me on my mental island of drugged alienation, an island where I was neither safe nor secure.

Under these psychotropic assaults I probably lent credence to the racist notion that I was subhuman. I believed I was supposed to accept the tribulations inflicted on me while in captivity. So I gritted my teeth and absorbed the injustices just as many of my slave ancestors had accepted their plight. There were fleeting moments when I railed against the sheriffs' madness, but most of the time I was either too drugged to resist or too acclimated to my outcast status to know that I should challenge what was unjust. Even I, a person who lived as foul as could be, deserved justice. Yet I experienced only a great separation between the system of law and the ethics of justice. Since life for me had always been callous, what was the difference now? If the system wanted to exterminate me, I thought, so what, feel free to do so. Perhaps I'd fare better in death than in life.

Part Two

Black Redemption

———————

TWENTY-SEVEN

The Missing Years

In my life, truth, justice and liberty were absent.

The druggings inflicted on me during my incarceration in High Power were compliments of the District Attorney's acquisition of a court order to have me placed in the medical unit. The order would also permit the monitoring of all my visits and telephone calls to obtain incriminating statements. Perhaps the D.A. thought I was able to use the phone and visit while comatose. This was the type of irrational thinking and duplicity, in concert with the questionable justice system, that I was up against.

This is not a conspiracy theory, phobic anxiety or delusion. America will not allow justice to embrace the likes of me. I was expected to acquiesce, to accept this one-sided version of justice. I wasn't able to perceive that "anything less than justice is an absolute injustice." The pathetic reality was that although I had no concept of justice, I knew the vulgar variations of *injustice* intimately. This book allows me to voice a legitimate grievance that most Americans cannot understand or even begin to approach.

My stint in High Power from 1979 to 1981 flew by with the speed of light. I sleepwalked numbly through most of it. I can recall no specific details about the trial proceedings, nor do I remember engaging in strategic dialogues with any of my several briefly glimpsed attorneys (two different public defenders and two different private lawyers). Lynn hired the first of my private attorneys, Harry Weiss, who handled the preliminary phase and then vanished. After that my mother and stepfather tried to hire two black attorneys, Carl Jones and Charles Lloyd, who both declined on the basis that the case was too hot. Then they hired Joe Ingber, an attorney I had heard about and foolishly suggested. This ineffective attorney would knowingly deliver spurious testimony at the federal deposition that assisted the Attorney General against me.

The witnesses against me were mostly snitches out to avoid prosecution for their own crimes by sacrificing me. James and Esther Garrett, Alfred "Blackie" Coward, Samuel "Capone" Coleman and George Oglesby all struck deals for lesser charges or immunity. Another fellow, Tony "Li'l Bamm" Simms, was thrown into the mix after being manipulated by his buddy Alfred Coward to lie about me. It backfired on Simms, as law books have since substantiated. Literally selling their souls, none of these career criminals had any compunction about ruining my life to save their own scrawny necks.

In the midst of this madness, Michelle came to visit me with my stepbrother Wayne. He was arrested for possessing a loaded weapon in the visiting room. Detectives turned the incident into a conspiracy, depicting me having Wayne attempt to break me out of jail. To compound matters I was accused of another escape plot, fabricated by the upper jailhouse snitch, Oglesby, in tandem with sheriffs and D.A. This quixotic scheme involved me and other Crips – of course – high-powered weaponry and, of all things, dynamite. The mention of dynamite and black folks in the same breath should have automatically been dismissed as highly unlikely. How many blacks in America have access to dynamite, and what company would sell explosives to a black man or woman without notifying the cops?

I was unable to exercise to relieve all of the pent-up tension, to get the blood circulating throughout my body and brain. Most people around who knew me expressed concern. Doc Holiday, a reputed Black Guerrilla Family leader, was housed in the cell next to mine. Often he would tell me about his son, also a Crip. Doc and I initiated a push-up routine five or six times a week, but I couldn't maintain it because I was always too tired, drowsy or asleep. Doc would holler over and ask, "Say, Took, how come you don't work out anymore? Are those people drugging you?" I'm sure I mumbled something incoherent. When I was on other rows, individuals I knew such as McFarlane and Dale Evans were puzzled by my condition and assumed I was still whacked out on PCP. When I spoke, no one could decipher my words, not even me.

Throughout the two years of being disoriented I completely forgot that Raymond Washington was murdered in August of 1979, five months after my incarceration. I believe it was Criplette Jackie who visited me and broke the unbelievable news. Her version of what had taken place was sketchy, and I can't remember too much about what we talked about. As with Buddha, I couldn't picture Raymond dead. How could that have possibly happened?

Raymond's death remains a mystery, but when the Crips became a media magnet, it seemed like everybody was Raymond's closest homeboy, his comrade, his loved one, his buddying co-founder of the Crips. Preposterous! How many of those same individuals were turning over every rock in society to locate his assassin? How many are in pursuit today, or how many truly care? It reminds me of young Odie's funeral, when individuals tossed all kinds of memorabilia into his casket. Had he been alive, he would have been hard-pressed to borrow change for a telephone call from most of them.

Raymond and I were brought together for a purpose beyond our limited understanding, and somewhere along the way we veered off the righteous course. It was a youthful mistake that chased us into adulthood, where we left a legacy of pain and tears among grieving black mothers and other loved ones. Fools of heart, we had no legitimate dream or attainable vision, only a cruel future, one capable only of poisoning our souls. I never knew Raymond's aspirations, but in our small world, ambitions were rare, and mostly fantasy.

Raymond was a black man with hidden potential overlooked by the old guard black leadership, who could have used his street savvy, organizational dexterity, and his popularity. He and I co-founded the Crips, a legacy of blood, rage, and death; but if his true worth and his potential contribution to the political struggle had been tapped into, his life may have been different. We'll never know. May Raymond, Buddha, and the countless others who senselessly lost their lives to violence rest in peace.

Several months before my court trial, I had been uprooted and housed alone, incommunicado, on G-Row in High Power. This was a place designed for disciplinary actions, and though I had violated no rules, I would reside on G-Row until the jury rendered its decision. I knew the verdict beforehand. I knew the moment I was abducted from society on these trumped-up charges. I knew the moment I looked in the mirror and saw a black face staring back at me. Yes, I knew.

The all-white jury marched single file into the courtroom like a firing squad and blasted me into cinders. They found me guilty of all charges. On April 15, 1981, I stood before the Torrance court judge bound in the usual judicial chains and cuffs as the penalty was read aloud: death. The judge sentenced me to die in San Quentin's death chamber.

Once again I was dealt a dead man's hand in life and was shuttled back to the County jail to await transfer to San Quentin prison. I sat on a bunk in the last cell on the tier by myself, punch-drunk from psychotropic drugs that were supposed to have murdered my mind but failed. Though it has been said I received numerous visits, only a handful come to mind. Besides my mother appearing to spread solace and some sense of stability to that chaotic setting, others mostly came bearing tidings of deceit or gloom. Once when Michelle came, she told me that she ran into Jimel in the visiting room claiming to be waiting to visit me. It was news to me. During my entire captivity, not once did he visit. Michelle went on to say that Jimel had asked, "Why did you pick Tookie over me when I met you first? You turned me down." He answered his own question. I wasn't shocked. There were countless men who salivated over Michelle but failed to capture her interest before or after I came into the picture. I recall Jimel asking his own woman, "Who looks the best, Tookie or me?" All she did was laugh nervously but refuse to answer. My homeboy Jackie stood there shaking his head in disbelief.

I shrugged it off and said, "Well, I guess Godfather and others' opinions about him were right."

That's when she lowered the boom, "Ah, by the way baby, I've found somebody else because you're not out here for me."

Well, she was right: I wasn't out there in society for her. There was a pang of regret for losing her, but I sucked it in and blew it out, knowing I had to move on. Though I never fashioned myself as a lothario, I had made myself available to other females to soften the impact of a "Dear John" drama. During the same time I was hooked up with Michelle, I was fornicating with Wynetta and other black beauties. It was a surprise when Wynetta and Jackie hooked up; although it pissed me off at first. At least he had the decency to break the news to me face-to-face.

I'll never recapture the void of those missing years. Although through most of my life I was a willing sinner of the highest magnitude, in my voice to God's ear I prayed earnestly for the strength to survive my social drug use and the involuntary druggings. I vowed never again to get intoxicated. My decision to repudiate drugs was the beginning of my redemption, something that would bear fruit, for children, nearly a decade later.

TWENTY-EIGHT

Inside the Beast

Early in the morning I was again shackled around the waist, wrists and ankles and hustled to a black and white County bus. En route to the infamous San Quentin prison, I made a point of sitting in the back of the bus to guard against enemy attacks. No doubt defending myself would've been next to impossible; I was the only person fully shackled while the other thirty or more men wore regular handcuffs with hands in front. I felt nervous, angry, and hyped. Though my mind swirled there was nothing wrong with my vision; I was hawking everybody's movements. The majority of the people on the bus were blacks and Mexicans, with a few Caucasians and several flamboyant homosexuals.

There was a lot of focus on the female impersonators who giggled and laughed like teenage schoolgirls. The conversations drifted from criminal cases, drugs, women, weapons, jokes, and gory prison tales to talk about Folsom, Soledad, and San Quentin. Each story was bloodier and more violent than the last. As I sat listening I remembered my stepfather Fred warning me to be careful: "Prison is no joke. Make sure when you use the toilet, always take your underwear and pants completely off. Better to fight with no pants and drawers than to be hindered with them around your ankles." It made sense, so I adopted this habit. I vowed to beat down anyone challenging me, even though I didn't know the first thing about prison life except through word of mouth. I actually believed convicts fought toe-to-toe, gladiator-style, with shanks and knives, a naïve notion capable of getting me killed. Hell, there were more knifing drive-bys in prison than on the streets. I listened to the stories and braced myself.

It was obvious the bus was nearing San Quentin, because the boisterous crowd began to talk less and less. I guess the full impact of having to face the beast was enough to temper their chitchat. The bus pulled inside a medieval-looking stone fortress. The ambience was eerie and gloomy. From Receiving and Release, I was marched in shackles and leg irons to the hospital for a physical examination. I sat in a caged-off area alone until the nurses were ready for me. After an hour, guards wearing oxygen masks started filing in, dragging prisoners between them. Each guy looked drenched with sweat or water and appeared half-dead. When they passed by me there was an unfamiliar foul scent that first irritated my nose, then caused both my eyes to sting and water. I learned later there was a riot in "the Hole" (the Adjustment Center, abbreviated as AC), and the guards used tear gas. The guards continued to drag in convict after convict. Each one smelled as though they had been swimming in gas.

This was my first day in San Quentin, christened with the noxious scent of tear gas. Once the examination was complete, I was escorted to North Seg, where I'd be housed on death row. To reach the top floor we had to use an elevator. The lighting upstairs was so dim it made the place look haunted. There was the usual humiliation of being strip-searched by strangers, then I was handcuffed and escorted to a cell. Death row had two sides, north and south, with thirty-four cells each. I was to be housed on the north side in Cell 32, way in the back. I was the forty-fifth person on death row. It may have been my first time in prison but it definitely wasn't my first confrontation with death. There wasn't too much of a psychological adjustment for me to make. Any setting where treachery and violence dominate was nothing new to me – all I had to do was carve out a niche.

Being on death row was the proverbial end of the line. Unlike prisons in general where inmates fight for freedom, civil liberties, and the dignity to be treated like a man, here we fight with limited time, opposing the death chamber to stay alive. I wasn't sentenced to death row to be rehabilitated. Whether it was my preference or not, I had to engage in battle with the court of appeals to prove my innocence. Though nobody believed me, I proclaimed my innocence from the beginning, and I'll never stop doing so. But many years would slip by as I languished in the utter darkness of apathy and dys-education. To sit in a death row cell was not a moment to reflect on my life; it was more an insult to my fervour to survive, another roadblock. The combination of ignorance and the hazy lingering effects of the druggings prevented me from attacking the law books. Instead I readily gravitated to the perils of disorder and the posture of a hardened convict, which required only minor adjusting on my part.

In the cell next to me was a native Indian from the Mono tribe called Chief. A young Crip on death row, Little L, had told Chief about me. He reached out with some stationery and personal care items. This Indian was down for anything. The first time I saw him, he was being escorted on his tiptoes, with officers pulling his handcuffed wrists up high. As they passed by, Chief's long black hair draped all over his face, and he smiled like a madman. I figured it was only a matter of time before I ended up in the same uncomfortable position. Though I didn't know what to expect, I was hyped up. Bring on the madness!

The programme for the condemned was simple enough. There was a two-grade system of status. Grade-A meant that one was afforded privileges – phone calls, contact visits, and a few other amenities. Grade-B offered no privileges and less yard time to exercise. On the first day I received grade-A, I got into a brief dispute with a Mexican guy over the phone time. Unfortunately for me, the death row counsellor happened to be walking on the gunrail side and witnessed it. The counsellor seemed to take it personally and after expressing displeasure at my refusal to stop beating the guy, he vowed to keep me on B grade until he retired or was transferred.

He proved to be a man of his word. The Hole is a place for men involved in revolutionary movements, gangs, escape attempts, protective custody, or other circumstances. It is also a place where some men have been killed, or had entered with a backbone but left with it bent or broken. Naturally there were defiant exceptions. Exactly ten years earlier, a charismatic black man, George Jackson, had a vision to elevate his spirit. His consciousness of self and others defied the status quo. He was murdered by a prison sniper's bullet but his spirit was emancipated. He had often stated he'd never leave prison alive.

When I stepped into this penal colony, I was faced with that grim possibility of never leaving alive. The notion of liberation was poised between doubt, apathy, and the slender and naïve possibility of "maybe." I took a deep breath then plunged into this segregated unit of isolation. The Hole is a detached building with three tiers on two sides, and back then one side of the third tier was for the condemned. My first day on the yard I met Black from the Long Beach Crips, Big Bub, his brother GeeGee from the Jordon Down Crips, Big Chief, Hootie, and an Asian guy, Choosoo. We were a cast of characters that probably would not have met under any other circumstances, but inside prison, on death row, we shared a common denominator.

After a scan of the three yards, I discovered that there were no weights! Choosoo introduced me to the 602 inmate appeal form and I submitted an appeal for weights. To my surprise, one month later weights were placed on the condemned yard, then later on the other yards. I was ready to regain the size and the weight I had lost in the county jail. At twenty-seven I was still brawny enough to bench 370 lbs for ten repetitions and in a short period of driving iron with Big Bub and Chief, I was back on double swoll. Though overall I was bigger than Bub, he was no joke, weighting 240 lbs with over twenty-inch arms. Proud of his shiny bald head, Bub was a dedicated Crip who was consistently in trouble. But then again that's what all Crips were – sheer trouble.

While I was in the Hole, so many individuals were coming in and out it was like a train station. I had a chance to briefly kick it with homeboy named Hoover Joe; he was a muscular Crip with a curly handlebar moustache that reminded me of a book cover portrait of W.E.B. Dubois. Huddled on opposite sides of the fenced yards, we briefly discussed progressive possibilities. The conversations were interesting though our ideological approach differed, mine being apolitical and on the ganghood level: take no prisoners! Seek, seize, suppress. The conversations would have been even more interesting had Hoover Joe not been transferred. There were plenty of other Crips passing through AC like Bad Habit Rabbit, a former Crip from the Imperial Court projects. Although he mentioned many Crip episodes that occurred in the projects, for the life of me I couldn't remember him. Every time I saw Rabbit we went through a ritual of trying to get me to remember him. No doubt the County jail druggings had a lot to do with my memory loss, but I regret that Rabbit and the many other Crips slipped through my mental net into oblivion.

Every now and then, triumphant moments occurred on death row. Two individuals, Choosoo and Hootie, got a full reversal of their cases and went home. Both were fortunate to have had the aid of their family, efficient attorneys, and their ethnic community to back them up. I would have been hard-pressed to expect the black community to embrace the likes of me. I symbolized all that had gone bad, and like a multitude of other imprisoned blacks, I was written off as worthless. The way I behaved back then, I can't blame them.

My only concern dwelt on what I was intimately familiar with: crippin'. I found comfort in idiocy that required no effort or intellectual rigour. To Crip or not to Crip was not the question, it was the answer. To me life after crippin' could only mean one thing: I was dead.

Most of my time in the hole was spent driving iron,

reminiscing, and watching the hypnotic tube (TV). Over the airwaves, whether interested or not, I got an earful of uncut versions of revolutionary theories, religious doctrines, Communist dogmas, and Afrocentric philosophy. Though I could read, people were sending me literary material(s) beyond my comprehension. It was akin to feeding a newborn baby solid foods. The attempt by some of them to wake me up was doomed to fail. Intellectually I was bankrupt, and as quickly as they passed books down to me, I sent them back.

No dogma was powerful enough to permeate my thick cranium nor threaten my allegiance to Cripdom. I knew many hardcore Crips who played their role to the hilt, but I took it beyond the limit. Crip was my religion. I was its co-creator and star-crossed prophet, and I critiqued all other Crips by my own standards. With a weary eye I scrutinized individuals professing to be a Crip because I knew some were frauds.

Life would never be as I remembered it, nor would the revered Crip connection. Despite my lack of discipline and my underfed intellect, I recognized the institution's racial favouritism that excluded all blacks except those who were informants on other blacks. The Hole was a place of communal dysfunction, whose quick and violent dramas were nothing like the gladiator tales told to me by Big Rock when I was a child. This was survival of the fittest, and I was familiar with the requirements of this game.

At that time there were no mesh fences on the outer cell bars to stop a prison-made blow-dart gun, a fashioned spear, a match bomb, a zip-gun, or a simple but deadly dousing of scalding liquid consisting of syrup, battery acid, or whatever else was available. Usually when an incident occurred on the tier, I found myself blamed. In one instance a death row snitch was being escorted down the tier by a female guard when a boiling hot concoction was thrown from one of the cells. The solution burned the inmate and some of it landed on the guard, resulting in severe burns and a sick leave. A guard stated on record, "I saw Williams' arm stretched outside the cell bars, then he threw some kind of liquid on the inmate." The accusation was false, absurd and impossible, considering that my arms were too large to squeeze through the narrow bars. I filed a 602 appeal form but, although innocent, I lost.

Strange things happened behind these lurid walls. Once I smelled smoke while writing a letter. Peering through the slits of the cell bars, I saw greyish-white smoke belching from the cell of an inmate who was out to court. The smoke began to hug the ceiling, then crept down the tier towards the front where I was housed. Within minutes the entire tier was engulfed in smoke – and all the windows that were usually opened were shut. Along with Bub, Black, and GeeGee, I hollered out for the guard to open the windows, but for fifteen minutes it was in vain. By the time the guards arrived the entire tier had turned greyish black with thick soot floating in the air covering the walls and everything else in the cell.

The smoke had me blowing my nose and coughing up jet-black mucus. I dropped to my knees with my head inside the toilet and threw up. Emanating with each flush was a welcoming surge of air for my smoke-filled lungs. It was ironic: the breeze carrying the oxygen of life to my lungs was the same inimical gust of cold air beneath me whenever I used the toilet.

The guards finally opened all the windows and placed a giant fan on the tier to blow out the smoke. Then they systematically used an oxygen tank with a mask held up against the square window and bars for whoever needed it. As I stood there inhaling fresh oxygen, I couldn't help wondering if this experience of asphyxiation was a vile precursor to being gassed in the chamber. That evening I actually thought all of us were going to die.

Despite these melancholy moments in the Hole, I was able to hone my knowledge of prison interactions. I became a student of sociology and psychology, owing to my keen observation of others. People can be creatures of habit, and it was necessary for me to be aware of such behaviour. The parasitical environment was contagious and I was infected.

But occasionally conflict arose between crippin' and the intrusive question, "Where do I go from here?" The question was odd. I possessed no conscience, so why would I entertain such a thought? In retrospect it was a moment of scepticism that challenged the Crip reality I held to more than anything. But I was diametrically opposed to self-change or to anything I felt would diminish my Crip image.

I was always willing to aid a Crip in distress – that was a given. But for some reason other than impulsive stupidity I opted to assist another black man who was under siege by guards. I didn't know this guy Coleman, had never met him, but it offended me to see one of the guards outside his cell preparing to shoot him with Big Bertha, a sawed-off shotgun that fires a thick plastic wad, and very painfully. They used it and prepared to rush in to seize Coleman.

"Why don't you cowards come down here and try to shoot me with that gun?" I hollered.

A sergeant shot back, "Who's that talking with the big mouth?"

"Stanley Williams, C29300, I'm in cell fifty-eight."

Within seconds a crowd of guards stood in front of the cell gawking at me. As the sergeant walked up, I heard him say, "Let me see who this big mouth is?" I stood there with my shirt off and prepared for an attack. The sergeant peered in at me.

"Well, well, well, look who we have here, it's Tookie. What's the problem?"

"If you plan to shoot that black man down there, then prepare to shoot me right now."

While the sergeant and I eyed one another, a guard in the crowd said, "Sarge, let's shoot him, too."

Looking at me, the sergeant told the guard, "Shut up, you don't know what's going on here." He then said, "All right, Tookie, we don't want a riot, but if we have to come back to deal with Coleman, and you interfere, then you're going down too."

"Fair enough."

The next day while I was on the yard, Mahfahali hollered

out from the Black Guerrilla Family yard, "Brother Tookie, that was a courageous gesture to stand up for that brother. Black man, you should be proud." Mahfahali was a thin, six-foot-three spiritual revolutionary notorious for stabbing guards.

I smiled and said, "Mahfahali, it's nothing but a Crip thing."

He smiled and shook his head, knowing that all of the revolutionary chats we engaged in had had no effect on me. Every conversation we had was unilateral. He talked while I watched TV. Some time later, the counsellor who had threatened to keep me on grade-B was transferred to another prison. With him out of the way, the classification committee restored my grade-A status, and I was sent back to North Seg. Arriving there was like starting all over again as far as the weights were concerned. There were just two lightweight barbells and one set of forty pound dumbbells. Once again I filed a 602 appeal form and a stockpile of heavy barbells, dumbbells, and weight benches were brought up to death row. Within months I was tying dumbbells on a 370-lb bar, more that 560 lbs total, for doing reps.

Occasionally guards would show up on the opposite side of the gun-rail fence and watch in amazement as I lifted the monstrous weight with relative ease. A few of them tried unsuccessfully to seek approval for me to enter the San Quentin weight-lifting contest. They had no doubt I'd win. Though I was driving iron on a regular basis, I was still bored. Curious, I took up drawing, which became a pleasant pastime. I began by drawing animals and birds, then people. With no assistance I developed a style enabling me to do pencil portraits of my mother, Martin L. King, Sojourner Truth, Malcolm X, Coretta Scott King, Frederick Douglass, Dorothy Height and others. Drawing acted like music on, calming the beast within. Hours flew by as I lost myself in the godlike power of creating life on paper. It amazed me that a person like me could pick up drawing and succeed. I relished the personal dexterity, like lifting weights.

Another skill I discovered by serendipity was memorizing

large numbers of words and their definitions. It frustrated me to be unable to comprehend legal terms and other words I came across while reading newspapers, magazines, and books. I was tired of skipping over certain words, or having to stop and jot down a word to look up later on. In time I started browsing through the dictionary and became fascinated with words, definitions, and foreign phrases.

In a short period I developed a style of mnemonics for memorizing long lists of words on one side of a sheet of paper, then folding it with the definitions on the opposite side. The more words I retained, the better I was able to understand what I perused. Months earlier I had been given an old pocket-sized dictionary with most of the pages scotch-taped together or missing. I tried to hustle the prison chaplain out of a dictionary, but he was more than willing to find one for me. A few weeks later he surprised me with a large Webster's Collegiate Dictionary. After I expressed my gratitude, the chaplain said, "I know you'll put that book to good use – but use the Lord's book, too." Shortly afterwards I asked a prison Imam for a thesaurus, which he provided. I tried Malcolm X's alphabetical technique for remembering words, which I found to be tedious. Instead I randomly selected words from the dictionary, thesaurus, and other books. In spite of my former schoolteachers' assertion that I was uneducable, my intent was to memorize the entire dictionary.

This was the early Eighties. The Crip population was increasing, becoming a force to be reckoned with throughout the prison departments. Whenever I was escorted to the dentist or to the clinic, I'd pass a large crowd of Crips hanging out on the mainline. It felt good being recognized by other Crips, whether they personally knew me or not. In spite of being handcuffed behind my back, I exhibited a posture of dignity and Crip defiance. I was still only barely bursting through a violent drug haze but remained a street folk hero of the wrong path.

San Quentin was hundreds of miles from where I used to stroll like a peacock, wild and unchecked, buoyed up by the illusion of freedom. Years earlier there had been a Watts Stax concert at the Los Angeles Coliseum. Hundreds of Crips attended from west and east, and some from Compton, prancing around, numerically strong, cocky and seemingly invincible. I felt the illusion of being free that day, however briefly. Big Country from the Brinks Gang was stomped and beaten down the escalator for giving East Side Crip Syles a black eye. When some Crips jacked people for their drugs and money, someone hollered over the microphone, "Will the Crips please come down and clear the field of these troublemakers?" I looked at Raymond, Bimbo and Caesar and we burst into laughter. It was our homeboys down there creating the madness. Times such as that made me feel invincible, free, in control of my destiny. It was a foolhardy delusion.

Here I was now, at San Quentin, freedom-less, confined to death row, wondering if I looked as strange to some of these characters as they did to me. There was a Caucasian guy who thought he was a vampire and avoided bright lights by wearing a blanket over his head. He was rumoured to eat raw meat and drink blood, which was highly unlikely unless he was self-anthropophagic – a cannibal. The would-be vampire was later found dead in his cell, supposedly by his own hands. Suicide never struck me as an option even during the worst of times. I never knew anyone personally who attempted or committed suicide.

While in North Seg, I became acquainted with a few blacks – Blue, Peanut, Ed, Ex-lax, Bedbug, Gangster, Milton, J.P., Snow, Zoom, Little L, Maddog, P.R. and Grandpa. Having given Maddog and Gangster their a.k.a.s, I also gave Grandpa his moniker. He was an elderly black man, six-foot-two, muscular and agile enough to play basketball with any of us. Sometimes after driving iron, I'd kick back in a small group and listen while they engaged in a session of "bullology" (braggadocio about women, sex, money, drugs and war). Being a private person and cautious, my conversation was limited. It was amusing to hear Grandpa launch into a political diatribe about death row being a racist slaughterhouse for society's blacks and other poverty-stricken people. He'd go on and on about governmental collusions, assassinations, tainted history, Cointelpro (the Counter-intelligence Program, an FBI operation to neutralize political dissidents, particularly the Black Panthers) and the black struggle. There was rarely anything comforting in what Grandpa said, nor was there meant to be. Most of the conversations I heard went in one ear and out the other. My interests lay in being vigilant and restricting my trust to a very few cohorts.

I started experiencing bouts of claustrophobia at least once or twice a week – a relapse, I feared, into the abyss of psychotropic insanity. I felt I was losing my mind when the walls appeared to be closing in on me. Panic-stricken and drenched with sweat, I'd grab hold of the bars with a vice-like grip and try to rip them apart to free myself. Regardless of my strength, the bars refused to budge.

I fought a silent battle to maintain my sanity. I found solace in driving iron, drawing portraits, reminiscing, and doing whatever gobbled up the hours. Big Bub and GeeGee had gotten their grade A, and were placed on the tier side with me. To my dismay, Bub had lost a lot of weight after having a major operation. The doctor had to cut into his chest cavity to remove a malignant cancer, leaving a long scar. Bub was a shell of himself but managed to keep his predatory instinct intact. Though he could barely walk and limped with a cane, he instilled fear in others and was active in chaos.

Rumours began to circulate that there was Crip intimidation and petty jacking in North Seg. Bub and his brother GeeGee were the first to become suspects: they were charged with strong-arming a guy for his tape player and tapes. Both were sent back to the Hole.

While I sat in my cell, drawing and minding my own business, Ed showed up with his face and lips turned ashy grey as if he had seen a ghost. Blood streaked on his tee-shirt.

"Cuz, those racist Aryan devils cut me with a razor," he nervously said.

Gangster looked stunned. When the bars were racked open and I stepped out, Ed pointed at the culprits standing bunched together at the end of the tier.

"I can whip all of them, and I don't want any help," I bragged.

Standing off to the side was a crowd of blacks, mostly Ed's homeboys. Gangster asked Ed, "Why don't they help?"

"Those niggers were too scared to move," he said.

I Crip-strolled down the tier toward the large group of whites. I bumped into one who was inebriated, said to be their leader.

"Watch where you're going, nigger," the guy slurred.

When I turned around he threw a jab that I avoided, then countered. He fell unconscious on the floor. I stooped down and used my fist as a hammer to bash his face in. A guard behind the fence pointed a gun at my head. With each punch I growled viciously and asked, "Is he out?"

The guard hollered, "Yes, Tookie, he's out, please stop, I don't want to shoot you."

Though I intended to continue, another guard from the back of the tier started shooting. That caught my attention.

Back in the cell I found a fractured bone protruding upward beneath the skin on my swollen hand. The doctor later put a cast on my hand and forearm – which I soon took off. The next day in the counsellor's office there was no mention of taking me to the Hole. All he wanted to know was whether I was willing to quash the conflict. I assumed the counsellor expected the incident to escalate into a bloody racial war. I responded with an imitative accent, "No problemo." After the unit lock-down, the white guy openly apologized and then privately thanked me because I could have killed him in the name of self-defence. In prison it's known as a "freebie killing" – justifiable homicide.

The conflict was resolved. For a while the unit operated as smoothly as a prison setting could. But of course we black folks tend to argue and fight amongst ourselves. As I recall, Grandpa and this fellow Troy "TJ" Jones started arguing over the weights, and TJ called Grandpa a homosexual. A fight broke out, and TJ tried to flee but got trapped between the weight benches. His blood splattered on the wall and floor. It was reported that a knife was involved so both of them were transferred to the Hole. Though in his late forties Grandpa handled himself quite well. Maybe all the years he had spent in California prisons had something to do with it. The penal system has a knack for eliciting the beast in man.

TWENTY-NINE

Things Happen

In 1985 I was back in the Los Angeles County Jail for an evidentiary hearing relevant to my automatic appeal. It wasn't until I was again sitting in the jail cell on G-row that memories of the medical unit's druggings and other dastardly plots resurfaced. I was uncomfortable being back in a predicament beyond my control. At the Torrance court where I was held in a glass booth, the guards put the snitch Oglesby in an adjacent booth. Even though I never really knew what Oglesby looked like, I remembered his name from reading my trial transcripts, plus I overheard a guard saying, "George Oglesby is here for the Williams case." Hearing that name, fury grew within me. I envisioned myself picking up the non-functioning water fountain next to me and hurling it through the big glass window at him. Oglesby must have sensed something, because when I stood up, he immediately started banging on the glass and hollering for the guards to take him out of the booth. That court date was the last time I saw Oglesby.

I was in the County jail for two weeks and it seemed like several months. Periodically sheriffs would stroll by and gawp at me. The more inquisitive ones stopped and asked, "Are you big Tookie from death row?" All I could do was ignore them and turn my head. I despised being viewed as a monkey in a menagerie, held captive for the amusement of others, and was more than satisfied when the court hearing was over and I left the jail. Awaiting me back at San Quentin, however, were allegations of extortion, intimidation, and conspiring to commit violence. Of course it was easy for staff to find some fool who was willing to sell his soul for peanuts. They found an ideal stool pigeon in TJ, the same black inmate Grandpa had properly touched up.

As a result of TJ's fears and untruths, I was soon transferred to C-section, where the larger overflow of death row's condemned men were housed. Once I settled in, the first person to reach out to me with a care package was Evil, a spearhead of the Raymond Avenue Crips. When I was finally cleared for the grade-A yard, I spent time driving iron with Evil while digesting his analysis of the prison politics in C-section. Firsthand knowledge of your surroundings can prevent your being triple-crossed, hurt, or killed.

From the moment Evil and I introduced ourselves, we clicked like biological siblings. He reminded me of my stepbrother Wayne. At five-foot-six, dark-complected, with long tresses, his short stature belied his body strength. We shared a common interest in vocabulary development, so we exchanged lists, while quizzing each other on enunciation, orthography, semantics, and correct use of each word in a sentence. Evil introduced me to black history with a book entitled *Destruction of Black Civilization* by Chancellor Williams. The study of black history, law, psychology, math, religion, Swahili, spirituality, and other subjects became a staple part of our daily discipline in the scheme of survival.

I had been in C-section for about three weeks when a sergeant was murdered, prompting an immediate lockdown. For more than a month everybody was subject to disruptive cell searches and occasional harassment by antagonistic guards. Rumour had it that there were so many inmates willing to snitch about the sergeant's murder that staff started to turn snitches away. It's pathetic how some grown men deem themselves to be men, yet break down like little boys and inform on others. The prison mystique was being stripped naked before my eyes.

During the lockdown there was still a lot of interaction. Every morning large segments in the unit exercised as one physical machine that resonated loudly in numerical cadence. Being an iron driver, I disliked the burpee exercises, military-style calisthenics with an innovative prison twist consisting of push-ups and kick-ins. But the atmosphere was so energetic that I got caught up in the exercises.

Crips were all over the place. Above me on the third and fourth tiers were Treach from R.A.C, Bub, and other Crips on grade-B. Being on that status I knew they were limited on food, so when I received my food package I sent them a pillowcase swollen with food. No guard's assistance was necessary because we used a line to pass the pillowcase up to where they were housed. I'd learn later that they were as free-hearted as I was.

Once the investigations had subsided and the suspects been rounded, San Quentin was off lockdown. In C-section were two yards, one for death row and the other one for the AD Seg prisoners, mostly parolees and others doing hard time. On occasion I was able to "Crip-reminisce" through the fence with young Hawkeye, Clarence Hoover, Spud, Tomcat, Rebo, Woodrat, Turtle, and others from Los Angeles. Seeing so many Crip homeboys brought back memories. It was reassuring to know that if it came down to an all-out war against any enemies, the strength and numbers were there. Then again, misery loves company, and I had plenty of it. It was pathetic how many of us Crips were languishing behind bars with no prospects.

Back in those days, when death row prisoners were escorted to the yard, the shower, or anywhere inside the unit, they were not handcuffed. One day while heading toward the shower I stopped off to talk with my homeboy Ghetto. I caught sight of TJ strolling down the tier, with a guard several yards behind him. If a camera had been available the lens would have captured the fury in my stare. The first thing Ghetto said was, "Cuz, it might be a setup." I thought the same thing, seeing TJ walking towards me with one hand thrust inside his prison coat pocket. There were no gunmen in sight, and the escort had disappeared. Whether TJ's intent was harmless or not, I beat him to the punch. He fell like a sack of potatoes and ended up with half his body dangling over the tier between the bottom trail. I tried to get at him until I found myself staring into a rifle barrel the size of a grapefruit.

"Stop hitting him, Tookie, or I'll shoot," yelled the black guard.

As crazy as the guard looked, I knew he would shoot, so I slowly raised up, then backed away. Several other guards approached, I was handcuffed, and then escorted to D-section, another disciplinary lock-up unit for grade-B condemned and others.

In D-section I was housed next door to Grandpa. He was there for having another run-in with TJ weeks before. On a line, he sent over the violation report that quoted TJ stating I was the Godfather of the Crips and Grandpa was a member. He went on to say that we wanted him to pay rent and when he refused, I ordered Grandpa to move on him. The accusations were indicative of the snitches and their masters who hounded me.

My life, though insignificant as it is to the world, continued to be plagued by plots linked to my past. I wasn't in D-section a week when I received a document (dated May 24, 1985) accusing me of a possible escape attempt. The prison handlers and their snitches had concocted yet another implausible story in which I plotted an escape with a man who had been dead for years. But I was Tookie – a man who could use a dead man and still be successful. Later these bogus charges were dropped.

Other bizarre things occurred. This black guy, Sticks, presented himself as an affable fellow, eager to engage in political conversations. On occasions he'd ask for a book, and I'd send him one to read. Sticks often talked about being proud to be a vegetarian, but he took every meat product served on the food cart.

One day I stopped by Sticks's cell to drop off a book, and he was in the back of the cell naked using a slice of bologna and cheese to wipe between his butt cheeks. I quickly turned my head and walked away.

"Brother Tookie, let me explain," he hollered.

"To each his own," I replied. "I'm not tripping."

I had ended the conversation, but Sticks continued defending his kinky behaviour. He pleaded, "Tookie, I'm not a pervert or a homo, and I wasn't flashing my buns at you. I wipe my butt with the meat then give it to my neighbour who I hate with a passion. Since I can't get my hands on that scumbag's throat, I do the next best thing to retaliate." Sticks carried on his one-sided talk about all of the despicable things he did to the food he passed to his greedy neighbour.

About a week later, Sticks had the audacity to call over and ask did I want some cookies out of his food packge. No matter how hungry I was, I remained silent. Minutes later he asked, "Bro, do you want one of these Gallo dry salamis?"

Fed up, I said, "Hell, no, and don't ask me again."

Sticks's voice quivered. "If that's the you way you want it . . ."

I was harsh – but better to offend him than eat food sautéed in his faeces.

Grandpa, my neighbour, was transferred back to C-section, and Evil's close homeboy Treach moved in next door. Immediately he and I clicked as Evil and I had done. This was the beginning of an inseparable triad of minds. I discovered Treach also possessed an affinity for study. Our first dialectical exchange – one of many to come – centred on who most deserved a national holiday in his honour, Martin Luther King Jr or Malcolm X. Treach defended his position on Malcolm X and I on King. I didn't know much about either of these black men, but was less familiar with Malcolm's history. However, the hours spent defending our philosophical positions were memorable, and we gained new insight and respect for both slain black activists. I also gained respect for this young Crip who articulated himself with aplomb. Though Treach's skin hue of burnt sienna was darker than Malcolm X, he resembled him in disciplined composure, height, goatee, and ferocious intellect.

Treach asked if I was doing any writing.

"Sure," I said, "I write missives from time to time."

He let out a hearty, deep laugh and said, "Not that kind of writing, cuz. I'm talking about literary writings, compositions, essays."

I told him it never dawned on me to capture my thoughts on paper.

Treach responded, "You know, Cuz, a man with your vocabulary should have a collection of essays. One day your work may prove to be a valuable asset."

I didn't envision the possibilities then, but he inspired me to write my first essay, "Black Unrest", and then plenty of others. I started off with a style of writing intended to impress people with my flair for words. But in time I toned it down, breaking the stereotype of a prisoner being grandiose in his use of language and vocabulary for the sake of appearing intelligent. Studying was noble. My prison cage was transformed into a study laboratory; a secluded place of challenge to mould an educated mind; a quasi-university where I could increase my familiarity with my culture as well as politics, religion, criminal law, and the world – and get in touch with myself.

Seeking to re-educate myself was the first step toward reasoning. Without a conscience I'd remain an educated fool doomed to repeat his mistakes. I didn't know why I was driven to study. Was I destined for something outside of crippin'?

When I wasn't studying or debating with Treach, we were on the exercise yard three days a week driving iron with a huge segment of Crips, representing many sets from South Central. The yard was replete with diehards: Cool Breeze, Crazy Crip, Turtle, Bobcat, Timebomb, Crusher, TeeDee, and others I can't remember. Being in D-section afforded me the opportunity to hear about what was going on with other Crips in San Quentin and throughout the penal system. There were plenty of war stories. I was told my homeboy Black Johnny had lost his mind. I couldn't help thinking about the omen I had about him and Buddha.

There was also mention of the ambushing of several homeboys, which infuriated me. Usually with the assistance of a rogue guard, a non-black prisoner would be allowed to hide in a black prisoner's cell underneath the bunk. Once the handcuffed black man entered the cell and the door was locked, the ambusher would quietly crawl out and stab him thirty or forty times. This deadly warfare – a dishonest guard aiding a non-black prison group – is a reality every black prisoner is aware of. Although some individuals survived these attacks, most died. I always checked under the bunk before entering my cell. To hear about these kinds of set-ups where a Crip, Blood, or another black man was carried out on a gurney paralysed, moribund or dead, was enough to enrage rage. How can a man defend himself while handcuffed and locked in a cell, with a hands-free enemy on a mission to stop his heart from beating?

There was a time, after yard, that I returned to the cell and all was clear under the bunk. But while leaning on the bars, talking to Treach, the cell door swung open. Hurriedly I closed it and whispered over to Treach that the door was unlocked. Treach's immediate response was, "Cuz, it's probably a set-up, don't come out." When a guard came to the cell two gun-rail guards stood slightly off to the side watching. I told the guard the door was unlocked and he simply smiled, then locked the door. Before leaving, the guard said, "Tookie, you're fortunate you didn't step outside, because they were waiting for you." It didn't surprise me.

There are subtle moments of humour squeezed in between the prison madness. I knew quite a few Crips who were jokesters, but none as hilarious as TeeDee from the Harlem Crips. He was a maestro of jokes, playing the dozens and capping on somebody. TeeDee had an animated flair that either made you want to kill him or laugh. He could look a guy straight in the eye and compliment his intellect, while secretly tapping someone else to indicate he's jiving. Or TeeDee would call a homeboy "handsome homie" knowing darn well he meant the opposite. I was never the joking and laughing type, but TeeDee had Treach and me rolling with laughter. Unlike Black Johnny, a pressure-hold headlock didn't work on TeeDee; he'd just come back for more. He was also good at engaging in private bull sessions.

During one such chat he said, "Tookie, I need several photos of you as soon as possible."

I asked him for what?

"Cuz, you're the only celebrity I know," was his insane response. He said, "I can have pictures of you blown up to poster size, then sell them at the Inglewood Forum." I told him that was ridiculous.

But he said, "You're the most famous person in prison since George Jackson. I'm going to make some money."

I figured TeeDee was joking. But after paroling, that nut actually did sell posters of me.

THIRTY

Change Will Come

Plenty of people have claimed to have had an epiphany that radically altered their lives. I wasn't fortunate enough to encounter dazzling light, visions, or a voice of infinite wisdom to shake my world to its foundation. Being brick-headed, it would've taken the sky falling on me for me to notice the need for a change in my life.

I failed continually to see the bigger picture. I trudged through life with no purpose or direction. All I saw were steel bars, thick walls, armed guards, and madness. Fighting the good fight was my motto, so, in lieu of sitting around in D-section on grade-B, I decided to challenge the violation report with a 602 appeal. Months later I won the appeal, and my grade-A status was restored. It was bittersweet leaving Treach in D-section, thinking he'd arrive later. I had no idea years would pass before I'd see him again. I relished our Crip reminiscences, dialectics, and philosophical exchanges.

Back in C-section I was able to regain enough strength to bench a 500-lb bar that had Chief's name soldered on it in bold letters, though he couldn't bench the weight. The day I benched the weight with ease for reps, Crip Slim threw his beanie up in the air and started jumping up and down as if he'd won the lottery. Slim told me that he was proud and happy that a Crip – and nobody else – was able to lift the weight. There was also dust gathering on a set of 130-lb dumbbells I started using for standing or sitting shoulder presses, curls, and back-arms for ten to fifteen reps. My true feat of strength was being able to perform seated, behind-the-neck shoulder presses for reps with a 375-lb bar. Some guards were still trying for permission for me to compete in the San Quentin weight-lifting contests, but the higher echelon vetoed it.

While we drove iron, watchful eyes always scanned the area. In the background was an unassuming Crip, Maddog, one of the most loyal and most deadly. He was a wily Army veteran who looked like a tall and burly black mountain man. Like sentries, he and the stocky faithful Crip Ghetto stood around ready for any intruders, prepared to smash whomever was foolish enough to violate our territory.

The population of death row for minorities was disproportionately increasing, mostly for black men and Mexicans from South Central Los Angeles. The first Bloods from different sets were Smallwood, Peewee and Ace, and then later, Big Time, Bopete, Monster, Shoes, Big Reg, Fat Rat, others. Smallwood ended up going back to court and getting his sentence reduced. Later, other young Bloods started arriving: Maria, Boon, J-Rock, others. The interactions between Crips and Bloods on the row was in sharp contrast to the bloody exchanges back in society. Though we drove iron side-by-side, I can't say we trusted one another. Nevertheless we did share common backgrounds, and we were pitted against the same alien penal setting of death. With the exception of squabbling between Gangster and Peewee, we were never at war. We did our thing and they did theirs.

During a renovation, C-section's death row population was moved to D-section, which was evacuated for our arrival. There was no difference between the units; I was locked up and forced to battle my demons. Most of the time I spent concentrating on drawing, which shielded me mentally from the chaos of prison life. When I was drawing, time was irrelevant; not much else mattered. I had no idea drawing was a defensive mechanism for me to combat the negative elements of an idle mind and hands. I was adopting an alien concept: productivity.

On the condemned yard was a huge weight pile and small universal-type bench press machine attached to the back wall. Right next to us was the Max-A yard containing Crips, Bloods, the Black Guerrilla Family, the Aryan Brotherhood, and other gang factions. The Max-A yard was a potpourri of unstable lunacy that could erupt at any time. Back then, a politicized version of the Crips, the Consolidated Crips Organization (CCO) gained considerable notoriety. Perhaps in the beginning its intentions were honourable, but later allegations of coercive recruiting, cronyism, intimidation, manipulation by the Black Guerrilla Family, and improprieties against other Crips cast a long shadow over the CCO. One of its biggest canards was that I sat on its board. This was a ploy to attract more Crips. Evil pointed out that if I was at the top of the CCO, other forces could not have subverted it as they did. If it had transformed itself into a political prison entity and cast out the gangster mentality, it would have been the most powerful black group in the prison system.

The CCO's rapid deterioration was hastened by internal conflicts and external antagonism from numerous Crip factions. Crip scrimmages were played out on the Max-A yard and throughout other California prisons with deadly force. Many of the CCO leadership jumped to the formidable opposing side. In San Quentin it was pathetic to hear or catch sight of Crips engaged in a blow-for-blow campaign for dominance. In the final analysis there were no winners, only disunity.

Aggression between prisoners – or between a guard and a prisoner – were potentially deadly in these close quarters. While working out on the bench press machine, I caught sight of Freaky Pete, another death row prisoner a few feet away, backing up quickly from the fence. I knew something was amiss. On the Max-A yard I saw a black man and a Southern Mexican guy engaged in battle, with the black man having the upper hand. The tower gunman fired a couple of rounds, and the black man crumbled to the ground, killed instantly. The Mexican guy died later at the hospital.

It was a moment of cold-blooded brutality that captured the attention of every prisoner present. Even after the guards ordered everyone on the Max-A yard to hit the dirt, blacks and Mexicans made half-hearted attempts to fight, but more shots ended such notions. On the condemned yard we too were ordered to get down on the ground. A nervous black guard who seemed to have lost his mind, screamed, "Tookie, you better hit the ground right now if you want to live!" I stood looking up at the guard as if daring him to shoot, before Ghetto and Maddog pulled me down.

Later I wondered how was it possible for such an attack to occur in the midst of other black men. It was irrelevant whether Percy was a Black Guerrilla Family Crip or a Blood. Where were his friends and comrades? I remember asking Ghetto, "Cuz, what was wrong with that picture?"

His response was, "No USALAMA (security) whatsoever. If that man had homeboys, they all froze." Then he said, "Cuz, you never have to worry about that. I'll be there for you."

I voiced the same sentiment to him. I knew my life wasn't worth a plugged nickel in here.

It came as no surprise when the state-level court denied my appeal. Once the prison staff found out, they took the unprecedented step of sending me to the Hole. Other than to harass me, it was difficult to understand their reasoning. Since then, no one else has undergone such treatment. After numerous requests to phone the state-appointed attorney, I was able to make contact and convince him to call the warden. I was returned to D-section where the entire death row unit was preparing to move back to C-section.

In June 1987, I was uprooted and placed in the Hole under suspicion of another escape plot. This time the so-called conspiracy had me teamed up with a cast of unknown Crips. The next day I was provided with a document that revealed a phone conversation between a person identifying himself as a Crip and a San Quentin operator. Not able to speak to me directly, he told the operator, "The Los Angeles Crips have a job to get Tookie out of there." He left his full name, address, and three phone numbers. Every lying syllable uttered about me was likely considered gospel by the staff. They were eager to believe the worst about me.

At the unit classification it was clear that I'd remain in the Hole pending an investigation. I was assigned to the same yard as my homeboy Evil and met Owl, Double Life, Tee, Little Owl, G and about twenty other Crips. I just missed Treach; he had been called down to the Los Angeles County jail by Crip Kato's attorney. Each designated yard was then split in half with different yard schedules. As a result Evil and I ended up on separate yards, with our homeboys split up. The same was done to the Southern and white yard, and the BGF and Northern yard.

This allowed me to become better acquainted with the homeboys. Double Life, G and I engaged in a study group to expand our political dialectics and vocabulary. To better understand politics and other topics, we needed to learn hundreds and thousands of new words. Following our workouts on the yard, Double Life didn't hesitate to pull out a long list of words to test me. There was never a moment that I missed the orthography or definition of a word. Studying had opened a new world for me.

One day out of curiosity I asked what the initial G stood for and he said, "God." Other than being born in God's image, he didn't have a leg to stand on. I'm sure it annoyed G when I asked why he wasn't able to liberate himself or me, since he was God. But who was I to challenge another man's belief, regardless of its oddity?

After a few weeks all the separated yards were restored. In several lengthy discussions with Evil, we concluded that crippin' wasn't what it used to be. There was nothing worse than Crips giving Crip a bad name. It was stunning to realize our brainchild was turning into caricature.

In the Hole there were no weights on the yard, so I improvised with push-ups, chin-ups, and basketball. Since I didn't want to lose my yokes, I avoided the burpee exercises which would have trimmed me down like a greyhound. Prison burpees are the hardest exercise known to man, and I disliked them so much I refused to do any until years later. Basketball was a frustration releaser and it was a pity to see so much raw talent deflected from greater opportunities.

On the prison grapevine, news travelled fast, especially when someone turned informer. We received word that Crime Dog McGruff from the Rolling Sixties was a snitch and was headed to death row. According to Buthalezi, his crimie McGruff had snitched on him, and he intended to snuff him. The day McGruff was placed on the Crip yard, Buthalezi had a decision to make. At his disposal were enough knives for a small ninja army but he blurted out an obscure excuse, "Cuz, I'm going to bust on him, but I need some steel to do the job right." Perhaps he was still rattled after witnessing his CCO homeboy getting a hit on the basketball court days before. Buthalezi was given ample time to handle McGruff himself or other arrangements would be made, to which he agreed. If Buthalezi violated his Crip word, it would render his voice forever unworthy.

Later that week the counsellor announced that the investigation into my alleged escape plan had been revealed as a teenage prank. With a brief warning to stay out of trouble, my grade-A was immediately restored and I was transferred to C-section. But it was like playing musical chairs: I wasn't there more than a month when C-section was moved to East Block. Outside the unit were six fenced yards with weight piles for death row prisoners. Gone were the days when friends or warring foes either exercised on the same Grade A yard or stayed locked up in their cells.

East Block was laid back. I found myself reading less, although occasionally I worked on expanding my vocabulary. The central focus in my life was to develop bigger muscles than I had when I was in society, but because I was shuffled back and forth to the Hole, my goal eluded me. With Bub out of commission, Ghetto's newly arrived cousin, Herk, became my workout partner. Standing over six feet, he was a yoked-up, cocoa brown, lothario thug with a cooler-than-cool stroll. The County jail had sapped his size and strength, but persistent workouts got him back on track. Each day we eagerly looked forward to the gates being racked open to do battle with the weight pile.

A buzz circulated that McGruff had received grade-A and was on his way to East Block. His crime partner Buthalezi had been talking long smack about what he planned to do. Now it was time to put up or shut up. I personally offered to assist him but Buthalezi did nothing. His failure to follow through enraged another Crip so much that he took on the task. McGruff was soon stretched out on the cement with multiple knife wounds. Buthalezi ran off to the other side of the yard.

The following day I received a copy of a CIDF (confidential information disclosure form), a bureaucratic euphemism for an unnamed person snitching on someone. I was accused of being the leader of the Blue Note Crips, actively recruiting others and having inmates assaulted. In the next preposterous CIDF I received, a Crip power struggle was allegedly brewing between Buthalezi and me. The administration's attempt to characterize Buthalezi as a controlled pawn against me was a fiasco from the start, ruined by Buthalezi's lack of conviction, his inability to honour his word, and fear that rendered him incompetent and foolish.

Though not all of Buthalezi's violations have been mentioned here, his misdeeds continue to eat away at his soul.

THIRTY-ONE

Trials, Tribulations

It was foolish of me to believe that my grandmother would live forever, but I felt the same about my father, Fred Holiwell, who died in 1988. I remember listening to this once strong, proud black man who was now dying of cancer. He whispered in quivering tones that tore at my heart; "Tookie, call the police, somebody's breaking into the house." Hearing him made me cringe in despair. I could do absolutely nothing for this man who had so often helped me.

Though Fred wasn't my biological father, he was the paternal fixture in my life, a man I could always call upon in times of trouble or need. After hearing of his death, I stretched out on the mattress on the floor and thought of a eulogy. I wasn't his real son, but Fred did for me what he'd do for any of his four children. He tried desperately to protect me from mistakes growing up and from the racist system of the law, an impossible aspiration for any black man.

The best thing I can say about Fred is that he loved my mother and was always there for her, and for that I give him high praise. His effect on my life is forever etched in my mind. Rest in peace, my father.

On occasions the inevitable question "why me?" came to me. I wondered how this crooked cycle of misfortune could be reversed. For years I obliged this system designed to destroy me. Clearly, as long as I continued functioning out of criminal intent and robotic stupidity, I'd be helping the system in its destructive intent. Later I'd learn that to buck the awful conditions with any positive agenda would only trigger efforts to discourage me. As a guard once told me, "You're here [only] to die."

There's enough intrigue in prison to put the C.I.A. to shame. I was not shocked when the classification committee lowered my status to grade-B, along with Ghetto, who was fingered as one of my bodyguards. Just weeks earlier the staff had converted part of East Block's second tier to serve as a lock-up for grade-B condemned prisoners. When Ghetto and I arrived, Evil, Treach, and a few others were already housed on the tier. Though we weren't allowed any weights on the exercise yard, it felt good being around Crip allies.

I was housed in a cell adjacent to Evil, which enabled us to resume conversations. He talked about this black actor, Phillip Michael Thomas, who had mentioned during a radio interview a book entitled *The Perennial Psychology of the Bhagavad Gita*. Evil, Treach, and I obtained a copy. Though it didn't alter my life as I thought it might, it did cause me to challenge my stance on personal thoughts, behaviour, and the conditions around me. But I was still torn between my fealty to crippin' and becoming a new being. Did Buddha, Raymond, Mac Thomas, Ode and all the rest die in vain?

I was embarking upon a task that had broken other men – to alter the course of my life. One stumbling block was the shallow concern of how other Crips would view my change. To say I wasn't interested in what my peers thought of me would be a lie. I wasn't about to lower my convictions. Though I was no longer an impulsive reactionary, I was neither a pacifist nor would I turn the other cheek if physically threatened. The natural do-or-die instinct of self-defence is a necessity I'll forever adhere to. Still, the scariest thing to me was life after crippin', the idea of developing a conscience to counter my own ignorance.

In 1989 I received a court order for a Los Angeles County child custody hearing for my son Stan. When I arrived at High Power I was placed on B-row. Around the corner on

A-row was Evil, who had been called down by Kato's attorney months earlier. Evil reached out to me the following day with a huge plastic bag filled with food, personal care items, and books. Although I was unable to see him or Kato, we communicated through the wall vent, an improvised telephone. Over the years of travelling back and forth to the Los Angeles County Jail, I ran into Crazy Dee, Timmy Tucker, Animal, Big Bamm, and Little Kill-Kill. Other than strolling down Crip memory lane with them, I found solace in having Animal test me on numerous words, and I returned the favour.

Shackled and seated in the courtroom, I saw my stepsister Demetri. I hadn't seen her in nearly a decade. I had hoped to see my son, whom I hadn't seen since 1979. Finally the judge entered the room, sat shuffling papers for a few minutes, and then rescheduled my hearing for an unspecified date, since neither my son nor his mother Beverly was present.

I was still shell-shocked from being in the Los Angeles County Jail in 1979-81. Before my departure Evil hollered through the vent to ask if I wanted to stay down there a little longer. I shot back, "No way, cuz, I'm ready to split!" Even though I was in good company with Evil and other Crips, I wanted out of there, and soon wasn't quick enough.

Arriving back at San Quentin, though no delight, was better than being in the County jail. In East Block I was housed a couple of cells from Treach. He soon started sending me books by authors such as Chancellor Williams, Runoko Rashidi, Danita R. Redd, Cheikh A. Diop, Francis Cress Welsing, Dr. Ben Jochannon, A. J. Rodgers, Ivan V. Sertima and John H. Clarke. These writers helped reveal the truth about the history of our culture. The more I read, the more I discovered the contradictions in myself and in the world I thought I knew.

Somewhere I read, "Nothing remains the same, and everything changes." Needless to say my change would be invisible to the vindictive and myopic staff and others who preferred I remain fossilized in the amber of the Crip legacy. It was slow and difficult for me to shake loose the

Machiavellian mentality that served for years as my apologia for manhood. I had always scraped and struggled for the tiniest of morsels, even self-change. The mental and behavioural evolution that Treach, Evil, and I were seeking transcended ourselves; it was larger than any one of us as individuals. We wanted to set a standard others could follow, create a natural transition from criminal to black man of learning. We wanted most to understand why we Crips chose this path in life. We wanted to kick the door wide open so any imprisoned black man could enter and begin to initiate a productive change within himself.

Sometime in 1990 those of us on grade-B in East Block were moved to The Hole in AC, with our property on carts trailing behind. Though everybody else had been scattered on different tiers, Treach and I were on the same tier with an open cell between us. Not long after our arrival, a man from India calling himself Mahindi was placed in that empty cell. Treach was quietly memorizing names of prisoners for future cell soldiering.

It was obvious to us that Mahindi was a J-Cat when he started ear-hustling and trying to interject into everybody's conversation. From past experience both Treach and I knew it was futile to argue with a man who wasn't wrapped too tight. There was no doubt in my mind he was intentionally placed next to us. For weeks Mahindi angered everybody on the tier with his abrupt intrusions, using his makeshift fishline to snatch up others. He stole fishlines so regularly some of the Aryan Brotherhood members tried to establish a truce by buying him off with cigarettes and candy, which didn't last long. Though everybody shined Mahindi on, he started banging on the steel toilet and the wall during all hours of the day and night. Several guards tried to calm him down, but as soon as they left, he'd bang in rhythm to some imaginary tune in his head. When Mahindi wasn't banging, he held one-sided conversations with Treach or me. Other times he'd wait until we started talking, then lash out, calling us niggers and other expletives. In his whiny, nasal voice he'd sometimes say, "Hey, Tookie, how come you look like Black Hercules, but you speak with a soft voice like a woman. Hell, you should switch voices with Treach. But maybe you two are playing games with my mind by throwing your voices like a ventriloquist. I'm not crazy, you know. Tookie ... Treach ... is that what you're trying to do, make me lose my mind? Answer me, *answer me!*"

Treach and I sometimes wished for the opportunity to snatch Mahindi by the collar and beat some sanity into him. Darn near everybody on the tier was waiting to catch him during cell search, when each person stands handcuffed outside the cell. With no hands available, feet would have worked just as well. But he was no fool. Mahindi never came out of his cell for searches, yard, or to shower. Since no one was willing to bite when Mahindi sold wolf tickets, it started driving him batty. At first he began to mumble to himself, then he'd loudly speak out in detail about his uncle molesting him as a child, or give accounts of other bizarre sex stories. This man needed treatment, to be housed in a medical ward, not in the Hole. I returned from the yard one day to see a guard cleaning out Mahindi's cell. From what I heard, he tried to commit suicide and almost succeeded. As cold as it may sound, his departure was a relief for everybody.

In the midst of these distractions I still possessed the enthusiasm to reinvent myself. It was difficult to transform my criminal mentality into a mind-set with a conscience. Everything was working against me: I was an imprisoned black man, condemned to die, co-founder of the infamous and hated Crips, and no one believed I'd ever change. Even I had doubts.

At least I now had knowledge of what *not* to do. I studied the lives of numerous men professing to be revolutionists – Christian, Muslim, Buddhist, Rastafarian, Erudite, ex-drug addict or former gang member, while still acting out their gangster fantasies. I had read about George Jackson and his comrades, about their courageous attempts to convert the black criminal into the ultimate revolutionary. They were stifled by individuals straddling the fence between revolutionary duties and criminal gain. It would be a harder challenge for me to transfigure my Machiavellian mode to an educated and redemptive mindset. You cannot serve two gods.

The recording of human errors must be a vivid reminder of what to avoid repeating. Often during yard time, in my discussions with Treach and Evil, we harped upon the foreseeable pitfalls and our determination to sidestep them. But despite the books we read, we knew that our life-altering transition had to be based on our own personal initiative or a relapse would be imminent. Only after undergoing personal transformations could we individually meet at the crossroads to compare notes. Until then, everything we pondered was pure speculation.

In the meantime, Bad News from the Rolling Sixties Crips moved in to the cell on the other side of me. He had accidentally cut off his fingers with a saw while working in the prison industry. Luckily, Marin Hospital was able to re-attach his fingers with reconstructive surgery. It was also around this time that I began to exchange letters and photos with a Puerto Rican woman name Rosa. She was attractive, generous and intelligent and an expert computer trouble-shooter for a large corporation. We slowly developed a cordial relationship although, judging from her few photos, Rosa appeared to be tipsy, no, a sloppy drunk. But I felt self-conscious and hypocritical about questioning her behaviour because of my own past, so I tried to be indifferent.

I received a missive from Leon Bing, a woman writer working on a book entitled *Do or Die*. Monster Kody from the Eight Tray Gangster Crips had told her about me, and she wanted to learn more about the history of the Crips. I decided to call Leon when Kato's attorney summoned Treach, Heron, and me to the Los Angeles County Jail. The first time I met Ms. Bing, it struck me as odd that a white woman would be interested in writing a book about street thugs like us. I was sceptical of her motives and unwilling to divulge the info I planned to use for my own memoirs. Though Leon was congenial enough, I believed it impossible for anyone – white, black, Mexican or other – to chronicle the specific black tragedy when he or she had not lived it. She would inevitably lack understanding of the essence and subtle contradictions of the experience. There is already too much misinformation being propagated. I politely suggested at the end of our first and only visit that she talk to Treach, who might be willing to help her.

Perhaps had I not been expecting a food package already en route to San Quentin, I would have stayed a little longer with Treach, Kato, and Heron in the County jail. The package I expected was sent to my neighbour, Bad News, since I had already received one for that quarter. Rosa was quite reliable in taking care of my needs. She was impressed with my eagerness to read, and provided me with all the books I wanted. From the outside, the relationship appeared to be running smoothly. Evil was curious as to whether I'd marry her. He looked perplexed when I said marriage was out of the equation, period. Rosa was a handful. She had issues and wasn't keen on accepting advice. I knew she had a drink problem, but I was caught off guard when she admitted that she was a kleptomaniac and had contemplated suicide. Then she mentioned that a psychologist was charging her $250 an hour to discuss her problems. "Two hundred and fifty dollars?" I quipped. "Hell, you'd do better paying me to resolve your problems instead of some quack."

Each visit was trying. I had to determine whether I'd wear the hat of a psychologist, friend, physician, father, counsellor, brother, lover, or objective listener. In Rosa's mind her problems far outweighed the seriousness of my pending execution. Though Rosa was affable and sweet, she was spoiled, expecting everything to go her way. One day Rosa said, "Since I'm looking out for you, Tookie, you can't complain or criticize me." That was our final visit. The materialistic items she rained down upon me were a blessing, but I wasn't hard up enough to kiss anybody's butt for them. No matter how many women slipped in and out of my life, my mother was always the superior constant.

To relieve my pent-up frustration I started doing burpees with Evil out on the yard. Pushing the envelope, I created higher burpee counts, along with double, triple, and quad-count Jashiri burpees with a pause, and crunch burpees. Though the routine started off with just Evil and me, others began to join in. Before long the entire yard was, in prison parlance, "busting down." Even Mario, a Blood, participated in our routines and didn't miss a workout. His presence on the yard was no oddity, because Crips and Bloods had been coexisting on death row for years with no serious conflict.

But of course, with a bunch of men playing basketball ("shish rugby"), there are bound to be disagreements. On the basketball court one day, I saw out of the corner of my eye a flashing silhouette, a hand going upside Little Man's head. He and Mario squared off to fight. I stood between them demanding to know the problem. Mario spat out, "Tookie, this dude Little Man has been dogging me ever since I've been on the court. I told him I'm no chump and to stop dogging me, but he kept doing it, so I popped him." Pulling Mario to the side, I asked was he willing to fight Little Man head up, and he quickly responded, "Yes." However, when I asked the bigger and more muscular Crip, Little Man, about fighting Mario, he responded, "Can you have somebody make a knife for me?" Disgusted I said, "Hell, no! This is a simple fight with no knives, so either you fight him toe-to-toe, or not at all." Little Man opted not to fight Mario, stating he'd take care of it in East Block, whatever that meant.

Only later did I realize that, at that moment, I initiated the beginning of fair play fighting. It made no difference to me that Mario and Little Man were gang rivals. Each deserved equal footing in a fight. Imagine me, developing a conscience – and with a Blood, a sworn enemy of what I stood for. Years previously, things would have turned out entirely differently, with a free-for-all. But my judicious even-handedness earned Mario and Little Man's respect.

This was a bad time for the disenfranchised. California's criminal judiciary was handing out death penalties like government food stamps in a depression. A youngster from the Lynwood Crips, Kerm was driven up from the County jail and was immediately placed in the Hole with us. His first day on the yard, I watched as he cautiously surveyed the territory and us. Kerm was a slender Crip with barely suppressed rage. I was impressed with his gung-ho attitude towards exercising and studying. Soon Chico, from the Eight Tray Gangster Crips, arrived. He too was thrown in The Hole for evaluation. He and Kerm had to remain there until the committee determined whether or not they would receive grade-A.

During a chat with Chico I discovered he lived just several blocks from where I had lived on 69th. He was one of many youngsters, along with Monster Kody, who sat around gawking at my homeboys and me driving iron. Chico was now taller than me and quite muscular. I could sense his fiery spunk – but more importantly, Chico had a penchant for study and exercise.

Occasionally I'd cross paths with a Crip with something to hide. Such was the case with Otabenga from the Long Beach Crips (LBC), who had been on death row for a few years. He seemed to have a huge chip on his shoulder ever since Gangster had attacked him for calling him a punk. As he and I strolled on the yard, Otabenga voiced his disagreement with the rule for exercising. I assured him that there was no obligation to exercise.

Apparently Otabenga mistook my humility for weakness. He blurted, "I hope I don't have to hurt anybody over this exercising thing, because I *will*." Ordinarily I would have clipped his chin without a second thought, but this time I merely warned him about his hostility – somebody might take it as a threat. His response was, "I don't care." His hand flinched upward, perhaps as a nervous tic or an attempt to strike. I defended myself with a slap across his face that sounded with a sharp crack. He stood there, shocked. One of the gunmen heard the slap and ordered us to stand still. He told Otabenga to walk towards the caged entrance. As he passed he made a half-hearted attempt to swing in slow motion from eight feet away.

Evil, standing nearby, took this as aggression against me and rushed the much larger Otabenga inside the caged area.

It was natural for Evil to retaliate on my behalf, as it was for Treach and me to run from opposite sides of the yard to assist him when necessary. The other gunman fired a shot inches from my foot. Nevertheless, I met Treach shoulder to shoulder at the entrance of the cage. It was impossible for all of us to fit inside the tight space. Evil continued his attack as Otabenga pleaded with him to stop.

At that time, none of us was aware that Otabenga had snitched on his crimie (criminal partner).

After a ten-day lock-down for the incident, we found out Tan Tan must have panicked, then jumped ship. He was now assigned to the A.C. walk-alone security yard with McGruff, Buthalezi, Dodo, Pineapple, and a few other Crips they had managed to dupe. Whether Tan Tan had something to hide I don't know. Foolishly, he asked if Evil or I planned to stab or hit him. I never did understand why he switched yards like that, because he was cool with everybody.

I started corresponding with another female, Benita, a fitness instructor from Los Angeles. Ever since I've been on death row, I envisioned one day meeting a beautiful sister with a huge Afro and her fist raised high in a symbolic gesture of black power, or at least meet a woman who looked black. Benita was a Caucasian with fiery red hair, the antithesis of my ideal woman. But she was responsive to me, more than willing to help.

I've often questioned why there are so many black men in the visiting room hooked up with white women. I have come to understand that there is a paucity of sisters willing to come visit black men behind bars. But white women – and especially those from foreign countries – visit black men in large numbers. And behind these walls, when compassion comes knocking – as it rarely does – you open the door.

THIRTY-TWO

Let There Be Light

It was 1992. I was preparing to leave for another evidentiary hearing in the Los Angeles County Court building downtown. Before my departure, Treach, Evil, and I collaborated on a book of poems entitled, *Unchained Voices*, with hopes of getting it published. Benita had contacted a noted black historian and author, Runoko Rashidi, who agreed to edit our work and try to find a publisher. The possibility of having our literary work in print and bearing fruits of wisdom for our homeboys and society had all three of us hyped up.

Early in the morning as the black and white sheriffs County bus drove away from San Quentin, I reflected upon the prospects of our project. I was also trying to digest the latest news about a riot in South Central, a reaction to white Los Angeles cops being acquitted for beating black motorist Rodney King. It was a *felix culpa* (fortunate fault) that a citizen with a video camera captured the public flogging. Mainstream society would not have believed the police brutality that black people know all too well. Yet, the LAPD described the brutal beating as an "isolated incident."

The unshocking fact that a predominantly Caucasian jury acquitted the four cops had South Central inhabitants bracing for a response. Though my bus was miles away from Los Angeles, the air had a caustic, charred smell. In the far distance a thick, black cloud of smoke hovered over South Central like a suffocating blanket.

At Los Angeles County Jail I was placed in a one-man holding tank. I saw the words "Crips and Bloods united forever," scrawled on the wall in big black letters. The proclamation wasn't surprising. Throughout most California prisons, Crips and Bloods have existed in an unspoken truce for over a decade, especially on death row. Yet, in society, for more than three decades, Crips and Bloods have been hunting each other down like animals. Regardless of how much we celebrated each strike against the other, in the long run, we all suffered a loss.

My hearing turned out to be the usual lopsided version of justice. For a defendant it's a legal crapshoot, especially when your state-appointed attorney's preparation and case management are perfunctory. But during the few weeks of court proceedings I did manage to contact Runoko Rashidi. It was an awkward moment when Runoko brought up an incident during which my homeboys and I jacked him up for money. This was probably true, but I could neither deny nor confirm it. I did express my gratitude for his offer to help us.

Although I went to court each weekday, it didn't hinder my visits or phone calls. Benita visited on a regular basis and made sure I had more than enough money for canteen. She turned out to be a dedicated woman who even looked out for Evil and Treach. Even after Benita got married, she still came to visit me. During one visit we were interrupted by Baboon, a West Side Crip from way back. He acted a complete fool, hollering, "Hey, Tookie, long time no see, cousin." Armed with an expression resembling a baboon, he wanted the world to know he was a g-h-e-t-t-o thug through and through. After Baboon calmed down for all but ten seconds, he said boisterously, "Wait a minute, cuz, I got a surprise for you, be right back." He returned in a moment with Li'l Pamm, who was beaming from ear to ear. Pamm revealed that she was now a legal investigator and would be visiting me in the attorney room. Both Pamm and Baboon gave me their phone numbers, suggesting I call often.

Days later I was told Baboon had been gunned down in retaliation for another murder. There was a heated war going on between some Crips and local Mexicans. When blacks weren't killing one another, trigger-happy cops or other people were trying to wipe us out. This ghetto martyrdom had gotten out of hand, with Bloods, other blacks, and my homeboys disappearing fast. I'm talking about hundreds of homeboys I knew personally, murdered for an illegitimate legacy of embedded cultural racism. From Buddha on down to each dead Crip, we acted invincible – but knew in our gut that we wouldn't live long.

When Pamm came to see me again, her investigator's licence had expired and she was arrested on the spot for trying to visit with an invalid licence. On the telephone later that night her voice quivered as she described how they had interrogated her about me. This wasn't the same brash Pamm I knew from over a decade ago; she was scared to death. She asked, "What in the world have you been doing, Tookie, that caused those crazy people to question me about you?" I told her I hadn't been doing anything, but that my past would forever be used against me. I could tell she had to distance herself from me, and I understood. We never spoke again.

While in High Power, I began to revisit the devils of my past. This critical reflection exposed a litany of fiascos, scandals, mayhem, nihilism and deaths of my homeboys, ending with the Crips entity fading into obscurity. At that moment I knew that my life as a Crip had come to an end. In a cold sweat I shook myself out of this awful reverie, consumed by sadness – not for crippin', but for the lives of all the Crips who had died, for the innocent black lives hurt in the crossfire, for the decades of young lives ruined for a cause-less cause.

I lay wide awake, thinking about how, most of my life, I lived for Crip, but the Crip God had abandoned me. I had poked so many holes in the thin fabric of my thug experience that I could no longer sustain a conscious apologia for Crippen.

During the bus ride back to San Quentin, I realized I was wading into uncharted territory that would bring unwanted attention on me from prison authorities. They would try at every turn to discredit – but I was game. In this setting – authority versus prisoners – the odds against my success were long indeed. But I didn't have to stand alone. Treach and Evil were undergoing the same transition, from thug to thinking black man with purpose. This is a concept – redemption – that criminologists, prison authorities, psychologists and law enforcement officers refuse to believe unless the transformation is accomplished under their "spirit breaking" guidelines.

Back in the Hole, I was placed in the first cell on the second tier, one cell away from Ghetto. I began studying more black history. I attribute the restoration of my self-confidence and self-worth to reading about my ancestors in America and Africa. I began to see that all I had learned from Caucasians about the black reflections of myself was a tissue of lies.

Recapturing a more accurate picture of black history inspired all of us on the yard to teach ourselves to speak Swahili. We had to become autodidactic – self-taught – and continue learning from one another as well. Outside on the yard, after each exhaustive workout of burpees and "Kenya laps" (very fast laps), we'd walk around in small groups and practise Swahili. When Young Kerm moved into the cell between Ghetto and me, we included him in an hour each weekday practising Swahili.

Studying was easy compared to controlling my temper. Since childhood my temper or rage was an explosive defence mechanism, whether triggered by threat or irritant. Controlling my temper would be a matter of resolution and discipline. I resolved to channel my rage into something more beneficial.

For decades I had participated in my own dehumanization. The word "menticide" – brainwashing – coined by black psychologist Bobby Wright, perfectly depicted my state of mind. I had been menticided about my culture, my ethnicity, and my purpose. There was much work that had to be done to reverse the damage. I'd have to rehumanize myself. I had no road map. Though I really didn't know how to accomplish the task, I knew not to indulge in hours of gazing into the hypnotic box (TV), dull my senses with drugs, gamble in any form, intentionally draw attention, or lose myself in the fantasy world of pornographic sex with two-dimensional females.

It was impossible for our peers to see by our mere appearance a change. But one result of the conversion was our ability to introduce autodidactics to the younger generation of Crips entering death row, lest they too be corrupted by the surrounding or by other duped or scandalous Crips. The premise was that any Crip armed with correct knowledge about himself, his culture, spirituality and the world would see the light and begin to change. There would always be exceptions but at least we were offering an option. Kicking back on the yard, Kerm thanked me for introducing him to scholastics. He explained how fortunate he was to have been assigned to our yard because we (Treach, Evil and I) helped him tremendously. Had he been sent to any other yard, he admitted, he would be gangbanging.

This was a refreshing moment: to see a man open up with no reservation, no fear of humiliation or ridicule. This illustrates how a young do-or-die Crip, not of my generation, was intelligent enough to acknowledge our teachings as a sign of strength. Moreover, it was a validation of the transition from being a Crip to an adult Afrocentric male. None of us could relate to other racial groups until we established a firm footing for our own – and then began to reach out.

Any form of positive awakening behind these walls of chaos can be considered a miracle. However, there are still in place the same prison mechanisms that engender racism, violence, collusion, deprivation, frame-ups, and other injustices. Though I was finding internal peace, I was not exempt from the external chaos. That was made perfectly clear the day I returned from the yard and learned that all my property had been confiscated. A note on the bunk informed me that due to a criminal investigation, my property had to be searched.

A week later when my property was returned, many pictures were missing from my photo albums. An attached note stated that after the photos had been copied, they'd be returned. Another confidential disclosure form was placed on the bars alleging that I had issued orders for certain staff and inmates in East Block to be hit. This was one of many examples of the authority's "dropping ice" that melts into lie.

Even death row is alive with snitches of all colours.

THIRTY-THREE

Human Angel

During my darkest moments, when the burdens seemed too heavy to bear, a human angel came into my life to lighten the load.

In late December 1992, as I was exercising, a guard placed a letter on the cell bars. I stopped and read the letter – from a black journalist and author, Barbara Becnel, then tossed it on the bunk and continued my burpee workout. Usually I'd tear up missives from journalists, authors, and the news media and flush them down the toilet. I sensed many of them were parasitical opportunists seeking to exploit the Crip legacy and line their pockets. But something urged me to re-read this letter.

Once I finished my workout and took a birdbath, I sat down and perused it again. It was both fate and good timing that induced me to even consider responding. Barbara assured me that her intentions were honourable. She was writing a book about the history of California's black gangs. Because of Raymond Washington's demise, she wrote, I was the sole surviving person who could provide an accurate account of the Crips' growth to become the most notorious black gang in California and to expand its reach across the USA, into South Africa and elsewhere. Though I didn't detect duplicity on Barbara's part, I still viewed her with suspicion.

The following month, January 1993, her first visit was scheduled in San Quentin's brown-panelled room where all media interviews were held. I was in chains with handcuffs and in a chair, awaiting Barbara's arrival. Two guards were stationed behind me and seated in the back of the room was the prison's black mouthpiece, Vernel Crittendon. A smiling Barbara entered the room – tall, svelte, elegantly dressed, and a beautiful brown-complexioned sister. She spoke with polite eloquence, neither cloying nor condescending. I had assumed she would be an uppity black bourgeois whom I'd browbeat or intellectually spar with to bring her back down to earth. I was a bit nervous and started to sweat profusely, as if I was about to be interrogated, but Barbara's manner set the tone for a pleasant dialogue. Her objective was to spend a single day gathering data about the Crips and me for the book. But this first interview encouraged her to schedule another meeting for the following day.

During that second interview I revealed to Barbara my interest in writing children's books to warn them about drugs, gangs, prison, and crime. Judging by her expression, my literary proffer blew her away. The more I explained my intent to deliver a positive message through books, the more the idea made sense to her – though I sensed a slight hesitation on her part to fully commit. Little did she know that my enthusiasm for writing children's books was even greater than my zeal had been for crippin'.

With each exchange in letters on the subject, the more Barbara got caught up in my literary vision. Still, she had reservations. I wished people could read me better instead of suspecting that I had an angle. Later, while strolling the yard with Hollaway, a friend not affiliated with gangs, I told him I wanted to do something positive with my life, to help children to stay out of this filthy hellhole and out of gangs. Besides Evil and Treach, Hollaway was the only other person who was able to feel the truth of my words.

Barbara and I began working on the first manuscript. She explained that I had to use the simplest language so that children could comprehend and enjoy reading the book. I discovered that writing had a sublime effect on me. It seemed to melt away the years of being desensitized and callous. I felt a sense of purpose: to create a book that might tap into the social pathology affecting black children. Though I held no academic degree, I had created my own college curriculum through years of studying, extrospection, and hard-knock experiences both on the streets of hell and in San Quentin. Though a role model I could never be, I could act as an African *griot* or Paul Revere, warning youths about what is coming down the crooked path.

Barbara liked how the book was turning out and managed to capture the interest of Harper's, a publishing company. Though they were interested, they preferred a book with stories of my past life, laced with blood, gore, and ghetto vernacular. They didn't want to hear about the refined Tookie; they wanted the beast, the Tookie of old. I told Barbara I wasn't that desperate. She wasn't sure whether my decision was the right one, but she respected my wishes and began looking elsewhere. Most other publishing companies considered my proposal to be too controversial, chiefly because I was on death row.

Barbara divided her time between finding a publisher for the children's books, writing her own book, and assisting in the Hands Across Watts (HAW) project, a programme designed to promote peace between warring LA gang factions and initiated by the PJs' Crip commander Tony Bogard and a Blood named Ty-Stick. Bogard grew up on the Crip legends about me battling rival gangs throughout the Westside, Compton PJs and JDs, stories he never forgot. He had told Barbara, "Every Crip knows that if you want to know the history of the Crips, contact Tookie on death row."

During this same period I received a missive from Jimel after fourteen years of silence. With no proper salutations or "long time no see," he launched into a broadside against HAW and Amer-I-Can, the programme set up by former gridiron football star Jim Brown to teach life management skills to gang members and prison inmates. Then he rattled on about Raymond, himself and me starting the Crips, saying therefore he and I should stick together. I figured the man was intoxicated, delusional, amnesic, or all three. His false claim was no different than those of other charlatans who claim to be co-founders of the Crips. Years later, I would read a book entitled *Uprising* that was ridiculed by every Crip and Blood on death row. One of the chapters, "Godfather Jimel Barnes," which features a lengthy interview with Jimel, was riddled with misinformation, with Jimel's guilty conscience compelling him to defend against "a lot of people saying I didn't pay my dues," or saying that "he was a perpetrator." Those are Jimel's words. Although in that chapter there were numerous contradictions and rambling, incoherent passages, I'll only address one example of misinformation. In the book, Jimel states, "Later, after Raymond passed away, I wanted a twin brother, I wanted somebody to replace Raymond, so I went out and found this guy Tookie and built him up from a little small guy to be a gladiator like me." In fact, I was incarcerated on March 15, 1979, *more than four months before Raymond's death* on August 9, 1979. It was not possible for Jimel to have met me and "built me up" after Raymond's murder. His misuse of Raymond's name to enhance his credibility, and his elevating himself by minimizing me and others, does not accord with the facts. My memoir should decontaminate the misinformation by Jimel and others.

During all the years I was acquainted with Jimel, not once did he ever mention the word "Crip" nor did he engage in Crip warfare. But now he wanted to be up front and centre. He had an agenda of some sort, and he was in need of support. I chose not to respond to the absurd missive.

Though I had known Barbara for a short period, I was more inclined to value her judgment about the HAW programme than the ravings of someone I hadn't heard from in over a decade. HAW was receiving positive coverage, particularly within the community and from the press. During a visit, Barbara asked if I wanted to be a part of an upcoming Los Angeles gang summit for peace. This was Barbara's method, I learned later, of determining if I was still crippin' and whether I was sincere about promoting peace. How was it possible for me to participate from death row? Barbara said that she could have my speech videotaped and shown on a huge screen before an audience. After I agreed to compose two speeches, one for adults and one for children, she scheduled the taping the following week, to be held in the panelling room at San Quentin.

When I arrived to meet Barbara for the taping, I found the room was packed, with a camera crew, guards and prison authorities dressed in suits – and wearing shocked expressions. How dare these strangers who knew me only by name, reputation, and documentation try to predict my response to a given situation. I was not an institutionalized animal, trained and predictable.

By completing both speeches, I cast off a great burden. But I could not predict whether my speech would be taken seriously, and I waited anxiously for the results. Some time later, Barbara told me that certain prison staff had even assured her I'd never show up to do a video that repudiated gangs because I was still the Crip Godfather. They told her, "That man will not even come out of the cell. You're wasting your time."

After a few days, an ecstatic Barbara told me that the moment the screen popped on with my reading, the entire audience became silent and watchful. And after the speech ended, there was a standing ovation! In a display of hypocrisy, even Jimel – who had suggested I distrust the non-profit HAW organization – happily nibbled on the event's *hors d'oeuvres*. His eventual disruptive behaviour and lies he told about me nearly led to his cap being peeled, first by Bogard, then by the other Crips and Bloods, who escorted him out of the building.

My (then) appellate attorneys had objected to the video being shown, but I overrode them. They acted as if I was a dirty secret that should remain unseen and unheard by the public. Their opinion didn't faze me. I was determined to get my message across to black youths about the perils of drugs, gangs, crime, violence, and prison life. What mattered most was the contribution I could make towards helping youths and the HAW. Barbara had her hands full trying to assist

Bogard in his transition from ganghood into the mainstream. Bogard thought he didn't need to be tutored or refined, that he could accomplish the impossible with his charm and street savvy. Like most Crips, he had a hair-trigger temper, cocked and ready for violence. On January 13, 1994, while in the PJs and not wearing his bulletproof vest, Bogard was shot and killed by another PJ Crip. May Bogard rest in peace.

1994 would be a year to remember. Barbara had it in her mind that I deserved grade-A and somehow she'd make sure I got it. Everybody on our yard figured my chances were slim and none, so for years I had refused each scheduled classification committee. Barbara refused to accept the status quo. She was a delicate-looking woman but a tenacious fighter with a fierce drive. She started a support campaign which included a number of notable citizens from mainstream society. Warden Vasquez and Associate Warden Nelson were bombarded with letters and email messages from credible advocates expressing their concerns and their belief in my conversion.

Associate Warden Nelson was the chief arbitrator for the classification committee in the Hole. It would be difficult to find a prisoner who would disagree that Nelson was the meanest and most unmerciful person on staff. There was no way he would allow me to have grade-A, but if by some miraculous intervention it did happen, everybody on the same yard had a shot.

The committee was composed of all Caucasians with the exception of one black counsellor, Hammond. Word had it Hammond was mean-spirited, anti-prisoner, and an Uncle Tom, but I reserved judgment. I was summoned to Hammond's office for a C-File (Central File) review and he expressed interest in the videotaped speech for the gang summit and the children's book I was working on. After making copies of documents in my C-File and discussing my children's project, Hammond admitted that I was nothing like what he had heard or read about in my files. I let him know that the prison files were a mere caricature of who I used to be, not who I was today. He caught me off guard when he asked why I thought I deserved to be on grade-A. I told him, "I've committed no rule violations to be in the Hole. I'm no longer crippin' and haven't had a disciplinary write-up in years. I've undergone a personal transformation." Hammond didn't say much, just that he hoped to see me in classification. I left the office thinking that the man appeared to be upfront. That was all I asked of anybody.

When I talked again with Barbara, she said I deserved grade-A because the speech I made for the LA gang summit was a public declaration of my repudiation of gang violence, gang membership and my leadership and participation in gang life. That speech was truly my forever farewell to Crip: I had chosen another path. I felt, however, that my video-taped speech from death row, though unprecedented, would have no effect on the committee. I agreed with Barbara that I would go to classification, held every sixty days, but I didn't believe a change in grade status was possible.

At the committee meeting, Hammond reminded the members that I hadn't had any disciplinary write-ups in years, and so he was recommending I receive grade-A. Nelson, the Associate Warden, vehemently objected, as did the others. One of them said, "The man's the co-founder of the Crips, for Christ's sake! His influence is too vast. He doesn't deserve a status change." Another counsellor proposed that I should "debrief."

Debriefing is a system used throughout the California Department of Corrections to barter the souls of prison gang members, revolutionists, or any prisoner, for information about their gang, its members, their hegemony, and any past and present criminal activities. Crips passing through the Hole used to talk about homeboys and prison gang members who had debriefed like it was the thing to do. Rumour had it the only way a man could get out of the Hole at Pelican Bay was by being paroled, debriefing, or in a casket.

Hammond explained that debriefing was for *prison* gang members, not a street gang like the Crips.

"Well, since Mr Williams wants grade-A he should have to debrief anyway," said another counsellor.

"I'm confident Mr Williams would refuse to debrief or to submit to a polygraph test," said Hammond, then looked over at me.

Through clinched teeth I said, "Of course I refuse. I value my life and dignity too much to debrief."

I left the room, steaming. Later, both Evil and Treach told me the committee brought up debriefing with them, which they too rejected.

I later explained to Barbara what debriefing meant. Offended by their suggestion that I debrief, she said her next step would be to contact Hammond and find out what could be done. I told her it wasn't enough I was facing execution; they also wanted to rip my dignity right out of my chest. I had doubted she had the wherewithal to have my speech videotaped, but she'd handled it. In time Barbara convinced me never to doubt her abilities. It was rare for me to trust anyone in society other than my mother, but I found myself trusting this woman, when I didn't even trust my attorneys. I marvelled at her trustworthiness and her dedication to follow through in a pinch.

Very few people in society are beating down these gates to go to bat for a death row prisoner. No other person on the face of this planet has offered to help me achieve a positive goal. But in a short time Barbara earned my respect and trust. Her energy was so infectious, I started thinking, "Well, perhaps there *is* a possibility of getting grade-A."

THIRTY-FOUR

Moto NDani
(The Fire Within)

There was a fire kindling in my mind, a fire that drove me to write books for children. It came from a source distinct from my usual rage. When I saw television or newspaper accounts of drive-by shootings with innocent children caught in the crossfire, I felt something that I am unable to articulate to this day. For the first time I was concerned not just for myself or those murdered children, but also for the welfare of other people's children, my children, grandchildren, nieces, and nephews. I found myself unable to eat after viewing children suffering in Africa, afflicted with disease, poverty, genocide, starvation, racism, despair, and death.

Decades ago I had built an emotional rampart against empathy for the hardships of others not close to me. This new, alien feeling of human compassion worried me. It was toppling one of the last bastions of the violent, misguided machismo that helped suppress my inner human feelings. I was maturing: becoming a person with a heart.

I began to gain fresh perspective on my unkind and puzzling life. It wasn't by chance I was born black in a world where my colour made me a pariah by definition, long before I was able to determine my character. Nor was it by accident that I was dys-educated, drug-addicted, enraged, bullet-riddled, pessimistic, cripping-bound, culturally unconscious, and wrongly convicted. My intimacy with the psychoses of this world could have damaged and defeated me, leaving me psychologically scarred, moribund. It was a belated effort on my part, but I was proving that even from the wretched abyss of death row, the impossible was possible. Perhaps merely demonstrating that this awakening was possible was my mission.

In the Hole nothing good is expected to happen. You enter the Hole without a fighting chance. When you leave it, months or years later, a part of you remains there forever. The Hole extracts something you can never regain. Call it hope. During that period, I could not rely upon charm or wit. I had to confront myself with the deepest, most undeniable self-truth. No matter how many thousands of men were unsuccessful before me, I felt I'd somehow excel. I wasn't special but my fighting spirit would not lie down. Since I no longer took mind-stimulating drugs, nothing save death could stop me elevating myself.

As for my recent classification rejection, I refused to worry about it. A man possessed, I pushed forward to achieve what the authorities perceived to be unachievable: transition toward redemption. Armed with a radical evolution of mind, body, and behaviour, I was being reshaped by the disciplines of consistent will power, knowledge, dedication, and spirituality. Serving as an ethical nutrient in my life, the "spirit act" of spirituality induced me to give beyond myself. Its cleansing effect introduced me to "Matt" (an Egyptian or Kamitic term for Truth, Justice, and Righteousness), and I discovered how to devote faith and praise to the one and only God.

In time I was able to deduce, through comparative studying of world religions, that no single person or religious sect has a monopoly on God or spiritual cultivation. I am not Christian, Muslim, Jew, Buddhist, or any other religious indoctrination, category or doctrine. I have no qualms about being non-denominational, for my intention is to connect with God on my own merits, to obtain spiritual enrichment rather than focusing on a particular church or religion. I will never turn away the spiritual knowledge of Metu Neter, Quran, Bible, the *Perennial Psychology of the Bhagavad*

Gita or any other worthy spiritual scripture. I construct my faith around facts that can best help me to redeem myself.

Over the years I have disciplined myself to fast, meditate, eliminate beef and pork from my diet, and wash up and purge prior to my own composed silent prayers. When I pray, I'm oriented towards Africa, the holy place where God permitted humanity to originate. While standing, I recite several composed prayers (Prayer of Mercy), and then kneel on a prayer rug, a pillow or blanket. I recite other composed prayers that bestow praises and thanks to the Creator. Throughout each day and evening I pray seven times or more, depending upon the spirit that moves me.

In the beginning it was difficult for me to pray on my knees. Still lingering was the macho tripping. If someone approached the cell while I was on my knees, I'd jump up and pretend to be doing something else. But once I understood the importance of prayer to my spiritual growth, it didn't matter if the entire prison population marched in a line past the cell during my prayers. I wouldn't budge an inch.

If not for that spiritual cultivation I would have succumbed to outside distractions. I was able to propel myself forward with a resolve never to give up, regardless of the odds or circumstances. I tested my practice of thought in the desolate climate of the Hole. As a result I was able to stand among men from any walk of life, and be confident of who I now define myself to be. Prison is no friend of mine. Its objective is to torment my body with years of isolation and seek to damage my mind with constant distractions, violence and sensory deprivation. I'm not immune to the chaos of prison but I have been able to confront and counter it.

I warn black men and women everywhere: beware of these tombs for the living called prison.

I am now finding an inner peace that has cooled the vapours of suspicion and defensiveness. Still, in prison it's tactical to be a little paranoid; it keeps me spry and on my toes. I also find solace in talking with Barbara about my innocence, my gang past, and about the plight of black people. To protect Barbara I always have avoided details of the black gang warfare or any self-incriminating acts. It is necessary to keep her safe and uninvolved in case she is summoned to court by the Attorney General, who would stoop to any level to procure evidence against me. The Attorney General's office subpoenaed Barbara once in an unsuccessful attempt to coerce incriminating evidence about me – evidence that did not exist. Barbara has become my intellectual sounding board when I choose to dwell upon the "psycho-philosophical" analysis of the when, what, how, and why, concerning gangs, politics, religion, underprivileged children, and my life.

Though I discussed many of the same topics with Evil and Treach, we had been locked up too long, and I needed an outside perspective. Feedback was important to me; I didn't want to be stuck in a time warp or be led astray by my own grand illusions. I was interested in how my book would fare in society, so I wanted bare facts to compare in order to form an analysis. I was determined despite Barbara's warning that I was exposing myself to the relentless stone throwers. Off-handedly during a conversation I told her that even if it were just a few Caucasian media people expressing their doubt and opposition, many blacks in the news business would treat me as a leper. It was a prophecy that would ring true.

In reality I had too much *moto ndani* in me to be hindered by black, Caucasian, Mexican, Asian or other myopic opinions based on superficial knowledge of me. I have become a man who will never buckle under controversy; in fact I now use it as fuel for my motivation. Naturally, there are other prisoners who have undergone major personal change and can appreciate what is required to lift oneself from the bowels of wretchedness. Through experience I knew the futility of trying to subvert or to outfox existing conditions. I would have to bend it to the will of my determination in order to rise above its madness. Of course there have been numerous prisoners who have failed, but that didn't faze me. I knew of a few black men – one in particular, Malcolm X – who underwent a miraculous change from seemingly permanent criminal to reborn black man. To me it didn't matter how prominent the individual. His or her achievements were of earthly means and therefore attainable for me and anyone else with the audacity to step forward. Who am I to even try? Just another black man, grounded, reaching for the stars with soaring thoughts and dreams.

Nothing outside of self-obstruction or death could stop my progression. I discovered time and again while reading black history that, regardless of a person's background, when one's mind, behaviour, circumstances, and spirit are aligned with destiny, the impossible can be achieved. Likewise, for a lowly person such as myself, there was a harmonized order, a dimly glimpsed path I could take to alter my negative existence. The isolation designed to emasculate me and cripple my spirit had failed. I was not the same man they had marched through the entrance to the A.C. years earlier. My rejection of the institution's contempt for humanity, and its pseudo-reform system – jumping through hoops to become a flunky or stool pigeon – was an affront to their mentality. For them my transition, my redemption, was bogus. I epitomized everything that they did not want a prisoner to be.

I was burdened no longer by the external chaos that surrounded me nor by my own miscarried thoughts. I was prepared to stand before the committee without the baggage of deception, doubt, or defeatism. During the next scheduled classification committee meeting, the dissenting members jockeyed with Hammond, who stood his ground in support of upgrading my status. Prior to the meeting, unknown to me, Hammond convinced Nelson to support the transfer. It seemed like an unshackling of heavy chains when Associate Warden Nelson agreed with Hammond in front of the entire committee.

I can visualize Nelson's hard-eyed expression when he asked, "Mr Williams, if you are given grade-A, do you plan to attack anyone in East Block?"

I assured him I did not. "In spite of what everyone thinks," I said, "I'm not a rabid animal. I don't have any plans to attack anyone. However, I want this committee to know that I am not a pacifist, and that I will defend myself under threatening circumstances. Other than that, you" – I directed my words to Nelson – "have my word as a man that I will not initiate untoward violence, nor violate my word." Then Nelson, the man most blacks and Mexicans in the Hole call the Grand Dragon of racism, approved my grade-A.

When Barbara next visited, I expressed my gratitude. Without her determination, the committee's decision would not have shifted in my favour. I knew that it was her compelling presentation that convinced counsellor Hammond. Without that, the committee would have rejected me again. She smiled broadly and said, "You're welcome."

Later that day I learned there would be a delay in my departure due to an incident in East Block. For years on death row, there have been racial flare-ups pitting blacks against Aryan Brotherhood and their allies, the Southern Mexicans (known as La Eme). This time a black man named Pride had scuffled with a wannabe Nazi who wore a swastika but looked more like an Asian or Portuguese. As a result Pride, who was said to have had his back turned, was shot dead. He was neither Crip nor Blood but a black man of controlled rage, intelligence, and a willingness to assist other blacks. When he and I used to drive iron his favourite topic was Afrocentricity and revolution. May he rest in peace.

The days of delay for my grade-A turned into weeks. There were rumours that I had ordered Pride to attack the Nazi. My transfer was suspended until the incident was investigated – some spineless inmates would say anything to prevent my arrival in East Block. While I was exercising on the yard, the prison mouthpiece Crittendon showed up, still styling a Jheri-curl Seventies hairdo. Standing outside the fence he said that there was talk of possibly allowing me to visit in East Block if I agreed to be fully shackled while the other death row prisoners roamed free in the visiting room.

He smiled at me like a reptile about to swallow a dove. With the composure of a seasoned snake handler I declined the suicidal offer.

More weeks passed. Hammond said an East Block lieutenant who had stated, "As long as I work in this condemned unit, Tookie cannot be housed here." The lieutenant apparently believed the myths documented in my C-File. Hammond told me there were numerous "kites" (notes written anonymously to prison officials by prisoners) protesting my transfer. Inmates would sometimes try reverse psychology to avoid facing their issues directly. Instead they would "warn" the prison staff in a kite that I would be attacked the moment I set foot on the yard – which the San Quentin officials would want to avoid. Little did I know what kind of weakness I was up against.

Barbara, bless her heart, believed that death row prisoners stuck together – one for one, all for all, like a college football team. In time she realized this wasn't so. When she asked why so many prisoners were opposed to me being housed in East Block, I replied, "Fear – not fear of me *per se*, but of the old me and my peers, the return of the monster presence." My peers and I were depicted as ruthless individuals pushing a rigid, compulsory programme of discipline, exercise, study, and zero tolerance for snitches. Though the zero tolerance had been true for years, the rest was a tactic to keep the rank-and-file from associating with us. When I finally entered the hornet's nest in East Block, my opponents were likely waiting to frame or fabricate incriminating statements, then report back to their masters. Not once did the possibility of being physically harmed enter my thoughts.

Still, I remained grade-A-housed under grade-B rules. Unfortunately more CIDF (confidential information disclosure form) documents were being added to my C-File with absurd allegations. Supposedly I was in collusion to "hit" certain prisoners and guards in East Block. I found myself experiencing a flashback, a "visual reckoning." I again reviewed my cataclysmic past, in vivid colour and in all its horror. The doomed life I had loved, praised, and was foolishly willing to die for began to fade into darkness. Sleeping one night, I saw a powerfully bright halo of light encircling enormous crowds of children. I hadn't the faintest idea what was going on. I awoke drenched in sweat, wondering if it was another omen, and why. There was no need for a warning. I couldn't forget the earthly hell, and I surely did not wish to return to it. I had made a covenant with Mwenyezi (Almighty) to embrace a complete change. The fervour of my determination would not allow me to deviate from that goal.

More than a month later, the lieutenant who had objected to my being in East Block was transferred, but there were still inmates whispering dissent into Hammond's ears. Fed up with the chickenhearted controversy, Hammond announced that whoever felt uncomfortable with my being on the yard should request reassignment to another yard. I heard there were quite a few yard jumpers. When the day arrived for my departure, I left a lot of books, food, and personal care items with Kerm to distribute among our peers. I wasn't worried about not seeing them again. I felt that once the prison authorities observed my behaviour for a year or two, my peers would leave the Hole as well.

The moment had finally come. I could vacate the hellhole that had stolen a small part of me and vandalized so many other lives. As I exited the building, a committee member who was absent the day I received my grade-A was walking in. He hysterically questioned the escorting guards.

"Where are you taking Tookie?"

"He's being rehoused in East Block," replied a guard.

The committee member's face contorted grotesquely. He spat out, "Tookie, you're very lucky I wasn't in classification that day. I would never have recommended grade-A for you."

"Being lucky had nothing to do with it," I responded. "Prayers work, especially when faced with the malicious minds of others."

THIRTY-FIVE

Redemption . . .
Step Forward

Arriving in East Block was an odd experience. I actually felt butterflies in my stomach. While I was being placed in a holding cell, Chico was being escorted out of an adjacent one. I asked him where was he going; "To the Hole, cuz," he responded. Though rough around the edges, with an explosive temper, Chico was cool. He was the flip-side of Young Kerm, who had unmistakable rage in his voice, posture and behaviour. What I respected most about Chico was his appetite for learning; he was a gifted mathematician. I jokingly called him "wild man."

I was housed in 3-EB-106 next door to an Indian I befriended named Apache. He conveniently ended up being in charge of the phone. The following morning on the yard I was cheerfully greeted by Herk, Mad Dog, Hollaway, Cricket, Taco, Wimp, Little L, Ex-Lax, Ant, Louisiana Smooth, Ocean, Square, Silent (Kwesi), Doggs, and Grandpa. When the hoopla died down, I was embraced by an evolving brother named K.C. whom I've known for many years. Though he wasn't into the gang life when we first met, he was a personable brother with heart. In addition to sharing the fact of being black and battling this killing machine called "capital punishment," we both strove for knowledge and freedom.

Scanning the yard, I saw that some were nervous – those who had something to hide. There was apprehension in their

little eyes and in their strained smiles. It didn't matter to me.
I planned to associate only with a few who had proven to be
stand-up men over the years. As long as I was left alone,
nobody had anything to worry about. I was harmless. If my
interest had been revenge, there were so many prison
provocateurs and riff-raff, I would have had to arm myself
with weapons in both hands, and some strapped to other
parts of my body, to make sure I didn't miss anybody. No
matter how deeply I despised particular individuals, they
were not worth my violating my spiritual resolve.

Later that same day I received a visit from Barbara. After
a brief hug, I dined on vending machine food while we
chatted about our children's books and other projects. I was
aware of being closely monitored by guards, not just in the
visiting room but also when I was on the yard, tier, and in
the cell. Barbara noticed that I was under critical surveillance
in the visiting area, and was appalled when I told her guards
were making side bets about how long I'd remain in East
Block. They had no way of knowing that I was no longer the
same dolt they believed they were betting on.

While those who opposed me were lost in their collusions
and hypotheticals about my next move, I forged ahead with
renewed enthusiasm. It was as though I was living in a
subjective world impervious to their negative vibes. Having
overcome my *own* ignorance, I can understand those who
remain blinded by the same dense veil that once covered my
eyes. I hope they will one day honour themselves with
knowledge, dignity and the wisdom to recognize the disguises
and trickery of the true enemy.

Returning to East Block was like jumping from the fire
into the frying pan but I rejected its old pecking-order
struggles and mind games. I had no plans to get caught up in
its stagnant conditioning. I didn't believe in existing just
because I had a pulse. There is more to life than steel bars,
senseless barbarity, prisoners, guards, gun towers, and the
other hokum. Though physically I could not leave, mentally
I could escape to Africa or beyond the sun's distance, ninety-
three million miles from earth.

Every aspect of my struggle was devised to overcome the elements that held me in bondage, beginning with myself, then working outward. I was beginning to understand that my experiences with these dysfunctional elements – the drug addiction, poverty, gangsterism, racism, and other roadblocks – were just excuses. No longer would my life, my being, be dictated by blind ignorance. Nor would I ever again allow the excuse of circumstances to dictate whom I should be. It was routine studying and questioning that prompted my soul searching. I began to develop a sense of critical reasoning from which sprang the first stirrings of conscience. This shocked me. This was the moment redemption fused with my life.

Until that moment I didn't have an inkling what was happening to me. There was no defining moment. I neither heard a voice of reason nor felt a jolt of energy. Even now, attempting to clarify this experience, I fall short. I don't expect anyone who's not had this sort of experience to comprehend it or be able to relate to the redemptive struggle of a condemned man.

Everywhere there are racists posing as liberals, conservatives, moderates and religious folks who believe black men are inferior, are incapable of atonement and an overall change. I know I'm expected to languish in violent stupidity on death row until my execution, but I cannot. This prison environment is not a reflection of me, nor am I addicted to its deadening and violent manipulations.

1995 saw a succession of arrivals on East Block: first Chico, then Treach, Ghetto, Evil, and Kerm. Each of these men entered with an intention to maintain the highest order of discipline. To have all of us on the same yard again was a joyous and proud moment for me, knowing I had held firm during this extended test of my discipline.

Meanwhile, Barbara attended the American Booksellers' Association annual meeting in Chicago. The convention centre was larger than a football field, and with multiple floors. It took Barbara two exhausting days to visit the 1,000 booths. Many publishers found favour with my work but shied away because of where I was incarcerated. One black man, Amos Wilson, was developing his own publishing company and showed an interest in my work. Wilson was a black psychologist and author of several books addressing the dilemma of black youth. But he died suddenly before we could connect again with him. May the brother rest in peace.

After walking the floors of the convention for two days, Barbara located a publisher, Rosen Publishing Group, whose books were aimed chiefly at schools and libraries. They agreed to publish my work. The process was tedious, having to meet the syntax standards of *two* editors – Barbara and the publisher's editors – but after months of correcting and rewriting, the book was ready. Barbara told me that the several chapters in my single children's book had been transformed into an eight-book series. The series was published in 1996.

The books quickly were accepted in poor black school districts, in classrooms and libraries, and in middle-class schools as well. Gangs had become a growth industry among middle-class white children as well as minority kids. In South Central Los Angeles at West Athens Elementary School, students asked if they could take the books home. Among educators, this sort of request is unprecedented. The West Athens school principal, Barbara Lake, was quoted in the *Los Angeles Times*, saying that she "could think of no other set of books that prompted parents to jam the school's switchboard, asking where they could buy their very own copies."

When the mainstream media got wind of anti-violence children's books authored by a death row prisoner, their curiosity triggered further investigation. NBC's *Today* show did a story on the books. Bryant Gumbel asked his reporter whether I received any money from the sales of the books. The reporter replied that I was donating all of my proceeds. After that reporters and journalists across America and around the world scrambled for telephone interviews with me and with Barbara.

Some journalists thought I had a hidden agenda and set out to expose me to the public. Others, after meeting me for an interview, would comment on my sincerity and intelligence – and then in their articles stick daggers into my back to appease the gods of "balanced" journalism. But no one could ignore the books' power to capture the attention of those troubled youth who disliked reading, but chose my books over many others. Magazines and newspaper articles displayed beaming faces of children, parents, teachers, and librarians endorsing the books. My colleagues and I have since collaborated on two other books, *The Sacred Eye Of The Falcon* and *Eye Of The Warrior*, in addition to *Unchained Voices*, and are pursuing a publisher for these as well.

In 1997, Barbara and I came up with an idea for an educational website (www.Tookie.com) which has had thousands of Internet visitors from all walks of life. Another children's book, *Life In Prison*, was written for junior and high school youths. While Barbara juggled her job, media interviews, and both of our literary projects, we were confronted with another battle. Rosen Publishing was not honouring its agreement to give a percentage of its profit on my books to Mothers Against Gangs, a non-profit organization headed by Sandra Davis. I wasn't surprised. After meeting Rosen himself for the first time, I told Barbara I didn't trust him. Having been wicked most of my life, I can sniff out iniquity in others. It came as no surprise when, years later, Rosen tried to take credit for the book in an interview. Barbara ended up hiring an attorney from New York to nullify the contract with Rosen. Barbara found another company eager to publish *Life In Prison*. After its 1998 publication, it went on to win two national book honours, including one from the American Library Association.

During this time I decided to embrace Swahili names. Treach and Evil chose several that best depicted the man I had become. Treach chose Ajamu, meaning, "He that fights for what he wants." Evil chose Niamke, "God's gift." The third name all three of us have adopted is Kamara/Camara:

"He who teaches from experience." Evil became Ajani, "He who fights for possession," and Treach became Adisa, "one who makes himself clear."

As part of my transition and redemption I'm extremely proud to have as my Swahili name, Ajamu Niamke Kamara, which resonates with who I am. I feel no allegiance or kinship to my slave names despite their being patronymic (a name descended from the father). Although I am on death row, my life has new meaning. I no longer feel as if my existence is of no consequence. It was only natural that in my reawakening and cleansing I discarded the old and adopted the new. With the exception of my mother and Barbara, everybody else had written me off the moment I was sentenced to die. And I was mentally dead up to the precise second I made the decision to redefine and redeem myself. And so...I am alive. The maze that once appeared to have no exit has been forced open for passage. Hear me, black man! Indian! Caucasian! Asian! Mexican! Jew! Arab! Others! There is a path out of desolation!

As my life continued to evolve I was still doing interviews over the phone and face-to-face. One of the best and most enlightening visits was with Barbara, David Evans, and three representatives of South Africa: Joanne Thomas, Mohau Magkobeyana, and Penny Foley, from the Center for Conflict Resolution Youth Project and the Johannesburg's Joint Enrichment Project. Two of the three arrived dressed in colourful African garb, but had to change into other clothes to meet San Quentin's clothing colour rules.

This did not spoil the visit. The experience was unforgettable. Adisa engaged in a dialogue with Mohau, and Ajani and I talked with David, Barbara, Joanne and Penny. I had read about the kindred spirit existing between blacks in America and the blacks in the Motherland, but I never expected to experience such a powerful feeling that drew me close to Joanne and Mohau. Other than our black faces and ancestry, we shared social blights: poverty, drugs, racism, disease, street gangs, illiteracy, rapid prison growth, Afrocide, and other madnesses.

I was taken aback by brother Mohau's humility and congenial disposition. Here was a black man from the Motherland who had no misunderstanding about what constituted his manhood, nor did he display street thug swagger. His words were articulate without venom. His fortitude, humble spirit and absence of arrogance was in total contrast to what I saw in America. His inner warrior shined with reserved dignity. Not once did the words "nigger" or "bitch" enter our dialogue. Meeting Mohau pointed me toward a deeper learning of the art of being humble while maintaining a resolute pride.

After taking a few group photos, we sat for thirty more minutes discussing our foundling project, the Internet Project For Street Peace. This would connect kids in the United States and in South Africa, to communicate, learn, and be mentored via email and computer chat room. I wanted children on both continents to evolve into culturally conscious adults, bridging the gap that we adults have failed to close. The encounter was refreshing, allowing me to reclaim the nexus severed since African slavery began to claim black lives, families and psyches. As my visitors rose to leave, we made plans to keep in touch and explore other ideas to bridge and benefit our continents.

Later that year I received a visit from actor Mike Farrell, a star of the comedy sitcom *MASH,* political activist and chairman of Death Penalty Focus. Barbara, Adisa, and an associate of Mike's were also present. We discussed the possibility of creating a movie out of my memoirs. I listened intently to the conversation, aware that this was an embryonic stage in what would become a long and challenging project. Actually I know of only one person capable of transforming our ideas into tangible realities: Barbara. I call her the human angel.

While walking around with Barbara and Mike inside the visiting area, the topic of my redemption surfaced. I stressed that had I not undertaken a dynamic interior change, there would be no atonement for me. I was able to eliminate the vile nature of my past – the impulsive behaviour, foul language, irrationality, vengeance, and non-spiritual existence – through reflection and prayer. No longer do I possess murderous dreams that killed my potential for having visions of hope and progress. But my redemption is small and self-serving if I fail to assist the violence-ridden communities from which I came. I wasn't sure Mike understood precisely what I was trying to say. But a person doesn't have to understand the structure of a rose to acknowledge its beauty. As long as he recognized I was not the same person I had been – that was good enough for me.

I told Mike and the others that my redemption was not a hazy fantasy in which a street thug becomes a good guy and lives happily ever after. I said that my mind was no longer polluted, and that the decades of personal vice and of crippin', of the deeply rooted psychological illness which drove me, had been resolved. But the cruel, desolate reality of prison is unforgiving. As long as I remain imprisoned, I will continue to be challenged to remain a human being and not a beast. Just because I chose to readjust my thoughts and behaviour, the small claustrophobic world of death row did not shift. Anyone in prison may suffer a quick, unexpected death by being in the wrong place at the wrong time. That reality is unchanged.

Death row is constructed for punishment and execution, not for reform.

THIRTY-SIX

A Woman Called Mother Africa

In 1998, Barbara told me that Nobel Peace Prize winner Archbishop Desmond Tutu of South Africa had written to me in support of my children's book series. I responded with a letter of gratitude and enclosed a pencil-drawn portrait of Desmond Tutu. Nothing is sweeter and more humbling than being accepted by your own people, those who can relate to your personal triumph over self and the insidious tentacles of colour prejudice. But without the dynamic of my inner rage, I would not have been able to overcome my past and the atrocious prison madness to move as far forward as I have. My brothers and sisters, wherever you may be throughout this world, I broke out of my mental prison years ago. Can you accept the challenge?

Working on my memoirs, the children's books, the portraits, and maintaining a low profile has not prevented prison authorities and their minions from lurking in the background. The day I was escorted by several guards after a visit straight to the Hole was no surprise to me. The following day I received a 115 rules violation report and a CIDF. It identified me in some off-the-wall conspiracy to provide inmates on East Block AD/Seg Yard-6 with a hacksaw blade (which never existed) to cut a portion of the AD/Seg Yard-5 fence to enter and attack the Aryan Brotherhood and the Eme (Southern Mexicans). The authorities concocted another story: the hacksaw blade was to be used in my attempt to escape from death row. Utter foolishness!

No matter how many times I end up in the Hole, the initial shock of its solitude and feelings of helplessness can weary the mind. It didn't matter how tough, peaceful, transformed, brave, or confident I was; the Hole was an immediate reminder of my insignificance in the penal hierarchy. There was nothing I could do. I knew my refutations would fall on deaf ears, and to present witnesses on my behalf was meaningless. It was not unlike being in criminal court, where I was presumed guilty and not about to be proven innocent. Literally, my hands were tied.

Barbara contacted Mike Farrell, who called Senator Tom Hayden and Jessie Jackson, Sr. The four of them, with other signatories, drafted and signed a letter of appeal which they mailed to the San Quentin warden and the Director of Corrections to question what had been done to me. I had been in the Hole for more than a month when I was taken to classification – and found not guilty. Though I was long since accustomed to such tactics, Barbara was shocked by them. Here on death row, I explained to Barbara, I'm the bogeyman, ogre, or the sacrificial lamb, depending on the requirements of the prison authorities. Nothing changes here.

In 1999, with Barbara, I developed the Internet Project For Street Peace. The programme was based on *Life In Prison* after it had attracted attention in America and a number of other countries with youth gang problems. Officials from several countries expressed an interest in setting up Internet Street Peace hubs to become a part of the network. To my astonishment Winnie Madikizela Mandela, Nelson Mandela's ex-wife and a member of South Africa's Parliament, expressed immediate interest. I had read articles about Winnie's struggle to free Nelson Mandela and to champion the people's cause for freedom. She was a beautiful Queen warrior who proudly stood up and spoke out against the apartheid system. Equally amazing was that from San Quentin's death row, the reverberations of my unchained words were heard by this remarkable woman called Mother

Africa. When Barbara told me Winnie was preparing to visit me in person – well, to say I was honoured was an understatement.

On October 28, 1999, Mrs Mandela crossed the Atlantic Ocean to grace me with her presence at San Quentin State Prison, to address my youth work and children's books and to attend fundraisers for the Internal Street Peace Network. Later I learned that our visit was delayed because Winnie's bodyguard didn't want the prison staff to touch her. The media awaited her arrival outside the prison walls. They were scrambling to interview her.

I wasn't certain how I should greet Winnie. Should I be formal or informal? But the moment I saw her, the ancestral ties were immediately felt, and instinctively we embraced with smiles and a kiss on each cheek. Her features, stature, mannerisms, and soft voice reminded me of my mother's. A black female guard had the entire visiting room rearranged to accommodate Winnie. Yes, even the black guards working that day, male and female, couldn't play down the fact that Mother Africa herself was visiting a death row prisoner.

With me, seated between Barbara and Winnie, present were Betty R. Soskin, Adisa, Ajani, Robin (an Associated Press journalist), California state political representatives, Winnie's spiritual adviser Shaka, and her bodyguard. While we sat around the connected tables, we broached the subject of the death penalty. Winnie was curious about the statistics and about the treatment of blacks on death row. She expressed her profound opposition to the barbarism of America's capital punishment apparatus. She vowed to visit whenever possible, until I regained my freedom.

I told Winnie about the time I was scheduled for execution in the late 1980s but my attorney went missing in action. I said he was probably at some Whites Only country club resort sipping pina coladas and it slipped his mind that his black client was scheduled to die. I was approached by a San Quentin representative who asked me if I understood the execution procedures to be carried out. Infuriated, I rolled my eyes and responded, "What's there to know?" Then I launched into a rapid description of the macabre ritual of capital punishment. "I know about the last meal, the priest's viaticum, the brand new state-issued clothing to die in, the Warden's inquiry about the prisoner's final words, the march to the gas chamber, being strapped in the death chair, the voyeuristic white strangers peeking at their own mortality vicariously through me, cyanide tablets being dropped into a liquid solution; then silent cheers for one less nigger." When I finished answering the questions, as I told Winnie, I suggested that the representative and the guards could "all go to hell."

Winnie responded hotly, in her lilting accented English, "The death penalty should be terminated across the board, wherever it exists."

When the conversation came around to gangs, I touched upon how a large percentage of blacks on death row were maintaining their own gang peace. I talked about the periodic eruption of racial wars in prisons that prompted blacks from diverse backgrounds and/or affiliations to band together to defend themselves. It would astonish middle-class blacks to know that the Crips and Bloods, those eternal enemies, have banded together along with other black men against their prison opposition. Many of these men, involved in the over three-decades-long gang rivalry, have real esteem for one another. Because of that ethnic solidarity I now see only black *men*, and no differences between Crips and Bloods. In prison blacks find themselves battling a discriminatory system, racist inmates, and guards who directly or indirectly support inmates' racial foolishness.

Talking to Winnie provided me with an opportunity to vent against the hypocritical, imprisoned "sick minds" that feel the need to despise blacks more than the institutional beast that can devour us all. I explained that in prison, racial war is indifferent to whether a black prisoner is peaceful, wise, respected, young or old. His colour will pull him into the madness. He has no choice but to fight . . . or die. When the guard on the gun rail fires into a crowd, only a prisoner dies – usually a black prisoner.

With time winding down, I suggested we take some photos. While we waited for the guard to take a picture, a tactful Barbara asked Winnie to convince me to keep my eyes open; I always close them before a photo is taken. After a few unsuccessful attempts, I managed to keep them open to a degree. Though most of the pictures taken were of Winnie and me, everybody in our entourage was able to join in. Several other black families asked if they could take a photo with us. Winnie was gracious, but I inquired about whether she was tired of taking pictures. Her response: "This is your moment. I came to see you, and I'll stand here and take pictures all day if you want."

After the photo sessions I asked Winnie if she wanted something to eat from the vending machines, to which she replied, "Just some bottled water." The machines don't stock bottled water – but to our surprise the San Quentin spokesman Crittendon volunteered to locate water and paper cups. His gesture caught me off-guard. Perhaps there is salvation after all for Crittendon, whom most prisoners and visitors consider to be an Uncle Tom.

How Barbara managed to overcome the political bureaucracy to bring Winnie to America, I can't imagine. God was working overtime through this woman. I was both grateful and proud of her. It was a gracious gesture for Mother Africa to visit me in this despicable place, not unlike one that had held her former husband captive for so many years.

Time was running out. Adisa and I tried to cram many questions into the few minutes left with Winnie. Then the speaker crackled loudly with a female voice: "Visiting is over, visiting is over." I was annoyed and wanted more time. Sensing my irritation, she lightly patted my hand and said, "Don't worry, Stan, there will be other times. I plan to give you a Swahili name too." The 7,200 seconds I spent with Winnie were more than an acknowledgement and a show of support. Her visit also created an everlasting nexus that linked us in a circle of kindred spirits. After our warm goodbyes – I thanked Winnie for the hundredth time –

Adisa, Ajari, and I filed into a long line of prisoners waiting to be escorted back to the cells.

Talking to Barbara later on the phone, she told me what had happened when they left the East Block visiting room. They heard what sounded like a hundred voices singing in Winnie's native tongue. A throng of prisoners, unable to see Winnie, were serenading her as she left the visiting room. I extend my thanks to all those Brothers, though I don't know who they were. *Asante santa!* Thank you very much.

That same night I smiled to myself, recalling that Winnie had said the highlight of her trip was seeing me. Being able to visit and talk with the woman called Mother Africa was a spiritual experience that profoundly touched my life. I'd never given my mortality any serious thought, but this night I made a decision. Whether my demise is of natural causes, or my soul is abruptly snatched by unnatural causes beyond my control, I want my body buried in Africa underneath a Yohimbe tree; or my cremated ashes scattered over Africa's Blue Nile river to feed the fishes and other organisms. Even in death, I can engender life. Peace and blessings to you, Ms Winnie Madikizela Mandela. I'm grateful and proud to have met you.

THIRTY-SEVEN

Black Phoenix Rising

Because I am guilty of being black, I have learned to expect the unexpected. After Winnie's visit I saw an increase in harassment, surveillance, confidential informant documents, and cell searches. In April 2000, I received a CDC 128-B chrono falsely accusing me of gang leadership, and all of my peers received a chrono for associating with me. A particular black lickspittle sergeant told Chico during a 602 hearing, "I don't care about you or any of the others. It's Tookie we want." After I filed an inmate appeal 602 form, the chrono was supposedly rescinded and destroyed.

In May 2000, I documented an officer positioned on the gunrail with a video camera focused on Yard-1 and taping *only my* movements and interactions. Obviously the video was meant to either capture a specific association or something untoward that could later be substantiated. I hadn't done anything improper for nearly a decade, and I associate with everybody on the yard: black, Indian, Cuban, Iranian, Caucasian, Mexican, Greek, Russian, and others.

That June, I received a CIDF labelling me a Crip leader and implicating me in an illogical conspiracy theory. The CIDF's allegation about me was as follows: "To attempt to gather support of other grade-A condemned prisoners of gang affiliation (i.e., Crips, Bloods, and Eme), to assault staff in retaliation for the death row contact visiting being discontinued." As a result I filed another appeal form stating that while the Warden and Associate Warden rejected the confidential informers' statements, they refused to remove the negative CIDF from my C-File and were unwilling to acknowledge my charges of being falsely gang-profiled and harassed.

In October 2000 I received another outlandish CIDF accusing me of having a position in a disruptive Crip group. Again I countered with a 602 form, still pending at this writing. Those staff members with vindictive minds could not imagine that I, a black with a gang past, could change.

The CDC, like any corrupt government, has *carte blanche* with prisoners – to harass, set up, brutalize, lie, cover up, demonize, and murder, in addition to conducting sanctioned executions. There are prison guards just as inhuman and irrational as some prisoners. A case in point: the 1971 Stanford Prison Experiment, which divided students into two groups. One group posed as prisoners, the other as guards, in a makeshift prison setting. The six-day experiment saw a barbaric transformation in attitude among those students role-playing as prison guards, resulting in the termination of the experiment. Yet that was but a scaled-down version of the full-blown madness behind these walls, where some of the most sadistic minds belong to guards. Some of the males and females working in prison go through a Jekyll and Hyde metamorphosis. Their own family members and friends would be appalled to discover how odious, conniving, mendacious, perverted, insidious, and animalistic they can be at work. Or perhaps not.

It's an act of *jujitsu*, fighting an institution that not only protects its own, but even *polices* itself when charges of malfeasance are brought forward. Where is the accountability? To address an injustice, I use whatever resources are at my disposal within the prison's jurisdiction, and when that fails – as it usually does – I seek recourse outside the wall. But regardless of the prison's tactics, the power of faith and perseverance has taken me higher. With all the shovelled dirt used to try to bury me alive, it was faith that enabled me to rise up. The more I'm targeted with their madness, the more people in society come on board to support my children's books, other projects, and me.

On November 18, 2001, Barbara excitedly told me that Mario Fehr, a member of the Swiss Parliament, had nominated me for the Nobel Peace Prize. Barbara warned me to prepare for the naysayers. That evening many of the major news stations on television and radio reported the nomination and Barbara was quickly inundated by print, radio and TV reporters requesting an interview with both of us. The circus atmosphere treated the nominations as if I had already won the Peace Prize. I braced myself for the same media to flip their script and undercut the nomination. How dare a destitute black man, non-Ivy Leaguer, co-founder of a notorious gang, and a death row prisoner, be nominated for the world's most prestigious award? It was an insult to racists, cynics, and sanctimonious people everywhere.

Coming out of the woodwork to vilify my nomination were law enforcement agencies, death penalty proponents, victim rights groups, newspaper columnists and San Quentin's mouthpiece, Crittendon. In the one-sided mudslinging I've been referred to as a criminal beast, a moral coward, a serial killer (please note that 99.9% of serial killers are *Caucasian*), an unrepentant thug, a black Hitler, and a few other unmentionable names reflecting America's toxic racism.

Not a few people were hot under the collar that Mr Fehr, a white European, had the audacity to nominate a black face from America's death row. Overlooked in the wailing was Fehr's courage in defying racism and the popular political slant which supports capital punishment. He did not prejudge me on the basis of colour, race, allegations, or circumstances. Instead Fehr focused on the merits of my transition and the efficacy of my redemptive output to help underprivileged children. I'm grateful for his courageous action.

My life mirrors the lives of numerous black men on San Quentin's death row. Many have arrived apathetic, distraught, fearful, enraged, and bent on further destruction. Their intent to survive at all costs can be rerouted and channelled into an intent to rise above one's own madness. Though I was trained on violence, I've discovered that strength can be found in the might of the intellect, in spirituality, in creativity, and in progress. I am not the violent genetic misfit incapable of change that the courts, society, media, law enforcement and prison administration believe I am. None of these people really know me. They only know *of* me.

By consistent discipline and practice I developed an instinctual consciousness that helps me to address any given situation. It was never easy to detach myself from the prison's procrustean effort to render me an automaton. The odds never favoured my staying alive, before I was imprisoned or after.

Neither my peers nor I could have anticipated the rising hunger for knowledge among both younger and older blacks undone by the draining force of ganghood. I believe behind these walls there is a conscious awakening – an untapped treasure of black minds, Crips, Bloods and others – capable of altering the mindset of a multitude. I have listened to their perspectives on life, politics, religion and the plight of black people, perspectives communicated with a keen sense of logic. Black society could benefit by studying those of us in prison, seeking creative perspectives to address ills that plague our communities. The crisis demands more than posturing from our black intelligentsia, think tanks, politicians, community leaders, religious sects, and the black citizenry. Whether in prison or behind the invisible bars of public society, no black face can run, hide, dismiss, or intellectualize the problem away. It requires more than theorizing, complaining, rapping, pointing fingers, or fighting among ourselves to make an impact.

Many of our men have been criminalized. They are spiritually deprived, cultural iconoclasts, woman abusers, neglectful fathers, drug-ridden, violent, illiterate and self-destructive. I suffered from these vices; they finally morphed into psychological illness. The infirm state of my mind was not genetic but rather psychological instability, a survival adaptation to an environment that promised much but delivered only degrees of failure. It wasn't too late for me to initiate my own self-therapy.

I have forever awakened the true black man within me. Burned in effigy, with no regrets, is my misconception of manhood, culture, education, life and the world. Death row became the Gethsemane where I overcame my hypocritical conscience and my self-hatred No longer the possessor of a radioactive mind polluted by self-destructiveness, I now exist with an analytical mentality and a thunderous heart that beats with inner peace, atonement and truth. Whether I'm dismissed from this physical world today or tomorrow, I take pleasure in knowing I defied the odds to embody a process of positive in me and other people.

In my hostile past I strove for thug greatness; now I am intent on helping children discover their inner potential. Black redemption is my *ankh*, in every form and fashion. I'm learning to "master self" while rising from the ashes of madness.

THIRTY-EIGHT

Sons of the Father

Because there are so many black fathers trapped within America's prison system, an entire nation could be grown from the roots of our abandoned children. Mass incarceration splits families and foments a son's resentment for his father. As a youth I often felt emptiness in my life, and not simply for lack of a father's presence. My biological father was a sad example of fatherhood. I yearned for an esteemed black male figure who projected a dynamic image I could strive to emulate or to surpass. In different circumstances my chances for success would have increased considerably.

My struggling mother was a true warrior for motherhood, but I could not absorb the male image from her. There are thousands of fatherless households where male youths grow up to become responsible adults. Perhaps I was just needier. In my early life, absent a strong fatherly presence, I launched a doomed odyssey for a maleness to fashion as my own. Although my mother and grandmother contributed fortitude, wisdom, dignity and love, my psyche rejected their femininity as a base on which to build my manhood.

My defiance was not an attack against my mother, but an effort to establish my manhood with no father around. I despised him for not being there to support our family. With my father missing in action, I picked up mixed messages about what constituted fatherhood. I promised myself I'd never be anything like my father, but along the way I too became selfish, forgetting my vow, and was incapable of taking care of a single son, never mind a second one. I'm past my disdain for the father I never knew. I've forgiven him, whether he accepts it or not. But could my sons forgive me?

Apart from my relationship with my mother, the closest family for me was the Crips. In the ultimate display of fatherly irresponsibility, I forsook my sons to barnstorm throughout South Central LA in the name of crippin'. I had only faint memories of Travon as a child, when I periodically showed up to have sex with his mother Bonnie. I was no more than a sperm donor: when that job was done, fathering wasn't necessary. From the moment of Travon's birth, on October 30, 1973, I can count on two hands the times I was in his presence, and on one hand the times I held him in my arms before I was incarcerated six years later.

I didn't begin to become a father to Travon until he was twenty. That's when he began to accompany my mother to visit me, which she did once or twice a year.

I remember his first visit to San Quentin vividly. The visiting area resonated with the sounds of screeching babies, children's laughter, and vocal admonitions from parents, mostly black and brown families visiting their loved ones. Many had travelled long distances for a few precious hours.

When I arrived, my mother was already sitting on the stool, using her handkerchief to clean the phone that usually smelled like bad breath. My hulking son stood impatiently behind her. Both my mother and Travon watched as the guard locked the steel-meshed door behind me and removed the modified handcuffs – a larger-than-normal pair of cuffs with a long linking chain in the middle to accommodate individuals too big for the standard cuffs. With the handcuffs off I felt a momentary sense of freedom. Despite being imprisoned, I experience other forms of freedom when I pray, type, meditate, exercise, shower, draw portraits, use the phone, study, assist youths – and during personal visits. I looked through the smudged, scratched window, marvelling at the beauty of my aging mother as she began to pray with her head slightly bowed. Her soft voice and angelic smile masked the grief of having a son on death row. I knew that under the cloak of darkness, back at home, the emotional camouflage disappeared as she crumbled into a weeping mother, sharing tears with a huge number of other lamenting mothers throughout South Central, as well as California and the nation.

Maintaining control is a common discipline among black mothers everywhere. They are accustomed to bearing the brunt of their son's or daughter's misfortunes. But my mother was genuinely happy to be talking with me face to face. Occasionally I'd glance at Travon, who kept throwing up his hands as if to say, "When's my turn?" I knew he was anxious, but I motioned for him to be patient.

Minutes later my mother handed the phone to Travon, who sat down on the stool. He was a mirror image of me, with thick black eyebrows, brown complexion, and massive size. It was awkward talking to my son, knowing I had neglected him for all of his young life. I told Travon I understood if he resented me, and I wanted to apologize for committing the ultimate sin, forsaking him to a fatherless childhood.

Back in the day, fatherhood scared me. Travon was not an unwanted son, but I was an unfit father, too immature to enlighten him about life. I admitted to him that I was ashamed for not being there for him. I had been plagued with a corrupt concept of manhood that would have jeopardized his future. I told Travon that at that time, I was no good for him or myself, and that I wasn't living. I was dying. I would have brought him down right with me.

I explained to my son that my maturity allowed me to present him with an olive branch and a message of wisdom. I gave him kudos for the wonderful job he was doing in taking care of his family. Though there was a lot for him to absorb during our visit, he appeared to appreciate my forthrightness. In between sharing the phone with my mother, I stressed to Travon that it was never his or Bonnie's fault, that the blame rested entirely on my shoulders. I wanted my son to know that I regretted not being there for him, that I would never forsake him again. My heart pounded, knowing I could hug neither my mother nor my son. But, I thought, one day it will happen. One day I will be able to say, "I love my son." It was impossible to make up for all the lost time, but I hoped he and I could establish a new beginning.

When the visit ended, we said our goodbyes and promised to keep in touch. Over the course of months and years of phone calls and annual visits with him and my mother, I tried my inexperienced hand at being a father from death row. Though I wanted desperately to assist Travon, I possessed nothing of material value. I had nothing but words – then again, what could I tell a son who was succeeding in life where I had blundered? In the back of my mind I often wondered, "Does Travon resent me?" He had every right to feel embittered, but one day he would have to give it up, or it will consume him.

Through Barbara I was in contact with Stan, another son whom I abandoned. His misfortune was in trying to follow the path I had trod. Stan was an Imperial Court Crip and had christened himself "Little Tookie" in my honour. Older Crips who knew Stan said his attitude was reminiscent of me at that age. Travon had told me that he had met Stan once, that they hung out for a while, and then parted ways. Other than being fathered by me, they seemed to be from different worlds. Needless to say Stan was out there crippin' like there was no tomorrow and masking his frustrations with intoxicants. Barbara offered to locate him so we could establish communication.

It was Tony Bogard who found Stan for us. Barbara provided him with a place to rehabilitate. He cleaned up nicely and seemed ready to start anew. I shuddered at the thought of Stan telling Barbara he wanted to end up on death row with his father, even after she explained that it was possible for him to visit me face-to-face. Barbara had even lined up a job for Stan – but he faded back into the madness of the streets, gone just like that, and this time no one could find him. I knew we were at a critical point, with a son announcing he is willing to give up his life to be in prison with his father. I hoped he was just "jaw-jackin'."

Later I learned that Stan had been convicted of murder and sentenced to life in prison. Prior to leaving the courtroom he addressed the jury: "My father Tookie will get every one of you!" Of course this statement triggered a report to San Quentin officials. I was in the Hole at that time and was allowed to view the document before it was placed in my C-File. I was trying to obtain grade-A and wanted no negatives for authorities to use against me.

Stan and I started corresponding through the very slow prison mail system. In the beginning I found it difficult to decipher my son's street vernacular. In time I convinced him to clarify his communications so that I could understand him. Like Travon, Stan was enthusiastic about increasing his vocabulary. However, Stan doubted his ability to read legal documents and relied upon others to do it for him. He even tried to foist this responsibility on me by sending his trial transcripts, which were lost in the mail. His hard-headedness was an unpleasant reminder of how I used to be.

Throughout the years I received bits of information about how Stan was doing. While TC, from the West Side Crips, was passing through San Quentin on his way to another prison, we talked about my incarcerated son. TC had met him at Mule Creek prison, and he had nothing but respect for him. He confirmed that Stan looked exactly like me, and he was a low-rider, meaning he was quick to indulge in violence. Another East Side Crip, Scrappy, arriving on death row, told me he knew Travon and that Stan was his cellie – cellmate – when they were in the Los Angeles County Jail.

Although I began to receive letters from Stan, corresponding between prisons was a slow and frustrating process. Our letters were often lost, destroyed, or confiscated. Missing are more than twenty irreplaceable photographs I sent to him over the years. After two decades of being trampled by the whimsy of the goon squad (a specialized prison gang unit), who have expropriated hundreds of pictures of me, alone and with others, I thought they'd have had enough by now. But it was a blessing being able to hear from both Travon and Stan. I hope that one day we can reconnect as father and sons in society.

On death row I have met numerous black men the same age as my sons or younger, like Whack, Jamal, Shawn, Asikiwe and Whiz. I didn't have to wonder why there were so many – young and old – on death row. Everywhere I turn, our black sons are milling around in this pit of death, waiting for a favourable outcome that may never be. Though ensnared in the web of the racist capital punishment system, I continue trying to set a noble example for my sons and others. Faith and discipline are the pillars of my resolve. I believe my sons can draw from those principles.

When I do talk with Travon or write to Stan, I try to enter their viewpoint in order to familiarize myself with their interior lives and their aspirations, to encourage them. My efforts with them recall my own childhood, when my mother tried in vain to impress her wisdom upon me. During an early conversation with Travon I learned that though he works in the medical field, his ambition was in music, to be a rapper, producer and lyricist. For a short period Travon had been influenced by his Crip legacy and had considered pursuing that disruptive life, but he spurned the enticements of the gang life. I applaud his triumph.

The situation was different with Stan. Both his mother and I were missing in parental action. He was raised by his mother's elderly grandfather and his grandmother (rest in peace), both of whom died while Stan was young. In spite of his grandfather's love, concern, and dedication, he went down this most unpromising road to imprisonment.

But Stan didn't wind up on death row. There are enough individuals here who *are* related by blood, such as Herk, whose Swahili name is Muata, and his cousins, Ghetto and Gangster Dee. It would have been cruel to find myself on death row with my son. After years of being shuttled between different prisons, Stan was sent to Pelican Bay, a state-of-the-art, often locked-down prison of well-documented cruelties and racial riots. Occasionally in our correspondence he'd mention the names of Puppet, TS, Double Life, HB, Turtle, and many others that showed him the ropes. More than a year later, I'd meet Loco and Ken Dog from the East Coast. They expressed respect for Stan and looked out for him. I humbly extend my gratitude to those black men and all the rest who provided my son the knowledge to survive these hellholes, chiefly TS and Puppet who, with his sister Linda, I've known the longest.

I'm not able to see Stan at all, and the few photos I have of him are not enough to substitute for his presence. But I am fortunate enough to receive visits from Travon and my mother, who once brought my grandson, little Tray, to visit me. When I first met Tray he was six, clean-cut and well-behaved. He impressed Adisa, Ajani, Muata, and me with his ability to read exceptionally well. As we strolled around the visiting room with my hand on his shoulder, I'd point to a sign, and with enthusiasm he'd read every word. When Tray was confronted with unfamiliar words he would break them down into syllables. Once Tray understood the patriarchal chain of command, he boldly asked, "Grandpa, since you are my father's father, will you beat him up for me?" He floored *everybody* with that question.

As four generations of us Williamses posed for pictures, I thought about Stan's absence. I wondered if the day would come when I'd meet him face-to-face, and I yearned to have both Travon and Stan in a family gathering. In every letter I wrote to Stan, I wanted to gain his acceptance into whatever kind of life he had established in prison. I knew there was nothing I could do. In prison, each man has to confront the isolation with his best and strongest desire to survive. It's not a cakewalk. In many of my letters to him I tapped into his views on gangs, politics, religion and black culture. There was a similarity in my sons' perspectives and mine. He was curious and asked a lot of profound questions.

I saw in his letters Stan's clear interest in shedding the self-destructive mentality in favour of becoming culturally conscious. The respect he had for me enabled him to incorporate my hard-earned wisdom into his transition. I was proud when he cleared the first hurdle, abandoning cryptic gang vernacular for more comprehensible language, coupled with an interest in retaining new vocabulary. As years passed and he acquired no rule violations, Stan wanted to transfer from Pelican Bay to another prison. He began to study law with the intent to fight for his freedom. Benita obtained a copy of his trial transcripts. The next step was to locate an attorney willing to help emancipate him.

Certain events can be termed God's will or the destiny of divine tutelage. I believe it was both that made the following possible. On a Wednesday evening of March 13, 2002, at 3:40pm, I was abruptly woken by my neighbour Adisa. He hollered over several times before I finally understood his urgency.

"Ajamu, Ajamu, your son is calling you!"

Groggily I asked, "What did you say, Bro?"

"Your son is downstairs calling you."

I jumped up, misinterpreting the statement as, "Your son is dead!" Then from downstairs boomed a voice, calling the word "father" in Swahili.

"Baba, Baba!"

Since I had never heard Stan's voice before, I asked, "Is that you, son?"

"Yes, Baba, it's me, your son. How are you doing, Baba?"

I let him know I was doing excellently because I was able to talk to him. Briefly we engaged in a ritual of salutations. Stan said he was passing through overnight, on a bus headed for Salinas Valley State Prison. As much as I wanted to, there was no way for us to hold a decent conversation with me hollering from the fourth tier down to him on the first tier, and being able to see him seemed impossible.

Adisa suggested I try to get one of the sergeants to allow me to go downstairs to talk with my son. Minutes later, when the rookie tier officer passed by, I told him it was an emergency, that I needed to see the sergeant. Assuming I had a complaint against him, the officer wanted to know why I needed the sergeant. I explained that I wanted to get downstairs to talk with my son, whom I had not seen since 1979.

"Is your son on death row?" the officer asked.

"No, he's just passing through on his way to Salinas Valley Prison."

I was taken aback when the officer said, "Okay, no problem. As soon as the four o'clock count is over."

After telling Stan I'd be seeing him just after count time, I began putting together a care package along with some photos. I could hear the excitement in Stan's voice as he talked to Scrappy a distance away on the second tier. After count time, at 4:10pm, I descended the stairs.

"How long has it been since you've seen your son?" asked the tier officer.

"Over twenty-three years," I said.

When we reached a holding tank area, Stan hollered out, "Over here, Baba!" Fate smiled on me this day: all the cells were empty except for one next to my son. As the officer placed me in the cage, I thanked him for making it possible. I was uncuffed, and faced Stan for the first time in more than two decades. It was like looking in a mirror.

With a huge smile on his face, young Stan stood there with arms folded genie-style across his chest. "Baba, you look good," he said. I reciprocated with the exact same words. Then we reached up to an upper corner where there was a gap between the cages to touch fingers in an ad-lib handshake. Standing with the mesh cage separating us was surreal. Styling a Kool-Aid grin, I told Stan, "This scenario in itself is a miracle." He explained that about fifteen of his peers were supposed to go to C-Section, but it was filled up. They were waiting in East Block's holding cages until other arrangements could be made. "I figured no matter where I went, somebody would know who you are, so I just started asking," he said.

When I handed Stan the photos, he thanked me profusely. I passed some food, candy and personal care items to him through the gap in the upper corner of our cages. A guard passed by and offered food from a food cart. Instead, Stan made several sandwiches from the peanut butter and jelly I gave him. In between bites, he bombarded me with questions. I seized the moment, as we faced each other, to initiate a father and son dialogue we could build upon. We needed for our peace of mind to see and hear, to physically confirm our family connection. This moment did more for us than a thousand letters of correspondence could ever do. It was a validation of our biological connection and a new beginning for our relationship.

There was no making up for my paternal negligence of Stan but I could at least try, as I do with Travon, to discover a common ground. Since time was limited I wanted to impress upon him what wisdom I possessed. I apologized for not being there for him.

He smiled and said, "Baba, I've already forgiven you. There's no need to explain. I understand the life you lived because I followed in your footsteps. You were Tookie, my father, the most notorious Crip. In my eyes you could do no wrong."

"I was wrong for not having the courage to be there for you."

"Fair enough, I accept your apology, Baba."

Waves of intense feeling surged through my body. Not that I was looking for an acceptance of my apology from anyone else in this unmerciful world, but no one has ever said to me, "I forgive you," other than Travon and Stan.

This expression of forgiveness was a huge boulder lifted off my shoulders. It was a cleansing that would allow me to reach out to the other sons and daughters of the world. It was atonement.

Staring at Stan, I saw that he projected the thug arrogance I had once exhibited, an arrogance capable of getting him killed. That unsettling thought made it vital that I speak on self-transition. When I discussed the need for introspection, humility and discipline, he mistook my emphasis on self-control as a pacifistic line, turning the other cheek.

"Baba, racial riots have broken out in every prison I've been in. I chose to fight rather than retreat or accept a beat-down."

I had no argument with defending oneself. I do the same. I told him I was referring to the senseless violence that we trigger without reflection on its consequences: the stupid stuff, the vicious canards, the thug stare-downs, the idle words of machismo that prick the ego.

"Son," I told him, "just because we exist around madness does not mean we have to function like mad dogs."

Most new prisoners greet the prison conditions with open belligerence. When pitted head-to-head against the force of the gun tower, guards, barbed wire, steel bars, discrimination, duplicity and double-standard prison rules, we lose. We must be motivated by our *moto ndani*, our fire within. We must rise above the grinding, rigid conditions by nourishing our intellect and spirituality. We must out-think negative situations with a common sense approach that radiates masterful countermeasures.

Stan vowed, before he left, to incorporate into his life the disciplines of education, spirituality, exercises, redemption and transition. He had heard that my peers and I had developed our own methodology to oppose the negative forces within and outside of ourselves. Since earlier in the conversation he had unabashedly admitted to following in my footsteps, I posed a question: "Son, are you willing to come anew?"

Without hesitation he said, "I have infinite love for you, Baba, and I'm determined to do what is necessary to change."

I was pleased to know Stan had the gumption to seek victory over his inner demons and that he trusted my judgment. I let him know that my word to him would never deviate from the truth, and that I would assist him in any way that I could. "My love for you and Travon," I said, "is undying." I reminded him not to be apprehensive about undergoing a transition, that his heart, conviction, and determination would not diminish but would only increase.

It was nearly time for us to say goodbye. We briefly discussed the children's books I had written, which he thought was a courageous effort on my part. Stan said when he read in the newspapers about my nomination for a Nobel

Peace Prize, it made him proud. In his words, "Everybody I know thought it was phenomenal that you were able to turn your life around, write children's books, get a visit from Winnie Mandela, and be nominated for a Nobel Prize. And you did it all from behind bars, on death row."

Suddenly the guard appeared. He gave notice to Stan it was time to go. But before Stan departed we reached up and touched fingers once again, as our eyes locked in a father and son bond. He was put back in handcuffs and walked by the cage I was in, turning his body so we could shake hands. Then almost as one, we spoke two words:

"Perfect love."

To gaze at my son walking away was like watching myself fade into the unknown. My fiery heart cried out with each step he took away from me. I now know and love Travon and Stan equally. At last, with my two sons' forgiveness, I felt redeemed.

Still, at this writing, my journey continues . . .

Afterthoughts

In 2002 I was nominated for the Nobel Prize for Literature by two people: Phil Casper, Associate Professor and Chair, Department of Philosophy at the College of Notre Dame, California, and Brown University Professor William Keach. Both professors defied the rule of political and social promotion of racial exclusion and negative stereotypes. Being nominated for the world's most prestigious award is an honour in itself. I do not position myself alongside Martin Luther King Jr, Nelson Mandela or Desmond Tutu. Each of these men under their own circumstances rose above racist adversity, opposition and predetermined outcomes to make their impact on the world.

I have emerged from a microcosm of fallibility, but as no less a human being than those esteemed men or any other man. Living under the duress of impending execution, I daily withstand hostile conditions, limitations, confidential informants, racial stereotyping and the self-appointed nay-sayers . . . to achieve the impossible.

Throughout California's prison complexes and on death row, I am branded a black bogeyman, the Crip Godfather, and whipping boy for any kind of prison controversy. Being a black prisoner, I'm automatically pitted against institutional racism, whereas black guards – regardless of rank – are themselves defenceless. They have to turn a blind eye to these kinds of injustices. Under such conditions, it is difficult for any man to overcome the odds, be he Indian, Asian, Mexican, Caucasian, or (chiefly) black. But like others, I dared to resist the institutional harassment, though it continues to escalate. The emperor has no clothes in the prison environment. His skin is white.

In the latest twist of penal aggression, I have been targeted for a literary public lynching. In July 2003, the *Los Angeles Times* printed an inflammatory front-page article entitled "Crips Target Of Prison Lockdown" by two highly duped *Times* staff writers. "Authorities at Corcoran State Prison have locked 1,300 African American general-population inmates in their cells with limited privileges as they investigate whether incarcerated members of the Crips street gang are conspiring to attack prison staffers in retaliation for the anticipated execution of the gang's co-founder."

The spurious article goes on to say that correctional officers at Corcoran discovered a so-called "kite" (a written message sent anonymously to the Warden) directing Crips to attack and kill high-ranking prison staff members. The article continues, quoting Corcoran officials, ". . . the anonymous kite (may) have been sent on behalf of Williams, whose court appeals are winding down." It is unprecedented that an anonymous, false prison kite can justify front-page coverage in a prestigious metropolitan newspaper and trigger the prison lockdown of thousands of prisoners in Corcoran, Pelican Bay and Salinas Valley Prison.

I agree with many of the opinions expressed by those who have sent messages to me at my website. They felt the *Times* article was a pretext hatched by the Attorney General's office, the CDC, and others to discredit my youth work, the Nobel Prize nominations, and primarily to influence the Ninth Circuit Court judges to ensure my execution. In fact, Russ Heimerich, a Department of Corrections spokesman in Sacramento, said, "Any time we have a Crip attack a staff member, we look for the link to Tookie." His words confirm that regardless of my transition, positive youth projects, peace initiatives, and more than a decade of committing *not a single disciplinary infraction*, I am always to be a suspect.

The vindictive objective to destroy me is so irrational that the CDC is willing to incite potential prison bedlam under the guise of preventing violence by locking down African Americans.

In spite of the synthetic *Times* article and other amateurish sources of false allegations and disinformation, I manage to rise above these malicious attempts to portray me negatively. Anxiety and defeatism are not an option. I will move onward. Barbara and her friend Shirley Neal, while pursuing several youth projects, have also contacted television networks to interest them in a documentary focusing on my crooked criminal trial; my innocence; prosecutorial misconduct; involuntary druggings; ineffective assistance of counsel; bias exclusion of black jurors; illegal/physical interrogation of witnesses; denial of exculpatory evidence; and on and on. Though it will be an uphill battle, I believe their perseverance will enable them to connect with a television network with the ethical guts to broach this controversial death penalty case.

Then there was talk of a movie project. Eventually Barbara negotiated with the Fox network to support a movie based on particular segments of my life, entitled *Redemption*, for its FX channel. Lynn Whitfield got the Barbara part. But when Jamie Foxx was signed to play me, I couldn't help but think that Fox executives weren't taking the project seriously. Most of my peers were scratching their heads, saying, "Bro, I don't get it. I can't see Jamie playing you." Only Adisa believed the brother could pull it off.

No one doubted Jamie's talent for mimicry. The question was whether he could make a portrayal of me believable. I reasoned that he didn't necessarily have to *look* like me. I knew it was impossible for him to pack on huge muscles in a short span of time. Would he have to wear padded muscles?

I was humbled by the fact that someone was interested in trying to capture the redemptive phases of my life, when many people think I'm irredeemable, incapable of transformation. Several months later Barbara and I met with the intended writer of the movie. In a few hours we covered many of the necessary topics. At the conclusion of this meeting, the writer promised I would not be demonized or misrepresented for melodramatic purposes. Shortly afterward, Barbara and I received and read the first draft of the movie. The script was littered with misrepresentations and black stereotypes. I think the problem lies with writer-producers and directors whose ideas of black experience are a blend of received information from news media, ethnic stereotypes, pulp fiction, music videos, magazines and books. Barbara vowed to address our complaints of blaxploitation. Although the writer and producer shared jubilation about the script, Fox executives rejected it again and again. I had little faith in either writer or producer or their ability to compose a realistic script. I thought Fox executives might eventually kick them off the project.

It was some time after reading the script that I received a visit from Barbara, who came with executive producer Rudy Langlais and his sidekick, both of whom tried to assure me that the movie would represent me in a redemptive light. Having viewed the rejected scripts, it was difficult for me to believe. I mentioned to Barbara later that all we could do was to pray that these characters would not develop acute amnesia about their announced intentions.

On July 12, 2003, I entered the visiting room to meet Vondie Curtis Hall, Jamie Foxx, and Jamie's manager, Marcus King, for the first time. After being uncuffed, I hugged Barbara and initiated brotherly handshakes all round. We talked about everything: street gangs, prison, politics, religion, families, entertainment and my life. I could see Jamie studying my mannerisms. When I brought up the subject of my youth mentoring programme, Jamie expressed his willingness to participate. He mentioned that he and rapper and producer P. Diddy often exchanged thoughts about helping youth and about the plight of black folks. He talked about how they had kicked around ideas for building a school for inner-city youths. Though there were comedic moments, Jamie was mostly observant and serious.

The conversation shifted to my thoughts about those in

society professing to be Crip godfathers and co-founders. I assured them that my memoirs would put into proper perspective the facts, and mentioned my distress about those who come forth making claims of being originators of this legacy of death. Too many black lives have been lost – and will continue to be lost – until the cycle is reversed. It is inconceivable that individuals would make claims with no substantiation rather than offer viable solutions to the problem. I am not proud of the roles that Raymond and I played, nor should anyone else be proud of their roles.

After two hours, there was a break. I went to the restroom while the others purchased more vending machine food. When we reentered the visiting cage, Vondi asked how I was able to maintain my sanity. I responded, "With extreme difficulty. I maintain my sanity through prayers, studying, exercising, drawing, reading, meditating, typing, visits and using the phone."

Jamie and Marcus wanted to know what was it that kept me motivated. "Faith in God," I replied. "*Dum spiro spero*. While I breathe, I hope."

Barbara asked, for the benefit of the others, what my thoughts were about those who were still crippin'. I said, "Unlike other former participants, I cannot be a hypocrite and denigrate any Crip, Blood, or anyone else who chooses to perpetuate the thug lifestyle – which is wrong, which is genocide. As long as I am alive I will continue to speak out against the violent toll of deaths and on behalf of life."

Near the end of the visit I asked Jamie if he was planning to visit me again. Both Jamie and Marcus said that they would be back the next Sunday and assured me that they were committed to their youth projects. During a brief conversation with Vondi, he vowed to represent me in the film with justice. I told him that I would definitely need it.

Following the photo session, I was escorted back to the hellhole. That night prior to dozing off, I revisited the moments of the day. Vondi and Marcus were extremely persuasive about Jamie having the talent to play the role. Jamie had proved to be down to earth, personable and attentive to the slightest detail of my concerns. He amazed us all by mimicking my voice and gestures with uncanny exactness. I thought perhaps this man can work his magic.

Barbara shortly thereafter sent me the second revision of *Redemption*, which lacked depth regarding my transition. The writer placed more emphasis on the person I used to be, rather than who I am today. Fox executives once again rejected the script. The burden to reconstruct the script now fell on Vondi. Since he was a black man, he could perhaps empathize with my transition. I hoped so.

Jamie and Marcus were men of their word. They showed up the following Sunday to visit me. Jamie talked extensively about the need to portray me as I am today. During the break, Jamie and Marcus had to leave to prepare for the trip to Canada where the movie set was being constructed. We paused to take more pictures, which Jamie signed, and I did likewise for him and Marcus. After they had left, Barbara, as usual, asked what did I think. I said, "If the script is rewritten well, I believe Jamie can deliver an excellent performance."

During August and early September, as the movie was being shot, I talked on the phone with Barbara, Jamie, Marcus and just about the entire movie crew. Prior to the close of shooting, I composed a taped message thanking the team for their dedicated work on the project. Several times I was able to converse with Lynn Whitfield, who played the role of Barbara. Amiable and kindhearted, Lynn promised to visit me despite her hectic schedule.

Barbara had travelled twice to Toronto, staying for a week each time. While there, she and Lynn established a strong rapport. On her final trip to Toronto, Barbara was accompanied by her mother Lillie, who came to watch the filming and enjoy the sights. Usually when I called, they were on the set, watching the goings-on. Even with Barbara present at the filming, I knew with all the executive testosterone unchecked her prudent suggestions might be patronized and ultimately neglected. Neither of us had any legal control. I remained concerned about the producer's "creative freedom" that permits him and others to embellish and put words in my mouth. Jamie, I learned, refused to do the original movie promo because he considered it to be uncharacteristic of me. Without Jamie's having my back, the executive producer would have had no reason to alter the promo. I doubt that any other black male actor or executive would have gone out on a limb for a man who is condemned to death.

I have great respect for Jamie Foxx.

Returning from Canada, Barbara told me that Lynn and Jamie had been exceptional in their roles. But I never received the final version, the third rewrite of the script. And the film had not been finalized for private viewing for Barbara, the focus test group, or others. (While imprisoned, I will not be able to see the movie.) But I pray the movie will reveal to all who see it that even the lowest of the lowlife – despite their circumstances – can transform and redeem himself.

No prisoner is safe within this tinderbox, where a mere spark of stupidity can explode into crazed violence. The institution itself can manipulate a given situation so that even a peaceful man faces an ultimate decision – defend himself vigorously or die.

Daily I face life's challenges with relentless faith and resolution. I'm a fighter of a different kind. I fight for the poor and wretched among us. Though it may be viewed by many as illogical on my part, I envision freedom outside these forbidding walls ... if not tangible freedom, then certainly in spirit.

Amani (Peace)

Special Acknowledgements

It is necessary to acknowledge individuals I neglected to mention within the body of my memoirs. This is in recognition of individuals in society and on death row (despite their history) who are true friends and are involved in progressive organizations, youth projects and self-evolutionary journeys, and who provided invaluable feedback for my Peace Protocol.

Frederick Douglass
Tony R
My sons
Winnie Mandela
Adisa
Jessie James
Haki
Wayne H
Kern
Ghetto
Nthato Robin Shaka
Kwesi
Big Cane
Malik
Little Ace
Scrappy
Big Time

Nelson Mandela
Wimpy
Ajani
Muata
Jamie Foxx
Marcus King
Vondie Hall
Kiilu Nyasha
Mumia Abu-Jaml
Chico
Kevin "KC" Cooper
Holloway
Nkpume
J. King Puppet
TS
Clint
Jay Dog

Jackie Watson
HB
Ojare
Warlock
Jelly Roll
Mustafa
Big Alton
Eric & Derrick
Peewee
Joe Marshall
Bahari-Ku
Oatmeal
Side Winder
Mario
Ice Tea
Big Al
Cool Breeze

Ajene

PR

Shoes

Fat Rat

Bopete

K. Dog

Pointblank

Big Tony

Willie Herb

Rebel

Mickey

Cricket

Barefoot Pookie

Snoop Dog

Little Dee

D. Moody

Ice Cube

Elu

Rusty

Shirley Neal

Chunga

Monster

Half Pint

Will Rock

Little Bruce

Khalifa

Melvin R

Chief

Apache

Ndio

Grandpa

Monkeyman

Asikiwe

Bobby Seale

Fadh

KI

Green Eyes

Bobo

Lynn Whitfield

Barbara Becnel

Cutes

Mouse

Eddie H

Geronimo Pratt

E-Moe

Little Money

Louisiana Smooth

Boon

Michael Christen

Big Reg

Big James

Snow

Romeo

T.S.

Stockton Mike

Walt

Skull

Big Vertice

Rudy Langlais

May all of you continue to promote self-transition, redemption, self-reliance, and above all, peace.

Appendix

The Tookie Protocol for Peace
A Local Street Peace Initiative
Stanley Tookie Williams

Peace Protocol Table of Contents

Introduction

To address the social emergency of urban violence, I have prepared this protocol for street peace – a comprehensive strategy for peace and reconstruction within the community. The design can be modified to meet the needs of a particular situation.

The United States government's approach to urban violence is often to launch one of its intermittent "wars" on crime and then trumpet success by pointing to wholesale incarcerations, yet fail to deter or rehabilitate the criminal mentality. But, for a generation of disgruntled youth and adults, living the thug life and going to prison have morphed into an underdog aspiration.

Placing blame is irrelevant. We must concentrate on a workable solution.

The approach to resolving an epidemic begins with understanding the origins of it, the causes and effects. To broach this issue I briefly draw on my life and gang experience as the co-founder of the infamous Crips. I grew up in South Central Los Angeles amid poverty, street gangs, pimps, prostitutes, police tyranny, illegal drugs, criminality and other social injustices. Here was a social vacuum without paternal guidance, without career-oriented pro-grammes, and without a nurturing village or community to support the male rite of passage toward becoming a responsible adult. Violence, gangs and street level socio-economic crimes (selling drugs, robbery, prostitution and theft) were – and continue to be – direct results of living in these conditions.

This social vacuum has spawned black urban nihilists like the Crips, the Bloods, and many other street gangs. Gangs serve as a weapon of rebellion against parental authority, culture, religion, community, law enforcement, the world, God, and other gangs. The muscular irrationality of a gang's instinct to survive is used to justify any wrongful act, even at the expense of a family member, stranger, friend or foe.

The phrase "by any means necessary" serves as a destructive rationale for street gangs to fend for themselves in society, without regard for anyone else. Each faction operates as an independent, lawless body that has no difficulty recruiting among the disenfranchised.

The absence of basic access to affordable housing, health care, quality education, secure employment and other necessities produces social instability. Any efforts to establish a peace policy will be doomed unless there is tangible social progress. Peace cannot be sustained without it. Poverty, racism and hopelessness foster an environment that supports the growth of toxic conditions.

Understanding Retaliation

From an illusory elitism of gang membership, a pattern of retaliation has emerged that perpetuates the pattern of murder-for-murder. In this scenario there are no winners. And the losers are too often buried in graveyards, maimed by gunfire, or incarcerated for their crimes.

Like a pendulum, retaliation swings back and forth with its inevitable, brutal payback.

Trying to stop belligerent gangs from retaliating against each other is difficult. Retaliation brings a sense of machismo and an earned street "reputation". Society sees only a cycle of senseless murders, an unending tragedy. It would amaze both gang members and others in society to hear that conflicts between Crips and Bloods on death row – where I live – are rare. These sworn enemies engage in non-hostile dialogues, banter, share food and books, study, and exercise together on the same prison yards without controversy.

If notorious rivals who have been exterminating one another for more than three decades can establish a truce in prison, then a cease-fire is surely possible in society. Throughout California prisons, Crips and Bloods coexist for the purpose of survival. That simple philosophy can be transmitted to rival gangs in society. Instead of our killing each other, that energy can be harnessed to oppose poverty, illiteracy, unemployment, discrimination, and other social and judiciary injustices.

There are many reasons why warring factions should avoid this cycle of violence and retaliation, of *lex talionis* (eye for an eye): innocents are injured or killed, and the psychic and social scars on adults and children are handed down to next generations.

Conclusion

There is no quick-fix remedy for the gang epidemic.

Here on death row I have discussed a street gang truce with individuals from different age groups, geographical locales, gangs, and mentalities. I discovered that my ideological and philosophical outlook on peace was in step with perspectives of the newer and the older generation. I also realized it is illogical to create a peace not based on an individual and collective improvement of the lives of community members. Failure to establish a truce that includes a social agenda will cause any negotiation for peace to relapse into war.

I am convinced that peace *is* possible, despite the many lives that have been lost from years of youth gang warfare. This document is designed to assist those whose aspirations are to create a cease-fire, end gang violence and restore social order. Although I have heard pessimistic individuals quote the English translation of the Latin phrase, *si vis pacem, para bellum* – if you desire peace, prepare for war – I strongly disagree.

Real peace will conquer war.

Signature Agreements

Perpetual Peace Accord For Opposing Gangs

Acknowledged here and now on this month _____,
day _____, and year _____, is a perpetual Peace Treaty
between the warring parties: _____
and _____. This word-of-honour agreement
binds the aforementioned rival factions to put aside their
differences, be they ideological, political, religious, philosophical,
racial, economical, geographical, criminal, material, personal
and collective retaliation, or any social reliance on violence or
murder. This document is an oath of responsibility for the
parties involved to co-exist in peace and reconciliation for the
security of our communities, their residents and offspring.

Signatory: _____

Date: _____

Observing Witness: _____

Point I:
Proclamation

A-1:   WE THE INVOLVED PARTIES WILL immediately cease fire and end any verbal, written, or physical violence against one another.

A-2:   WE THE INVOLVED PARTIES WILL cease and desist the perpetuation of drive-by shootings, walk-up shootings, set-up shootings, ambushes, murder, drug deals, robbery, vandalism, kidnapping, rape, extortion, female and child abuse, illegal profiteering, or any kind of violence or criminality.

A-3:   WE THE INVOLVED PARTIES WILL use every non-violent measure to resolve all past, present, or future conflicts between us.

A-4:   WE THE INVOLVED PARTIES WILL learn to respect one another and co-exist in peace within the community or elsewhere.

A-5:   WE THE INVOLVED PARTIES WILL help to restore order and to rebuild the community.

A-6:   WE THE INVOLVED PARTIES WILL not disrespect, instigate, or taunt each other or family members, relatives, wives, girlfriends, and acquaintances of the opposite parties.

A-7:   WE THE INVOLVED PARTIES WILL not encroach upon each other's community or neighbourhood without prior notice to avoid suspicion or conflict.

A-8:   WE THE INVOLVED PARTIES WILL help individually and collectively to keep the community safe from any improprieties.

A-9:   WE THE INVOLVED PARTIES WILL not use the Peace Accord as a camouflage to commit mayhem against each other.

A-10: WE THE INVOLVED PARTIES WILL neither seek out nor plot with acquaintances or outsiders (defined as parties not obligated to this Proclamation) to carry out vendettas against each other.

A-11: WE THE INVOLVED PARTIES WILL not allow mistreatment or harm to befall any individuals appointed as Peacekeepers or others involved in the peace process.

A-12: WE THE INVOLVED PARTIES will put forth effort to

become educated, computer-literate, and to learn a trade that will enable us to become productive in the reconstruction of our community.

A-13: WE THE INVOLVED PARTIES WILL eliminate any self-destructive behaviour and personal vices – illicit drug usage, drug dealing, abuse of alcohol, inhalants, etc. – that would intoxicate our minds, impair our judgment and jeopardize the peace negotiations.

A-14: WE THE INVOLVED PARTIES will work side by side to do whatever is ethical to uphold the Peace Accord and Proclamation, and we vow to live in harmony.

A-15: WE THE INVOLVED PARTIES recognize both the Peace Accord and Proclamation as being fair and attainable. We agree to its entire contents.

Signatory: _____

Date: _____

Observing Witness: _____

Point II:
Violations of Proclamation Clause

This written clause is designed to maintain fairness in the determination of possible violation of Point I: Proclamation, and to determine what, if any, will be the punitive measures. Violations committed by parties from either side will be adjudicated (via monetary fines, community labour, expulsion, etc.) ONLY by a selected nonpartisan Peacekeepers Committee, to avoid possible hostile reactions by a violator from either party. Violations will be recognized as follows:

I: To violate the cease-fire in any form;
II: To violate any of the provisions in the Proclamation, including A-1 through A-15;
III: To assist another party member to violate the Proclamation;
IV: To alter or rewrite the agreed-upon Proclamation to favour one party's interest over the other party's;

V: To obstruct any of the appointed Peacekeepers from performing their duties to maintain peace.

Signatory: _____

Date: _____

Observing Witness: _____

Point III:
Peacekeepers and Monitoring Committee

B-1:   Mediators, who could be members of local faith-based groups or other community-based organizations, initiate an outreach process to begin establishment of a Peacekeepers Committee. In the beginning they play a crucial role in identifying the founding members of the Peacekeepers Committee. Once this core group of founders is established, their outreach abilities are used to further expand the Peacekeepers Committee, and they become members of that Committee.

B-2:   Members of the Peacekeepers Committee will consist of several – preferably former – local gang leaders or influential gang members; church leaders or influential members of the church congregation; local political representatives; grassroots community leaders; concerned parents; and other reliable and interested people within the community.

B-3:   The Peacekeepers will assemble daily or less often – depending upon the severity of the situation – until there is peace and community stability. Meetings can be held in a specific home, basement, garage, church, gymnasium, or in any enclosed facility. To provide safety for all the people involved in the peace negotiations, implement "pat searches" and metal detectors.

B-4:   Selection of Peacekeepers Committee members can be held annually or biannually.

B-5.   All Peacekeepers will wear a specific-coloured armband and insignia of peace to identify them. Any vehicle driven by a Peacekeeper will have a visibly attached white flag prior to venturing into any recognized area of either party participating in the transition to peace.

B-6: All decisions related to peace strategies and/or violations of peace among either party must be voted on by the Peacekeepers Committee before any such measures are enacted.

B-7: Each Peacekeeper is required to allocate his or her time to monitor specific communities and war zones. Moreover, he or she is expected to keep in touch with members from either party.

B-8: Any Peacekeeper Committee member can be voted off the Committee if he or she is neglectful of duties or guilty of any wrongdoing – be it criminal or otherwise.

B-9: To prevent Peacekeepers from involvement in law enforcement issues, they are to leave the solving of serious crimes, including murder, to the authorities.

B-10: The Peacekeepers obligation is to implement and maintain peace and *not* to play the role of a police officer, a member of the Federal Bureau of Investigation, the Central Intelligence Agency or any other law enforcement agency.

B-11: The Peacekeepers Committee is expected to create Buffer Zones (see **Point V:** Buffer Zones) within the community to meet the needs of either party. These Buffer Zones are necessary for the provisions of peace meetings, socializing, sharing information and providing a sanctuary.

B-12: All Peacekeepers must recite and sign a written oath regarding their responsibility to establish peace.

B-13: No Peacekeeper will act as a vigilante or enforcer through means of violence, nor will any Peacekeeper suggest or rely upon representatives of either party to act as vigilantes or enforcers.

Signatory: _____

Date: _____

Observing Witness: _____

Point IV:
Peacekeepers Oath

I, _____, do solemnly
swear to uphold all the obligations of being a Peacekeepers
Committee member. Throughout the course of my appointed
duties I promise to be truthful and fair with either party. As a
Peacekeeper my responsibility is to establish and maintain peace
within the community. I vow to adhere to everything required
of me within the Peacekeepers Committee, Point III: B-1 through
B-12, and the Peacekeepers Oath.

Signatory: _____

Date: _____

Observing Witness: _____

Point V:
Buffer Zones

Both parties agree to designate neutral areas called Buffer Zones
that are monitored by the Peacekeepers Committee. These Buffer
Zones will be set up to provide either party with a safe haven
for peace talks, intermingling, relevant information sharing,
meetings, etc. Such Buffer Zones can be established in a church,
office, home, recreation centre, building, or any kind of structure
or territory, including a block or entire community. All members
from either party will agree to never violate the sanctity of the
Buffer Zones, which are created to assist in peaceful negotiations.

Signatory: _____

Date: _____

Observing Witness: _____

Point VI:
Gang Membership Renunciation

The long-term objective is for an eventual dismantling of all disruptive parties (gangs, sets, hoods, groups, organizations, empires, etc.) that are prone to create havoc within the community. There will be party members from either side interested in changing his or her lifestyle. Point VI is written to protect any person who decides, or is encouraged, to give up his or her membership from any disruptive group.

1: All parties agree to allow any member who chooses to disassociate himself or herself from membership or association with any disruptive group representing either party to do so without the threat or enactment of ridicule, violence or retaliation.

2: Former members of a disruptive group representing either party will be allowed to continue helping to establish peace without fear of repercussion.

3: Counselling and reorientation will be offered to any individual who decides to quit membership in a disruptive group representing either party.

4: For whatever reason, if any ex-member of a disruptive group rejoins his or her group, he or she will be excluded from the ongoing peace initiative.

Signatory: _____

Date:_____

Observing Witness: _____

Putting the
Theory of Peace into Practice

Establishing Peace

The process for creating peace among hostile factions requires a neutral mediator or mediators. The following is a process mediators should use to initiate a peace process:

Have as many supporters as possible on board prior to contacting either of the warring parties.

Schedule a meeting separately and together with the local churches, mosques, synagogues, temples, community-based organizations, violence prevention programmes, schools, veterans' groups, Masons, businesses and local politicians to discuss their participation in the grassroots struggle for peace. Present a proposed peace document to each of these entities that illustrates the critical role of each of these groups to the community peace process.

If a mediator (or mediators) is not familiar with either of the parties, then that mediator should seek assistance from a reliable source who is acquainted with both sides and is capable of setting up separate meetings with each of the most influential representatives of the opposing parties to recruit their participation in the development of the community's peace process.

Prior to the meeting, the mediator should learn as much as possible about the individuals the mediator is scheduled to meet.

Whenever the mediator (or mediators) determines that positive gains have been made during the dialogue with both sides, then the leaders of the opposing parties should be invited to attend a joint meeting in a neutral setting. Make it known that for security purposes, pat-searches and metal detectors will be implemented.

During those joint meetings, encourage both parties to express themselves while the mediator (or mediators) observes and listens carefully. Since both sides are protagonists in the peace process, make sure to embody their most reasonable suggestions in tandem with your ideas about peace.

Present both parties with a comprehensive peace strategy that is viable and attainable.

Seek assistance in the peace process from the parents, family members, relatives and other associates of the leaders and members of the opposing parties. With both parties aware that people they care about will also be present at each peace meeting, rally, march and other social functions, it should dissuade potential hostile actions.

To effectively address urban warfare the peace plan should address situations within a community, block-by-block, and expand as the project prevails.

Draw from influential sources such as Original Gangsters who are incarcerated from within either party. Redemption, integrity and aspirations can be found among the most wretched.

Do a background check on members of the Peacekeepers Committee to prevent possible infiltration and sabotage to your process by agents provocateurs. (There *will* be attempts by internal and external sources to disrupt the peace protocol. A viable peace policy supported by a staunch community can overcome its detractors' obstacles.)

Initiate study groups to familiarize both parties with the origins of their ancestors and culture. Help them to develop pride in themselves and in their heritage. Teach them how to renounce their self-hate that produces violence, and show them how to cleanse themselves with dignity, honesty, justice and righteousness.

With peace as the objective, fear or flight is not an option. When you reduce the human factor to its bare essentials, we all want to live. Everyone's life is on the line. It will require instinct, intellect, sponsors, and absolute courage to bring together a tractable peace agreement. With the majority of the community on board, peace can prevail.

Maintaining Peace

To establish peace is one reality, to maintain it is another; to preserve peace will require consistent discipline, upkeep, inter-action, and monitoring. Here are a few suggestions:

In addition to the Peacekeepers, select a Community Watch

Group organized with video cameras to monitor activity in the community. This is a precautionary – and interim – method to let police and everyone else know that they're being observed. Post large, visible signs to forewarn that these areas are being video-monitored.

Both the Peacekeepers and the Community Watch must work in shifts, around the clock, to monitor behaviour and maintain peace. Their availability is critical to uphold order.

Communal communication is necessary to supervise the war zone areas. Strategic points can be established throughout a neighbourhood provided with computers, cell phones, walkie-talkies, etc., to monitor social activities. Preferably during the day, at-home mothers and elderly folks are suitable candidates for Community Watch Groups. Whenever there appears to be improper activity, Watch Group members should contact the Peacekeepers to address the situation. The most serious incidents (shootings, murders, etc.) must be left up to law enforcement agencies. The Peacekeepers and Community Watch groups are not police officers.

All Peacekeepers and Community Watch Groups should interact with all people in the community. Throughout the neighbourhood, go door to door to discuss the peace policy or to distribute peace fliers. If there are people who refuse to discuss peace with you, leave a flier in their mailbox or underneath the windshield wiper of their car. *Let no community resident be ignorant of your peace initiative.*

Follow through on every policy that will create peace.

Maintain contact with all parties under the peace accord. Keep them abreast of progress being made, and/or any concerns, suggestions, etc., concerning the truce.

Remind all individuals participating in the peace process that they will be held accountable for their inappropriate behaviour. Established and agreeable guidelines for punitive damages will be enforced by Peacekeepers. Damages can range from monetary fines, community work, expulsion, or other requirements of the peace agreement.

Maintain a written report on the progress of the peace negotiations.

Always encourage all individuals involved in the peace process.

To preserve a truce, children must be educated on the premise of peace. The knowledge of peace combined with their direct participation will help to create a generation of peace idealists.

To disarm is the ultimate gesture of peace and a true moment of reckoning. Disarmament is not a coward's way out, but rather a wise person's way *in* for peace. However, for me it would be a disservice to suggest to anyone to disarm themselves when peace is still a theory and not a living practice.

It is a myth that manhood and womanhood can be defined through the barrel of a gun. Realistically, the majority of people who do possess weapons will not surrender them under any circumstances. Moreover, if a self-hate mentality is maintained among community residents, violence will continue, with or without the presence of guns.

For people to disarm themselves, they must first disarm their minds with education and enlightenment in support of an ultimate peace. Dare I entreat every man, woman and child to lower the barrel of their weapons in honour of peace?

Social Agenda For Peacekeepers

It is unrealistic in any attempt to establish a peace policy without including a social agenda. History has shown that communities and nations have either prospered or perished depending upon the viability of their social agenda – which is an orderly system that promotes prosperity for all its residents.

Throughout history, we see that the absence of peace and a workable social covenant can give rise to nihilistic settings. Here in America, the subculture of gangsterism and criminality continues to devastate communities with its lawless agenda. This social agenda, in the paragraphs below, has been designed to help reintegrate the so-called gangbangers, criminals, ex-cons, and other incorrigibles into society.

Education and Career Trade Programmes

This process is geared to provide each individual with the opportunity and information to earn a high school diploma or a G.E.D.

In addition to this fundamental education and certification, individuals with scholastic ambition are encouraged to pursue further education: in politics, socioeconomics, computer technology, architecture, sociology, psychology, mathematics, history or law sciences. Their education and skills will be valuable assets in the redevelopment of both themselves and their communities.

Establish a relationship with local schools, colleges, youth centres, and technological centres to request their assistance in bringing the individuals' education to fruition.

Create your own designated study groups and computer classes to be held in a home, church, garage, basement, youth centre, or other places.

Political Awareness

Stress the importance of being politically conscious. Encourage individuals to read relevant materials (newspapers, magazines, books, websites, etc.) to become politically literate, recognize their rights and the power of their votes.

Educate them on the duties and obligations of each local political representative to further their community involvement.

Teach residents to be alert to political dynamics that affect their lives. Impress upon them that if the politician representing their district has not made ground-breaking achievements that improve their lives and the community, then something is wrong. By "achievements," I mean available jobs, livable housing, health care, quality education, no addicts/drugs/homelessness, safe, clean neighbourhoods, and reduced poverty, violence and crime.

Employment Placement

When an individual has completed an educational process, he or she will need to find a job. An Employment Placing Panel can be created to help find a suitable job for each individual. This will require phone calls, emails and footwork to locate available jobs. This "recruiting" process is itself a useful skill.

Teach each individual etiquette and mannerisms: how to speak well, dress properly, maintain good personal hygiene, be prompt, patient, and develop a good work ethic. The objective, first, is to gain employment and then to begin to build a solid employment record.

Socioeconomic Commission

Establish a Socioeconomic Commission consisting of entre-preneurs, bankers, economists, stockbrokers, and other business professionals. Use every available means at your disposal to contact these people whose resources can be a valuable asset.

Your presentation to these business-oriented people must be cogent, reasonable and doable. Remember that the Peace Protocol and the Social Agenda is a unified package that includes the specific role of Socioeconomic Commission members.

The Commission's mission is to help create a system of small businesses that in turn promote ownership, local employment expansion, and overall community economic development. In addition, the commission's mission is to teach a grassroots individual how to administer a small business enterprise.

Encourage individuals to reduce their consumer spending and debt.

Peace March

Beginning with the famous August 28, 1963, march on Washington (climaxed by Martin Luther King's "I Have A Dream" speech), there have been numerous other peaceful marches that have momentarily seized our focus on relevant issues. The march of peace is akin to the march of war, because both are predicated on the notion of overcoming obstacles to success.

When we march in the name of peace, let us march with a

strategic purpose that will produce tangible accessibilities: the reality of a need for peace, employment, housing, health care, education, property ownership, and other amenities.

Community Cleanup

Another important reality is the need to clean up the community, block by block. I can already hear people moaning at the thought of having to clean up the community. There are run-down neighbourhoods that should be a priority and need immediate addressing, much as a person cleans his/her own home. Knock on every door on every block and ask for their participation in the clean-up project.

Street by street, groups of adults, children and youths can clean up filth, abandoned cars, graffiti, and other refuse. Naturally, to refurbish homes and apartments may require financial assistance from committed sponsors and others who have an interest in the community's development. But funds are not necessary when we can rely on our own hands and a little footwork. The clean-up project benefits everyone, because the area is clean and no longer an eyesore – and it raises property values!

Armed with brooms, trash cans, plastic bags, paint brushes and rollers, and water hoses, residents can purge their own communities. Upon the completion of the cleaning process, post fliers that emphasize the need for cleanliness and no littering. The rise or fall of any neighbourhood can be attributed to the residents' concern to keep the community clean, alive and well – or to continued indifference, lack of pride, and neglect.

Signature Agreement
Community Peace Accord

We the people of the community named here –
_____ – do solemnly swear to
participate in the Street Peace Protocol to restore decorum and
to provide safety for all residents. We agree to work side by side
with all other people whose goal is the pursuit of peace. We are
not a vigilante group, militia, nor are we working in the capacity
of a law enforcement agency. We function as an independent
peace group and as concerned citizens of our community. We
believe that peace can be established and maintained through
dedicated work.

**We agree to adhere to the standards of this document, without
fail.**

Signatory: _____

Date: _____

Observing Witness: _____

Postscript

A Final Note From Tookie

There are no books or manuals on how to create a peace policy for street gangs. I have drafted this peace protocol to serve as a prototype or framework on which to build. It is a common-sense approach that beckons the heart and invites your strong intention to assist those who live in chaos and fear, both children and adults. I hope that my insight will move society – and gang members – to draft from this peace protocol and make it work.

As you move in this direction, you will learn to construct a peace policy that will meet the necessities for peace in your neighbourhood, in your city, in your nation. There is much serious work ahead, and the entire community will depend upon each and every one of you. Keep in mind that even the warring souls of gang members yearn for peace but are blind to its path. Your faith, wisdom, concern, and guidance can help show them the way. Never allow yourself to be distracted or discouraged by detractors and dissenters whose views are counterproductive.

Finally, I call upon the pure energy of human beings and institutions – gangs, ex-cons, parents, churches and mosques, schools and universities, youth centres, think tanks, university professors and other educators, entrepreneurs, entertainers, human rights agencies, social organizations, politicians, rappers, newspapers, media broadcast outlets, the employed and unemployed, the wealthy and the poor, the young and the elderly, and anyone else who is interested in promoting street peace – to help create a new community of safety and well-being. This peace protocol is not the solution. Look in the mirror. There is the solution!

Peace Protocol Kit

To use Tookie's Protocol for Peace to help your community, print the document from Tookie's website at http://www.tookie.com/protocol/index.html.